CURRENT SCIENTIFIC TECHNIQUES IN ARCHAEOLOGY

CURRENT SCIENTIFIC TECHNIQUES IN ARCHAEOLOGY

P. A. PARKES

ST. MARTIN'S PRESS
New York

© 1986 P. A. Parkes
All rights reserved. For information, write:
Scholarly & Reference Division,
St. Martin's Press, Inc., 175 Fifth Avenue, New York, NY 10010
First published in the United States of America in 1987
Printed in Great Britain

Library of Congress Cataloging-in-Publication Data

Parkes, P.A. (Penelope), 1957-
  Current scientific techniques in archaeology

  Bibliography: p.
  Includes index
  1. Archaeology—Methodology. I. Title
CC75.P29   1986   930.1'028   86-17906
ISBN 0-312-00097-9

CONTENTS

UNITS

This list includes the main units found in archaeometry, though others may also be used if they are more convenient. Some quantities are so related that it is a simple matter to change from one unit to a totally different one if required. For example x-rays and γ-rays are normally described in terms of energy, visible light by its wavelength and short radiowaves by their frequency. However, as all are types of electromagnetic radiation it is very easy to calculate the wavelength of an x-ray of known energy etc. if required. The quantities measured by scientists range from the very big to the very small and so there are an agreed set of prefixes with abbreviations to indicate multiples and fractions of the basic units. The use of some such as kilo in kilogramme and milli in millimetre are already familiar but some of the others are not normally encountered in everyday life. With both units and prefixes it is important to distinguish between upper and lower case letters because they have different meanings.

Prefixes

G	giga	10^9
M	mega	10^6
k	kilo	10^3
c	centi	10^{-2}
m	milli	10^{-3}
μ	micro	10^{-6}
n	nano	10^{-9}

Units

Å	Angström	length (10^{-10} metres)
A	Ampere	electric current
Am^2	Ampere metre ^{2}	size of magnetic dipole

amu	atomic mass unit	mass of atoms and molecules
bit	binary digit	information content
byte		size of computer memory (8 bits)
°C	degrees Celsius	temperature (same as degrees Centigrade)
cm^{-1}	wavenumber	number of waves per unit length (cm)
eV	electronvolt	energy
g	gram(me)	mass
G	Gauss	intensity of magnetic field (10^{-4} Teslas[1])
γ	nanoTesla	intensity of magnetic field
Hz	Hertz	frequency (1 cycle per second)
K	Kelvin	temperature (° Celsius + 273)
m	metre	length
N	Newton	force
Ω	Ohm	resistance
O	Oersted	intensity of magnetic field (10^{-4} Teslas[1])
ppm	parts per million	concentration
rad	radiation absorbed dose	quantity of ionising radiation
T	Tesla	intensity of magnetic field
V	volt	electric voltage
yr	year	time

Note

1. Under some circumstances the Oersted and Gauss are not equal in size, but in much archaeometric work they can be taken to be equal.

ABBREVIATIONS AND SYMBOLS

This list contains the abbreviations and symbols used in this book and not in common everyday or archaeological use. The symbols for the elements are not included in this list but will be found in the Periodic Table at the end of the book; symbols for units are also listed separately. The use of upper and lower case letters has been determined by the most common usage in the original papers, but other authors may use upper and lower case letters differently. Some of the abbreviations have more than one meaning (not necessarily listed here).

a	total error (used in TL dating)
AAS or AA	atomic absorption spectroscopy
AES	Auger electron spectroscopy
af	alternating field
AMS	accelerator mass spectroscopy
$^{40}Ar/^{39}Ar$	argon−40/argon−39 technique for K/Ar dating
ARM	anhysteretic remanent magnetisation
CAM	Crassulacean acid metabolism
C_3	Calvin pathway ·
C_4	Hatch-Slack pathway
C−14	carbon−14 or radiocarbon
CRM	chemical remanent magnetisation
D	declination
d	distance (in mathematical formulae)
DRM	depositional or detrital remanent magnetisation
DTA	differential thermal analysis
DTG or DTGA	differential thermo-gravimetric analysis
e	electron
ED	energy dispersive (in x-ray fluorescence analysis)
EM	electromagnetic
EPR	electron paramagnetic resonance
ESR	electron spin resonance
F^A	ancient field (magnetic dating)

F^L	laboratory field (magnetic dating)
gc	gas chromatography
glc	gas liquid chromatography
GP	geophysical
HEMS	high energy mass spectroscopy
hplc	high pressure (or high performance) liquid chromatography
I	inclination (or dip)
ICP	inductively coupled plasma (spectroscopy)
INAA	instrumental neutron activation analysis
IR	infra-red
IRM	isothermal remanent magnetisation
K−Ar	potassium/argon (dating)
M^+	singly charged molecular ion
ms	mass spectroscopy
MS	Mössbauer spectroscopy
n	whole number
n	neutron
NAA	neutron activation analysis
nmr	nuclear magnetic resonance
NRM	natural remanent magnetisation
OES	optical emission spectroscopy
p	experimental error (used in TL dating)
p	proton
PCA	principal components analysis
PDB	PD belemnite (a standard for C–14 dating)
PIGME	particle (or proton) induced gamma-ray emission
PIXE	particle (or proton) induced x-ray emission
PMS	pyrolysis mass spectroscopy
PNAA	prompt neutron activation analysis
PTRM or pTRM	partial thermoremanent magnetisation
PDRM	post-depositional remanent magnetisation
SCM	soil conductivity meter (banjo)
SEM	scanning electron microscope
SIRM	saturated isothermal remanent magnetisation
SQUID	super-conducting quantum interference device
SRM	shear remanent magnetisation
TG or T_G	thermo-gravimetric analysis
TL	thermoluminescence
TRM	thermoremanent magnetisation

VDU	visual display unit
VRM	viscous remanent magnetisation
WD	wavelength dispersive (in x-ray fluorescence)
XPS	x-ray photoelectron spectroscopy
XRD	x-ray diffraction
XRF	x-ray fluorescence
δ	small quantity: used for isotopic fractionation
θ	an angle (in mathematical formulae)
λ	wavelength
σ	standard deviation
χ_m	magnetic susceptibility

Superscripts

*	excited state
+	positive charge
−	negative charge

ACKNOWLEDGEMENTS

Firstly I would like to thank the General Editor of this series, Professor L. Alcock, and my husband, Dr K. E. B. Parkes, for reading the manuscript of this book and making many helpful comments. I am also indebted to my husband for drawing some of the diagrams.

I would also like to thank Dr M. J. Aitken for the raw data for figure 3.2, Jeffrey May for information about Dragonby and access to the plans on which figures 9.10 and 9.11 are based, and Dr G. Pearson and Dr D. Sanderson for, as yet, unpublished data in their respective fields. In addition I am grateful to Professor L. Alcock for permission to reproduce figure 9.12, Dr A. J. Clarke and English Heritage for permission to reproduce figures 4.3 and 9.5b and Dr G. Lock for permission to reproduce figures 10.2 and 10.3. Finally, I would like to thank my typist, Mrs V. M. Madeley, for typing my manuscript so efficiently.

1 INTRODUCTION

This book provides an introduction and guide to techniques derived from the physical and chemical sciences for archaeologists with little or no scientific training: in short, the field of archaeometry. Techniques covered by other volumes in this series (e.g. dendrochronology[1] and materials science[2]) as well as those of the life and earth sciences have been deliberately excluded. An account of the archaeological uses of computers is, however, included.

Each chapter opens with a summary of the archaeological potential of the technique described in it, together with an explanation of any scientific principles necessary for its understanding. The basis of the technique is then described. Particular attention is given to common problems which may affect the accuracy or nature of the results obtained and to what constitutes a suitable sample. Discussion of laboratory procedures is kept to a minimum, except in the chapters on geophysical surveying and computers, because only in these two cases is the archaeologist likely to be actively involved in the experimental procedures. Finally, a range of examples illustrates the sort of problems where the techniques are useful. The examples were selected to illustrate both the scope and the limitations of the technique, and should not be taken as a guide to its relative importance.

In most cases, costs are not quoted. This is because, with the exception of C–14 dating, these techniques are not available on a service basis, but rather as part of a wider research project. Hence, ideally, when planning a project the archaeologist should decide which scientific techniques are likely to be of use in helping to solve the problems under consideration. He can then consult the appropriate specialists at this stage so that a collaborative research project can be planned and steps taken to ensure that the most useful samples are collected for analysis. Once an excavation is completed it is too late to decide that larger or different samples would have been better.

If, however, samples have to be selected once an excavation has been finished it is up to the archaeologist to ensure that the

1

samples chosen really are the most appropriate ones to have analysed. For example, when having samples dated, the archaeologist must be positive that they come from the context of interest. The scientist will not be pleased if, having put much effort into obtaining a date which upsets the archaeologist's hypotheses, he is then informed that maybe the sample had been re-used or had migrated from a different layer. In addition, the archaeologist should be clear about the information he would like, and should put as precise a question as possible to the scientist. For example, it is better to ask if all of a set of samples are the same age to within a given number of years, or from when in the Iron Age does a given pottery sherd date, rather than just to ask how old is the sample. Equally it is better to ask whether two brooches were made from the same metal, or from what clay was certain pottery made, rather than merely to enquire from what the object was made. It will then be easier for the scientist to decide whether he can provide the required information using the samples available and, if not, whether he or someone else could obtain any useful information. In some cases he may even be able to use smaller samples than would normally be required. The archaeologist should also explain to the scientist the archaeological background to the problem. Not only is it more interesting for the scientist if he knows why a particular date or analysis is required, but he may also be able to suggest to the archaeologist ways of obtaining information that could shed additional light on the problem. Finally, the archaeologist should give the scientist as much information as possible about the sample he is submitting. For example, if he wants dates for several samples he should make it clear if they are all expected to be of the same age or if some are known to be older than others.

Although the main purpose of archaeometry is solving archaeological problems, the physical and chemical analysis of archaeological artefacts can also provide information of great importance to other scientists. Thus the archaeologist may find himself approached with requests for samples with specific properties. For example, he may be asked for pottery samples of known age to help geophysicists understand the past behaviour of the Earth's magnetic field; or he may be asked for wood of known age for studies on how the rate of C–14 production has varied in the past. In such cases, while the information obtained may not be of immediate relevance to the archaeologist it may eventually enable more accurate dates to be obtained for archaeological samples. In such cases, if the archaeologist is doubtful as to whether the samples are suitable it may be better not to provide them, or at the very least, he should make clear to the scientist any uncertainties in their date or origin.

While this book provides an account of the techniques currently available (1985) new scientific techniques are constantly being developed and old ones improved. Thus, if the archaeologist is to make best use of the available possibilities, he needs to take note of future developments. Unfortunately, primary publications in the area of archaeometry are scattered through a large number of journals and will often require a considerable scientific background for their full appreciation. This book should, however, give the archaeologist sufficient feeling for the techniques currently being developed and used for him to follow most of the publications in the three main journals: *Archaeometry*,[3] *Journal of Archaeological Science*[4] and *Science and Archaeology*.[5] He may, nevertheless, find it preferable to rely on contacts with scientists working in the area for news of developments.

Finally, a few words of warning. For reasons explained in Chapter 2, C–14 dates may be quoted in either radiocarbon or calendar years, without any attempt to distinguish between the two, or it even being clear that the dates given for artefacts are based on C–14 dates. Thus, when a date for a sample in a paper is given as, say, 7,000 BP, it may be impossible to decide whether it is in calendar or radiocarbon years. Hence, although the author favours the practice, common in archaeological journals, of using upper case AD, BC and BP for dates in calendar years and lower case ad, bc and bp for dates in radiocarbon years, it has been necessary in this book to follow the exact usage in the original publications and so in some cases AD, BC and BP will be found to have been used for radiocarbon years. Secondly, while in general any word which is not specifically defined here can be taken to have its normal English meaning, it must be pointed out that in archaeometry 'non-destructive' frequently only means that the appearance of an object is unaffected: some of its other properties may, however, be changed. Thus, if an archaeologist wishes to have an object analysed using more than one technique, he should first check whether any of the techniques will make it impossible to use one of the other techniques. Finally, billion has been used throughout to mean 1,000 million (10^9).

Notes and Further Reading

Further examples of some of the techniques described in this book can be found in 'The Archaeologist and the Laboratory' *CBA Research Report* no. 58 edited by Patricia Phillips (Council for British Archaeology, 1985). The examples are grouped by material rather than technique and there is very little discussion of the different techniques as such. The general field of archaeometry is discussed further in *Future Directions in Archaeometry* edited by Jacqueline S. Olin (Smithsonian Institution, 1982).

1. M. G. L. Baillie, *Tree-ring Dating and Archaeology* (Croom Helm, 1982).
2. A book on materials science by E. A. Slater is in preparation.
3. *Archaeometry* is published twice yearly by the Research Laboratory for Archaeology and the History of Art, Oxford University.
4. The *Journal of Archaeological Science* is published six times a year by Academic Press. It contains articles on techniques derived from the earth and life sciences as well as physics and chemistry.
5. *Science and Archaeology* is published once a year by the Research Centre for Computer Archaeology and is the journal which most frequently contains articles on the uses of computers in archaeology.

2 RADIOCARBON OR CARBON–14 DATING

2.1 Introduction

Carbon–14 or C–14 dating, as it is often abbreviated, is the most widely used of the scientific techniques available to the archaeologist for several reasons. Firstly, it has been available for sufficient time to have become well-established, unlike some of the newer techniques. Secondly, for the dating process itself, all that is needed is a sample of carbon that can be directly related to the problem of interest. Thus, as carbon is present in all living things, samples for dating can be obtained from bones, wood (including charcoal), or the other organic remains frequently found on archaeological sites. Thirdly, at present, it can be used for samples up to about 50,000 years old and it is hoped that this limit can be extended back to around 100,000 years by the use of new techniques. For recent samples the major limitation is the uncertainty in the dates which, at best, is normally around 200 years. This means that in some periods, for example during Roman times, stylistic dating may offer a more precise date. Finally obtaining samples is a simple process because, compared to TL (thermoluminescence) dating, burial conditions are unimportant. It is thus possible (though not normally to be recommended) to send samples for dating many years after they were excavated.

Although C–14 dating has been around for a long time, the last few years have seen several important developments. The first arose out of the early realisation that the relationship between the measurements on the sample and its age were not as simple as was initially assumed. Hence, in order to make the uncertainty in the sample age as small as possible, it has been necessary to produce a calibration curve to enable the results of the measurements to be turned into sample age. Much effort recently has gone into producing an improved calibration curve. The other field in which major developments have occurred is in the actual measurement of the sample ages. New equipment, including accelerator mass spectrometers and mini-counters, has been developed to enable

5

smaller samples, such as seeds and fragments of bone, to be dated. In addition, when large samples are available, measuring techniques have been improved, so that 'high precision' dates, in which the uncertainties in the date are much smaller than with conventional techniques, are available.

2.2 Principles Behind C–14 Dating

2.2.1 Atoms and Isotopes

The smallest part into which matter can be broken by chemical means is the atom. Different types of atoms form the different elements, each of which has its own chemical properties. Atoms consist of a dense nucleus of positively charged particles (protons) and an approximately equal number of uncharged particles (neutrons) surrounded by a cloud of one or more negatively charged particles (electrons). Atoms contain the same number of protons and electrons and so are electrically neutral. Because the number of electrons determines the way an atom behaves in chemical reactions (i.e. its chemical properties), atoms with different numbers of protons form the different elements. There are approximately 100 different elements including carbon, nitrogen, oxygen, hydrogen and unalloyed metals (see periodic table at end for complete list). The atoms of these different elements join together to form the molecules and compounds which make up all matter, just as the 26 letters of the English alphabet can be combined to give the words which make up books.

To continue with the analogy, just as an A can be printed in several different ways, for example in Gothic or Roman script, so most elements have several different forms known as isotopes. The isotopes of an element all contain the same number of protons and electrons and so the basic chemical properties are fixed, but the number of neutrons varies. Thus the isotopes of carbon which are of importance in archaeology are those containing 6, 7 or 8 neutrons. The carbon will still behave as carbon whichever number of neutrons it contains, though properties such as boiling point, which depend partly on the mass of the atom will vary slightly between the isotopes. Different isotopes are normally distinguished in the following way. Firstly, the name of each element is abbreviated to 1 or 2 letters so carbon is commonly referred to just as C. (Beware: occasionally the abbreviation is not obvious because it is based on the Latin name of the element, e.g. iron becomes Fe and potassium K.) Then the total number of protons and neutrons in the isotope concerned is put as a superscript before the element name. Finally, the number of protons can be put as a subscript, also before the element name. Thus the isotopes of carbon already mentioned are $^{12}_{6}C$, $^{13}_{6}C$ and $^{14}_{6}C$, since all carbon atoms contain 6 protons. For isotopes frequently mentioned the form C–14 is often used: hence the term C–14 dating. The atomic number of an atom is the same as the number of protons it contains, while its mass number is the total number of protons and neutrons in the nucleus. Hence $^{12}_{6}C$ has an atomic number of 6 and a mass number of 12. Finally, nuclei containing different numbers of protons or neutrons are known as different nuclides, so $^{13}_{6}C$, $^{14}_{6}C$ and $^{14}_{7}N$ are all different nuclides.

2.2.2 Radioactive Decay

One of the ways in which the isotopes of an element differ from each other is in their lifetime. Most of those which occur naturally are stable and so appear to last for ever. This is because the number of neutrons is sufficient to counterbalance the repulsive force between the protons due to their positive charges. In a few isotopes this balance is not achieved and so they can change into different nuclides in a process known as radioactive decay. This normally involves the emission of one or more particles from the nucleus of the atom and results in the formation of a more stable nuclide. Two types of decay are particularly common. The first involves the emission of two protons and two neutrons, in a particle known as an α particle (the nucleus of the helium 4 atom), to leave an atom with an atomic number reduced by 2 and a mass number reduced by 4. An example of an α decay which is important archaeologically (see Chapters 3 and 5) is the decay of uranium 234 to thorium 230 which is often written

$$^{234}_{92}U \rightarrow \, ^{230}_{90}Th + ^{4}_{2}He$$

The other form of decay is the emission of a β particle, the electron produced when a neutron turns into a proton, which results in the atomic number of the nuclide increasing by 1 while the mass number stays the same. An important example of β emission is the decay of carbon 14 to nitrogen 14 which may be written

$$^{14}_{6}C \rightarrow \, ^{14}_{7}N + e^- \; \text{ or } \; ^{14}_{6}C \rightarrow \, ^{14}_{7}N + \beta^-$$

Figure 2.1 Fraction of initial ^{14}C (or other radioactive) nuclei remaining after successive half-lives

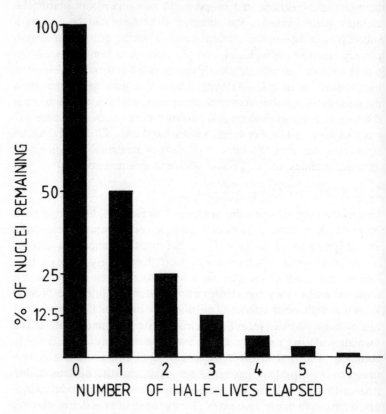

because both the mass and atomic number of the electron are zero. Often the emission of the particle leaves the nuclide in an excited state so this excess energy is lost as γ-rays, which are like very energetic (or short wavelength) X-rays, and the nuclide is left in a stable state. γ-rays are important in several areas of archaeological science (see Chapters 5 and 7). Colloquially, nuclides which undergo radioactive decay are known as radio-isotopes, so C–14 is often known as radiocarbon to distinguish it from the stable isotopes of carbon.

An important property of radio-isotopes is their half-life, which is the length of time it takes the number of atoms present of a given isotope to decrease to half its initial value. This half-life is independent of the number of atoms present, so if one counts the number remaining after a second half-life has passed one will find the half has decreased by a further half to leave a quarter of the original atoms (see Figure 2.1). Thus, if one starts with 16,000 atoms with a half-life of 10 years, after 10 years there will be 8,000 of the original atoms, after 20 years 4,000, after 30 years 2,000 and so on. Reversing the process provides a dating technique, because if one knows the original number of radioactive atoms in the sample and their half-life, and then counts the number of radioactive atoms remaining, it is easy to calculate the age of the sample. If one takes the above sample, and finds there are only 500 of the original radioactive atoms left, then one knows it is 50 years old. C–14 dating is based on this principle.

2.2.3 Basis of C–14 Dating

^{14}C is produced in the atmosphere when the neutrons associated with cosmic rays (high energy particles from outer space) collide with ^{14}N (nitrogen) nuclei in the atmosphere

$$^{14}_{7}N + ^{1}_{0}n \rightarrow\ ^{14}_{6}C + ^{1}_{1}H$$

where $^{1}_{0}n$ is a neutron and $^{1}_{1}H$ a proton or nucleus of a hydrogen atom.

This ^{14}C combines with oxygen in the atmosphere to form carbon dioxide and so becomes mixed with the stable ^{12}C and ^{13}C which are also present in the atmosphere as carbon dioxide. This carbon in the atmosphere, along with that in the rest of the biosphere (plants and animals and carbon dioxide dissolved in the oceans) form the carbon exchange reservoir. Carbon is continuously moving from one part of the reservoir to another so the concentration of ^{14}C throughout the reservoir is approximately constant. The processes involved in this exchange start with photosynthesis, in which plants take in carbon dioxide from the atmosphere and use it to make new material. The plants are then either eaten by animals, resulting in the transfer of carbon dioxide from the atmosphere to the animal, or they die and decompose so that the carbon dioxide returns to the atmosphere. The animals themselves either are eaten or die and decompose, so that the remaining carbon dioxide is returned to the atmosphere. In addition, the carbon dioxide dissolved in the oceans is continuously leaving them to re-enter the atmosphere and is replaced by fresh carbon dioxide from the atmosphere (see Figure 2.2). Carbon 'locked up' as carbonates in rocks like limestone or buried

Figure 2.2 The carbon cycle

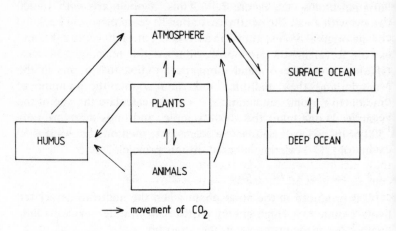

movement of CO_2

deep underground as oil and gas does not form part of the ex-change reservoir.

Within the exchange reservoir the production of ^{14}C is in equilibrium with its decay, because the production and decay of ^{14}C in the atmosphere has been occurring for much longer than the half-life of ^{14}C. Therefore, the amount of ^{14}C present in the reservoir remains approximately constant at 62 tons. This means that roughly 1 in 10^{12} atoms of carbon are ^{14}C rather than ^{12}C or ^{13}C. However, when living things die no new carbon enters them so, because ^{14}C is radioactive, the fraction of the carbon which is ^{14}C slowly decreases. Hence, by measuring the amount of ^{14}C present in dead materials it is possible to determine their age, because half-life of ^{14}C has been measured and found to be 5730 years. Thus, providing the ^{14}C content of materials can be accur-ately measured, the decay of ^{14}C provides a useful means of determining the age of archaeological materials.

2.2.4 Assumptions Behind C–14 Dating

(a) The rate of production of C–14 in the atmosphere is constant. This assumption is necessary to enable the initial ^{14}C content of the sample being dated to be calculated. If the rate of production of ^{14}C is constant then, since the decay of ^{14}C is in equilibrium with its production, the amount of ^{14}C in the carbon exchange reservoir will remain constant. Hence the initial ^{14}C content of ancient plant

and animal remains will be the same as that of similar modern material. In practice this assumption only holds approximately and the proportion of carbon in the exchange reservoir which is ^{14}C changes slightly from year to year. During the past century man's activities have had a drastic effect on the quantity of ^{14}C in the reservoir (see Section 2.2.5) but these effects can be allowed for. More serious problems for C–14 dating arise because the number of cosmic rays entering the Earth's atmosphere varies from year to year. When the number of cosmic rays per year is low, the rate of ^{14}C production will also be low and so the quantity of ^{14}C in the exchange reservoir will decrease. Measurements have shown that the concentration of ^{14}C in the atmosphere can change by 10 per cent over several thousand years. Thus, the initial ^{14}C concentration of old samples will be uncertain by this amount. This problem can, at least since the last glaciation, be overcome by the use of calibration curves in which the present day ^{14}C content of samples of known age is plotted against the age of the sample. The age of a sample of unknown date can then be found by finding the date (or dates) corresponding to the ^{14}C content of the sample. This means that C–14 dating can no longer be regarded as being an absolute dating method, but rather provides only relative dates which, in some cases, can be calibrated to give calendar dates.

(b) The sample freely exchanged carbon with the reservoir during its lifetime but no exchange occurred after death. Normally all the ^{14}C in living plants and animals does come from the atmosphere. The main exception is if the water supply contains dissolved carbonates, because in such carbonates the ^{14}C concentration will be less than that of the atmosphere. Hence the initial ^{14}C concentration of the sample will be lower than expected, leading to an overestimate of its age. This is a particular problem with shells and marine samples because the ^{14}C content of the deep oceans is about 2,000 years old. Hence special steps have to be taken to correct for this effect. The requirement that no ^{14}C enters the sample after death is more difficult to fulfil and is discussed in Section 2.3.2b.

(c) The half-life of ^{14}C does not change and is known accurately. It is generally accepted that the half-lives of radioactive nuclides do not change and are unaffected by external circumstances such as temperature. The accurate measurement of half-lives is more

difficult and, in fact, the value for the half-life initially used for C–14 dating was 5568 years which is 3 per cent lower than the currently accepted value of 5730 years. This results in an error of 100 years in a 3,000 year old sample where the quoted error is likely to be ±50 years. To avoid confusion the old half-life is always used when publishing dates.

(d) The concentration of ^{14}C in living things is the same as the concentration in the atmosphere. Again, in practice, this assumption only holds approximately and the ^{14}C concentration in plants is approximately 4 per cent lower than that in the atmosphere. This problem of 'fractionation' is discussed in more detail in Section 2.3.2a.

2.2.5 *The Effect of Man on the ^{14}C Concentration of the Atmosphere*

Over the past century man's activities have had a marked effect on the concentration of ^{14}C in the atmosphere. From 1850 onwards the burning of fossil fuels led to a decrease in the ^{14}C concentration because coal and oil are made from plants which died millions of years ago and so contain effectively no ^{14}C. Thus, the use of fossil fuels adds ^{12}C and ^{13}C to the atmosphere without adding any ^{14}C. This resulted in a 3 per cent decrease in the atmospheric ^{14}C concentration between 1850 and 1950. Since 1950 the testing of atomic weapons in the atmosphere has released particles which created extra ^{14}C and has resulted in a twofold increase in the concentration of ^{14}C in the atmosphere. The introduction of the atmospheric test ban treaty in 1964 means that the atmospheric ^{14}C concentration is no longer increasing. In fact, at present, it is decreasing because the extra ^{14}C is slowly being distributed through the whole carbon exchange reservoir. The movement of this extra ^{14}C is currently being studied to establish how ^{14}C moves from the atmosphere to the ocean. It is expected that when this distribution process is complete the final increase in the ^{14}C in the atmosphere will only be about 3 per cent. Thus references to the natural or modern atmospheric concentration of ^{14}C normally mean the concentration in 1850 before man's activities began to affect it.

2.3 Conventional Dating Techniques

2.3.1 *Samples and Laboratory Procedures*

The main requirement in samples for C–14 dating is that they contain sufficient carbon (normally between 1 and 2g) for the ^{14}C concentration to be easily determined. Thus wood, including charcoal, and other plant remains are the most convenient source because they contain large quantities of carbon. Some of the carbon in the sample is lost during the laboratory treatment of the sample, so for conventional dating about 30g of charcoal or 100g of dry wood is required from each sample to be dated. Bone is the other main source of samples, but here the proportion of the material which is carbon is less and the carbon content decreases as the bone ages. In addition, ribs contain less collagen than do other bones (the normal source of the carbon for dating bone) and so are less suitable for dating. Thus over a kilogram of bone may be required if a satisfactory date is to be obtained, though, in some cases, for recent bones 50g may be sufficient. This can be a serious limitation because the dating process involves the total destruction of the sample. Shells from both land and sea creatures have also been dated: here the minimum sample size is 100g. The second requirement is that the age of the sample can be directly related to the archaeological problem. This is particularly a problem with large timbers, because the wood from the centre of trees is often over 400 years old at the time of felling and timbers in buildings may either have been re-used or replaced, thus extending the uncertainty in date even further. For this reason twigs and other plant material, which would have been used within a few years of their death, are a better source of samples than thick timbers. The other requirement is that the samples are not contaminated with carbon of a different age. Thus any material which has been treated with a preservative is unlikely to provide satisfactory samples though, in exceptional circumstances, if it is known what preservatives have been used, it may be possible to remove them before dating the sample. Similarly, you should avoid smoking near the samples and touch them as little as possible to reduce the chance of introducing modern carbon into the samples. Also well preserved material is less likely to be contaminated than poorly preserved.

Again, to avoid contamination, samples should be wrapped in aluminium foil or polythene, or placed in aluminium, polythene or glass containers. Materials such as cotton wool and paper are unsuitable as it may be difficult to remove all of them from the sample when it is unpacked in the laboratory. Plastics, other than polythene, are also unsuitable because they may give off fumes which could contaminate the samples. Each sample should be wrapped separately and labelled clearly. Sample submission forms should be obtained from the laboratory which is to do the dating and one completed for each sample to be dated. Samples and forms should then be sent to the laboratory doing the dating.At some point, preferably before the samples are submitted, it is a good idea to discuss them with someone from the laboratory to check that the material is suitable for dating and also that there is sufficient of it to provide good samples. In addition the cost of the dating programme should be found out. At present (1985) most laboratories charge between £150 and £200 for each sample dated.

Once in the laboratory the sample is treated to remove likely forms of contamination (a process often referred to as pretreatment) and a series of chemical reactions carried out to separate the carbon from the other material and produce a simple chemical compound, which contains a high concentration of carbon. This may be either a gas or a liquid depending on the technique used for the actual dating. The basis of conventional C–14 dating is to count the β particles emitted by the ^{14}C while it decays radioactively, because the number of particles emitted per minute (or number of disintegrations per minute) is proportional to the concentration of ^{14}C in the sample. Hence, if this number is known, the age of the sample can be calculated. Two different types of instrument are used for the counting. In the first, the gas proportional counter, the carbon is used in the form of a gas, often carbon dioxide. This gas forms an important part of the instrument, because the passage of a β particle through it produces a signal which is detected and recorded electronically enabling the total number of particles emitted to be found. In the other instrument, the liquid scintillation counter, the carbon is turned into a liquid, often benzene. A liquid scintillator (a material which produces a flash of light whenever it is hit by a β particle or similar object) is then dissolved in it. Photomultipliers (instruments for measuring small quantities of light) are used to count the flashes of light produced and hence the number of β particles emitted can be measured. In both cases, while the counting is in progress, the samples must be carefully shielded. Otherwise cosmic rays or particles from the radioactive decay of materials other than the sample may enter the counter and, on being mistaken for β particles from the sample, be included in the count. This would lead to an underestimate of the sample age. Such shielding is easier to achieve with liquid scintillation counters, because the volume occupied by the sample is less, but this advantage is counterbalanced by carbon dioxide being easier to prepare than benzene. In both cases it is also necessary to measure standard samples containing a known amount of ^{14}C and the background level (i.e. the number of counts when no sample is present) so that the count rate for the sample can be accurately converted into the ^{14}C concentration of the sample and hence its age. In one gram of natural carbon there are approximately 15 disintegrations per minute, while to obtain an accurate age for a sample at least 10,000 disintegrations need to be counted. Thus, at least one day is needed to measure each sample, with longer times being required for older samples.

2.3.2 Experimental Problems

(a) Fractionation. This is the name given to the process by which during a chemical reaction ^{14}C reacts less readily than ^{12}C, and so alters the concentration of ^{14}C from that present before the reaction occurred. It can occur either whilst the sample material was alive or when it is processed in the laboratory. In the laboratory fractionation can be prevented by making sure that all the carbon in the initial sample is converted into the final product. By contrast, in living things only part of the available carbon is used and it has been found in plants that the ^{14}C concentration is 3 to 4 per cent lower than that in the atmosphere leading to an overestimate of the age of plant material by about 300 years. When the plants are eaten further fractionation occurs, so in bones the initial ^{14}C concentration is approximately 5 per cent lower than the atmospheric concentration. The exact amount of fractionation occurring depends on the species involved and so today it is customary to measure it for all samples which are being dated.

This is done by measuring the ratio of the two stable isotopes of carbon, ^{12}C and ^{13}C, using an instrument known as a mass spectrometer, which can measure the masses of atoms and molecules very accurately. If no fractionation occurred then the ratio ^{12}C: ^{13}C would always be the same, but any process which causes fractionation will change the ratio from that of the atmosphere. By assuming that the amount of fractionation depends only on the difference in mass between the isotopes, the fractionation produced in the ^{12}C: ^{14}C ratio can be calculated by doubling that measured for ^{12}C: ^{13}C ratio. Although this assumption appears to work well in practice, theoretical arguments suggest that it is an over-simplification, and a more detailed analysis may become necessary in the future. Any fractionation produced in the laboratory can also be measured in this way. The ^{12}C: ^{13}C ratio has also been used to provide information about ancient diets (see Chapter 6).

(b) Contamination. This section considers only those forms of contamination which may occur while the material is buried, and assumes that after excavation steps will be taken to avoid contaminating the samples. Depending on the source of the contamination it can either increase or decrease the concentration of ^{14}C in the sample, and so lead to either an under- or an overestimate of the sample age. More modern carbon can be introduced into samples either by soluble carbon compounds such as humic acids from the decomposition of more recent plant and animal remains being washed into the ancient material, or by plant roots growing into bone or wood, or by bacterial action changing the original carbon for new. These problems can be reduced by a careful selection of the samples: avoid wood with mould growing on it and bones with plant roots running through them. Also whenever possible choose solid lumps of charcoal, bone or wood rather than scrappy pieces because it will have been harder for contaminating carbon to penetrate them. In addition, if necessary, the surface layer can be removed because the centre is less likely to have been contaminated than the surface. As a further check, if possible, have two different materials dated, e.g. bone and wood, because if contamination has occurred it will have affected the two materials differently.

Older carbon can be introduced into samples as carbonates dissolved in the ground water. This may lead to the deposition of calcium carbonate within the dead material. Fortunately, in most cases, such contamination can easily be removed in the laboratory. More serious problems may arise if the main source of water for plants comes from underground reservoirs or is hard because then the concentration of ^{14}C in the water will be less than that of the atmosphere. This problem can only be overcome by comparing the age derived by C–14 dating with the known age of a similar species from the same place and using this figure to correct the ages of the samples being dated. This practice is often adopted with shells.

Recrystallisation is another source of contamination in bones and shells and results in some of the original carbonate in the material being replaced by new carbonate containing more modern carbon. This problem may be overcome by a careful examination of the samples so that any showing signs of recrystallisation are rejected, but a safer solution is to use only the organic component of the material for dating (collagen in bone and conchiolin in shells). An alternative solution arises with shells because calcium carbonate occurs in two forms: calcite and aragonite. Some species make shells containing only aragonite, but recrystallisation produces only calcite and so, by dating only aragonite, recrystallised material can be avoided.

2.4 Presentation of C–14 Dates and their Accuracy

2.4.1 Standard Form for Dates

Most laboratories which undertake C–14 dating publish their results in the journal *Radiocarbon*. The CBA (Council for British Archaeology) periodically publishes summaries of these C–14 dates, and any published elsewhere, for British sites. In *Radiocarbon* all dates are published in the same form:

	sample no.	site name	age (years bp)
			fractionation
		comment	
e.g.	X153	Avalon	3860 ± 50
			$\delta^{13}C = -24.8\%o$
		charcoal from	
		pit	

X153 is the sample number and starts with the code for the laboratory which carried out the measurements. $\delta^{13}C$ is the difference between the $^{12}C/^{13}C$ ratio for a standard sample and that measured for the sample being dated measured in parts per thousand (%o) and is used to correct for the ^{14}C fractionation that has occurred. 3860 ± 50 years bp is the part of most interest to the archaeologist because it is a measure of the age of the sample. Although, in the above form, it *appears* directly comparable with dates from other sources, there are two reasons why it is not. Firstly, although the age is given in years, they are 'radiocarbon' years not calendar years. The age in calendar years, which can be compared directly with dates from other sources, may be up to 800 years older than the radiocarbon age. The first cause of this discrepancy arises because the value of the half-life of ^{14}C used for the first dates was 3 per cent less than the currently accepted value. Therefore, to avoid confusion over what value had been used, it was agreed that all dates should be published using the original value for the half-life of 5568 years rather than the new value of 5730 years. The other cause is that the rate of production of ^{14}C has not been constant but the size of the changes is only known for the recent past so again, to avoid confusion, all dates are published on the assumption that the concentration has remained constant. To show that radiocarbon years are being used lower case letters are often used for the era, i.e. bp, bc and ad, with AD, BC and BP being reserved for calendar years. Unfortunately, this is not a universal practice so sometimes AD, BC and BP are used for radiocarbon years. In particular, scientific journals tend to use years BP for dates calculated using a standardised set of assumptions (see Gillespie[1]). For the recent past it is possible to convert radiocarbon years into calendar years, so articles in archaeological journals may contain radiocarbon dates in both radiocarbon and calendar years.

The other difference is in the error term which is the counting error and not a measure of the uncertainties in the age as it is with other dating techniques. The counting error is the uncertainty in the date which arises because the ^{14}C concentration and, hence the date, is calculated from counting the number of ^{14}C atoms which decay in a known time and assuming that this number enables an accurate estimate of the concentration to be made. The larger the fraction of ^{14}C atoms which are counted the closer the estimate will be to the actual ^{14}C concentration in the sample and hence to its age. This is because radioactive decay is a random process and so in any given period there may be more or less than the expected number of decays. A similar situation arises in throwing a dice. If it is thrown only six times it is very likely that one number (3 say) will be thrown twice while another (5 say) is not thrown at all. Thus it might incorrectly be concluded that the numbers on the dice were 1, 2, 3, 3, 4 and 6. If, instead, it is thrown one hundred times each of the six numbers will occur approximately the same number of times and so a much better idea will be obtained of the numbers on the dice.

It must also be remembered that the counting error quoted is one standard deviation (one sigma or 1σ) which gives the 68 per cent confidence limit. This means that the probability that the true

Figure 2.3 Typical range of measured ages that would be obtained by measuring 20 identical samples of age x

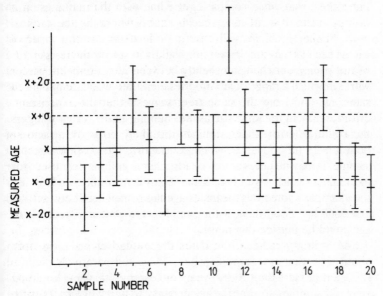

age of the sample lies between the quoted age plus the counting error and the quoted age minus the counting error is only 68 per cent. This is equivalent to saying that there is nearly a 1 in 3 chance that the true age of the sample is outside this range: for the example quoted that would be of the age of the sample lying outside the range 3910–3810 bp. To be reasonably certain that the true age is within the range covered one needs to use the 95 per cent confidence limit so that there is only a 1 in 20 chance that the true age lies outside this range. The 95 per cent confidence limit is equivalent to twice the standard deviation (i.e. the 2σ level) and so is found by doubling the quoted error (see Figure 2.3). For the sample quoted this increases the possible age range to 3960–3760 bp. For even greater certainty the 99 per cent confidence limit or 3σ level can be used.

A further complication is that the counting error is not the only source of error since experimental errors will also occur. Experimental errors arise because it is impossible to measure a quantity under exactly the same conditions on repeated occasions, and so slightly different values may be obtained on each occasion. If the length of a 10.0mm line is measured ten times the following values might be obtained 9.8, 10.1, 10.1, 9.9, 10.0, 10.2, 10.0, 9.9, 10.1 and 9.8mm. This does not mean that the line is changing length but rather, that when comparing the line with the markings on an ordinary ruler, it is difficult to decide exactly where the line starts and ends. Similar problems will arise in C–14 dating from a variety of causes such as the samples varying slightly in size or the temperature of the equipment changing slightly between measurements. Recent work, in which a range of laboratories measured wood samples of the same age and from the same tree, suggests that the experimental errors are about the same size as the counting errors.[2] Thus using just the counting error underestimates the likely error by a factor of between 2 and 3. Hence, when considering the possible age of a sample, it may be necessary to quadruple the counting error in order to obtain a realistic age range at the 95 per cent confidence limit. For the example quoted this means its age lies somewhere between 4060 and 3660 bp. Even then, if the sample were contaminated, its true age could lie outside this range.

For ordinary radiocarbon dates the quoted errors range from about ±50 years for samples where ^{14}C is comparatively plentiful (i.e. samples less than 10,000 years old) to ±2,000 years for 50,000 year old samples so that the uncertainty in age will vary between 400 and 8,000 years. It is also possible to obtain high precision dates (see section 2.5.2) where the uncertainty in age is much less (±20 years). To reduce the problems caused by the 1 in 20 'wild' dates, two or more dates should be obtained for each structure being dated because the larger the number of dates which agree the smaller the chance that they are wrong.

If two, or more, dates are obtained from the same sample such as a single skeleton or mass of charcoal, then the average value can be used as the date of the sample. This will result in a smaller uncertainty in the age of the sample because the error for the average is calculated using the following formula:

$$\frac{1}{E_A} = \sqrt{\frac{1}{\dfrac{1}{E_1^2} + \dfrac{1}{E_2^2}}}$$

where E_A is the error for the average and E_1 and E_2 the errors for the individual dates. Thus if dates of 1556±50 bp, 1519±50 bp and 1480±45 bp were obtained for a mass of charcoal they could be averaged to give a date

$$\frac{1556+1519+1490}{3} \pm \sqrt{\frac{1}{\frac{1}{50^2} + \frac{1}{50^2} + \frac{1}{45^2}}} = 1522 \pm 28 \text{ bp.}$$

Dates from different samples, even if from the same layer, should not be combined in this way because the two samples may be of different ages. For example two bits of wood, although found together, could differ in age by 400 years. A simple test of whether two dates from different objects (either from the same or different layers) are the same is to see whether their dates overlap at the 2σ level. If they do then they could be of the same date, while if they do not then they probably are not. For example dates of 2950 ± 100 bp and 2630 ± 100 bp cover a 2σ range of 3150–2750 bp and 2830–2430 bp and so could come from samples of the same age, while dates of 4635 ± 100 bp and 2546 ± 100 bp cover a 2σ range of 4835–4435 bp and 2746–2346 bp and so are extremely unlikely to come from samples of the same age. Gillespie[3] describes a more rigorous way of checking whether two or more dates could come from samples of the same age. The problems of interpreting radiocarbon dates and their errors are discussed further by Campbell et al.[4]

2.5 Recent Developments

2.5.1 Calibration Curves and the Bristlecone Pine Record

Originally it was assumed that radiocarbon years and calendar years were the same length, but as more samples, particularly from Egypt, were dated using the radiocarbon technique, it was found that although the radiocarbon dates back to about 1,000 BC in general agreed with the expected dates, for older samples the radiocarbon dates tended to be younger than expected. This led to disputes as to which method of dating was wrong and so measurements were carried out on a large number of wood samples of known age. This showed that it was the radiocarbon dates which were too young.

Initially this work was carried out using wood from bristlecone pine trees, which grow at high altitudes in the White Mountains of California where the climate is so dry that the dead trees can survive for thousands of years. Using dendrochronology it was possible to obtain wood from these trees whose year of growth was known exactly covering the period from the present back to 6,000 BC. Samples covering a 10 year time span were then dated using standard C–14 techniques and the age obtained compared with the known age of the samples. This showed that frequently the C–14 age was not the same as the expected age and that a radiocarbon year did not have a constant length. In particular, it was found that back to 1,000 BC the radiocarbon age and the calendar age differed by less than 200 years. The discrepancy then starts to grow until between 2,500 and 5,000 BC radiocarbon ages are younger than calendar ages by between 600 and 800 years. As well as the long-term trend, short-term fluctuations of 100 years or so were also visible, but there was much dispute as to whether these fluctuations were genuine or just the result of uncertainties in the measurements.

Recently, similar work[5] has been carried out on oak from Western Europe, dated by dendrochronology and covering the period from the present day back to 5,000 BC, to check that the bristlecone pine results were applicable worldwide and not just a result of the high altitude. They have shown a similar picture of short-term fluctuations superimposed on a longer term trend (see Figure 2.4). Furthermore, the fluctuations appear to be the same when plots for samples from different parts of the world are compared. This has two important consequences, in that firstly, normally, any radiocarbon year corresponds to the same calendar year everywhere in the world so that radiocarbon dates from all over the world can be compared directly with each other. Secondly, for that period (up to about 10,000 years ago, the end of the last ice age) when wood can be dated by dendrochronology it is possible to radiocarbon date samples of known age and build a calibration curve to enable radiocarbon years to be converted into calendar years. This enables radiocarbon dates to be compared directly with dates from other sources. At present several different calibration curves are in use, so when publishing calibrated dates it is essential to state which calibration curve has been used, but work is proceeding on the completion of more accurate measurements which will enable a single calibration curve to be produced.[6]

One complication when calibrating radiocarbon dates is that the scale of some of the fluctuations is such that a single radiocarbon year may correspond to two or more different calendar dates up to 400 years apart. This results in the uncertainty in the calendar age

Figure 2.4 Part of the radiocarbon calibration curve showing the existence of both short-term wiggles and long-term trends

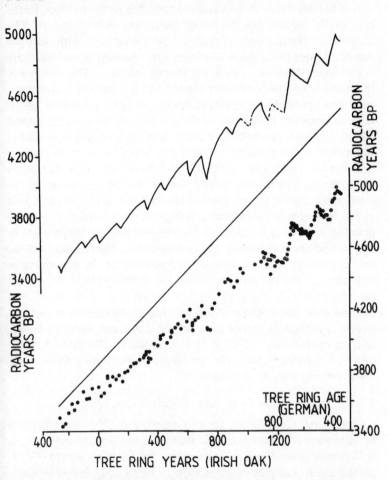

The straight line shows where the points would have to lie if radiocarbon years were equivalent to calendar years. The lower portion of the diagram shows the values obtained by measurement and the upper portion a curve fitted to the points (after G. Pearson, 'High precision radiocarbon dating by liquid scintillation counting applied to radiocarbon time-scale calibration', *Radiocarbon*, vol. 22 (1980) pp. 337–45)

being much greater than the uncertainty in the radiocarbon age. Even, if there is no ambiguity in the date, the calibration procedure will normally increase the uncertainty in the age, because the error in the calibration curve has to be added to the error in the radiocarbon age. Tables are available to enable radiocarbon years and errors to be converted to calendar years and errors.[7]

It is believed that these variations are due to fluctuations in the rate of ^{14}C production for which there are several causes. The short-term fluctuations appear to be correlated with sunspot activity,[8] since the number of cosmic rays reaching the atmosphere is less when there are a large number of sunspots. The maxima in the number of sunspots occur every 11 years, but their sizes vary, so it is not possible at present to deduce the past size of the short-term fluctuations in the rate of ^{14}C production. Thus in the period when it is not possible to obtain dendrochronologically dated samples it is not possible to build a calibration curve to convert radiocarbon years into calendar years. However, the longer-term trend in the rate of ^{14}C production is due to variations in the strength of the Earth's magnetic field and, as this can be measured in the period when dendrochronology is not possible, it may be possible to correct C–14 dates for this effect (see Chapter 4). In this period the importance of the short-term fluctuations will be less anyway as, because of the small amount of ^{14}C remaining in old samples, the uncertainty in the age is greater than the size of the short-term fluctuations. Thus a knowledge of them will not help to date the samples more accurately. Furthermore, in this period, even uncalibrated radiocarbon dates are likely to be the most accurate method of dating samples so the need for the calibration curve is less. The problems of calibrating C–14 dates are discussed further in Ottaway.[9]

2.5.2 High Precision Dates and 'Wiggle Matching'

Conventional C–14 dating aims to measure the ^{14}C concentration to within about ±0.6 per cent so that the quoted error on the age is ±50 years (one standard deviation) for samples where ^{14}C is plentiful (i.e. samples younger than 10,000 years). However such accuracy is not sufficient to enable maximum use to be made of calibration curves since the short-term fluctuations are comparable in size to the uncertainty in sample age and so are lost. It was thus desirable to be able to measure the sample age to ±20 years, corresponding to an uncertainty in its ^{14}C content of ±0.25 per cent. In principle the errors can be reduced by increasing the length of time during which the β particles emitted by the sample are counted, but this would result in fewer samples being measured each year and hence fewer dates being produced. Furthermore, as part of the error arises from uncertainties in the background count, longer counting times for the sample are likely to lead to an increase in this source of error rather than a decrease. Instead the origins of the errors were investigated and attempts made to reduce them. This has resulted in several of the laboratories carrying out C–14 dating specialising in the production of 'high precision' dates where the quoted errors are ± 0.25 per cent giving errors in the age of samples as small as ± 20 years. These errors are intended to be a realistic estimate of the total error, i.e. they are not just counting errors. In the scientific world precision and accuracy have different meanings. Precision refers to the closeness of the agreement between a set of measurements of the same quantity while accuracy refers to the closeness of the measured value to the real value. Thus the precision of a measurement is easier to determine but the accuracy is of more concern to the archaeologist. Pearson[10] has described the steps taken at Belfast to reduce errors to this level in the liquid scintillation counter there. He found it necessary to consider a variety of factors. These included changes in atmospheric pressure, because high pressure results in fewer cosmic rays getting through the atmosphere, and hence a lower background count. He also found that benzene was lost from the sample container during counting, resulting in a loss of ^{14}C from the sample, and hence an overestimate of the sample age unless allowance was made for this loss. Finally changes in the weight of the sample containers during counting made it difficult to estimate the loss of benzene. Counting errors were reduced both by using large samples containing over 10grams of carbon and by increasing the counting times.

The use of high precision data has shown that the short-term fluctuations do really exist, and are the same, at least, throughout the northern hemisphere[11] (see Figure 2.5). This has led to the development of the technique of 'wiggle matching' to reduce the errors associated with C–14 dates. For this technique a set of samples of known relative ages covering several hundred years is required. Large timbers are ideal since the relative dates of the annual rings can be found using dendrochronology. Samples can then be taken every 10 or 20 years and a high precision C–14 date obtained for each sample. This produces a set of dates which can be compared with the calibration curve. If there were no wiggles in

Figure 2.5 Comparison of radiocarbon ages of wood of identical dendrochronological age, but some from North American pines and the rest from Irish and Scottish oaks

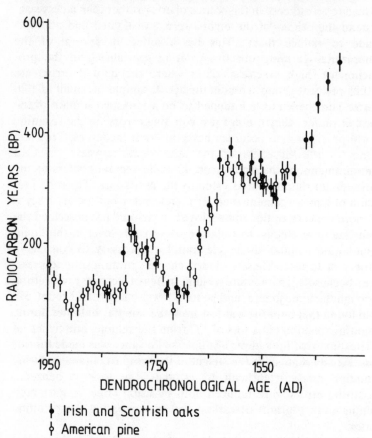

Irish and Scottish oaks
American pine

Source: After G. Pearson, 'High Precision radiocarbon dating by liquid scintillation counting applied to radiocarbon time-scale calibration', *Radiocarbon*, vol. 22 (1980), pp. 337–45

the calibration curve, then the radiocarbon age of the samples would increase steadily on moving from the youngest to the oldest sample as determined by dendrochronology. Instead, it may be found that the radiocarbon ages pass through a maximum (or minimum) producing a wiggle, which should be similar in shape to a wiggle on the calibration curve in the region expected from the uncalibrated radiocarbon dates. By carefully matching the wiggle in the radiocarbon dates with that on the calibration curve a very precise date could be obtained for the sample, with the uncertainty in the age being less than 10 years, and in particular there could be no ambiguity in the date as might arise if only a single sample from the timber had been dated. A wiggle matched date is naturally more expensive and time-consuming than a single date from a timber, but if several samples are being submitted for dating it may be possible to obtain a more precise and accurate date if the samples are chosen from a single timber so that wiggle matching is possible rather than from a variety of sources.

2.5.3 Small Samples and Accelerator Mass Spectrometry

One of the problems when using C–14 dating can be obtaining sufficient uncontaminated carbon from the sample to enable an accurate date to be obtained. Two methods have recently been developed which enable samples containing only a few milligrams of carbon to be dated, so samples which previously were too small can now be dated. New sources of samples include single seed grains, single threads from woven material and soot or food residues from pots. In addition, when plenty of carbon is available, it is possible to be more selective in choosing the carbon which is actually dated so that the chances of contaminated carbon being included are reduced.

The first method is a refinement of the gas proportional counting technique,[12] frequently used in conventional radiocarbon dating. It involves technical improvements to the equipment so that the counting of a single sample can be continued for several months until sufficient β particles have been counted, rather than having to be completed within a week. In addition, the smaller the sample that can be measured, the smaller the counter can be. This enables the background to be kept low, because it is both easier to screen a small counter from cosmic rays and also easier to build it out of non-radioactive materials. The development of these mini-counters, as they are known, enables samples containing only 20mg of carbon to be dated, so approximately 10 times less material is required than is needed for conventional dating. This technique is cheaper than the other technique for using small samples though, as long counting times are required, the technique is slow and the laboratory will need several counters if it is to count a reasonable number of samples in a year.

The other development, of high energy accelerator mass spectrometry[13] (often referred to as accelerator C–14 dating), is a more radical change, in that it involves actually counting the ^{14}C atoms present in the sample, rather than waiting for them to decay as is done in the other methods. It is a development of the ordinary mass spectrometry used to determine the $^{12}C/^{13}C$ ratio in fractionation studies. It makes it theoretically possible to count all the ^{14}C atoms present in a sample in under a day compared with conventional β counting techniques in which it would take over 80 years to count even 1 per cent of the ^{14}C atoms present. In practice, only about 1 per cent of the ^{14}C atoms are counted because not all of them are transported from the initial sample to the detector where the counting is done. The current aim is to determine the age of samples as accurately as can be done using conventional methods but using much less carbon. This requires that the age is determined with an error of ± 1 per cent. Hence, except for very old samples, only 1 mg of carbon (or less) need be measured. If such high accuracy is not needed (e.g. if the only requirement is to determine whether a seed is modern or ancient), then even less carbon can be used. A further consequence of actually counting the ^{14}C atoms present is that older samples can be dated. Currently background counts limit the age to about 60,000 years, but it is hoped that in the purpose-built machines this background can be reduced so that samples up to 100,000 years old can be dated. In this age range larger samples are required as 1 mg of 110,000 year old carbon contains only 50 ^{14}C atoms. The ultimate limit on the method may be set by the problems of obtaining such old samples free from contamination by more modern carbon. Another problem may be the creation of new ^{14}C from the nitrogen in bone by the background radiation, leading to ^{14}C content of very old bone staying constant instead of decreasing with age. The $^{12}C/^{14}C$ ratio for many samples can be measured in under an hour which, combined with the small sample required, means that it will be easier to measure several samples of the same expected age to check that reliable results are being obtained.

The other advantage of small sample size is that more materials can be dated, because carbon need only be present as a minor constituent of the sample. Thus it will become possible to date pottery by the C–14 method either by extracting food residues or soot left on it during cooking, or else by extracting the carbon introduced into the pot as plant temper during its manufacture. Iron, on average, contains 0.1 per cent carbon, most of which comes from the charcoal used as a fuel in the smithing furnace, so 1g of iron should provide sufficient carbon for dating. With plant and animal remains individual seeds or insects can be dated, making it possible to check whether controversial finds belong in the context in which they are found rather than having been brought down by natural means from a later level. In addition with bones and shells it will be possible to extract specific compounds so that the component least likely to be affected by contamination can be dated. For bone, work has been done on extracting hydroxyproline from the collagen[14] as it is found only in collagen and hence cannot be introduced by humic acid contamination or bacterial action; while for shells, it will be possible to date the protein conchiolin and thus avoid the problems of recrystallisation which occur when dating the carbonate fraction.

The possibility of using very small samples for dating does, however, increase the risk of producing misleading dates unless the archaeologist is extremely careful to ensure that the samples dated do belong in the context in which they are found. In general, it is better to have a small portion of a large object dated than all of a small one, particularly if it is the large object which is the main source of interest. For example, if a fragment of charcoal is associated with a human skull or a paleolithic bone tool it will be better to have a small piece of the bone dated, rather than all of the charcoal. Not only could the charcoal be intrusive, and hence more modern than the bone, but also by dating the bone it is the object of interest which is dated, so there can be no uncertainties caused by the charcoal having been produced from old wood. Under normal circumstances isolated seeds are probably a poor choice of sample, because they can easily move into the wrong context, and so give dates irrelevant to the feature being dated. Of course, a few seeds from a large number of seeds found together should provide a perfectly satisfactory sample provided any extra expense involved in using a small sample could be justified by the saving of the rest of the seeds for other studies.

The purpose-built accelerators for C–14 dating have only recently started to produce dates so the technique has still to develop its full potential. In particular the errors on the first dates published were much larger than the errors from conventional dating. These large errors were acceptable when the technique was being used to check whether controversial finds were ancient or modern (see section 2.6) but would limit the use of the technique as a routine dating method. However, in the latest date list from the Radiocarbon Accelerator Unit at Oxford,[15] which includes dates from the Paleolithic to the Bronze Age for sites in Britain, Europe and North America, the errors are comparable to those for conventional dating. For example, two samples of charred hazelnuts from Longmoor Inclosure gave dates of 8,930 ± 100 and 8,760 ± 110 BP where the errors are intended to be a realistic estimate of the uncertainty in the age rather than just counting errors. It would thus seem that accelerator C–14 dating is now capable of providing routine C–14 dates. At present it is not available on a commercial basis in the way that conventional C–14 dating is, but rather the laboratories using the technique will select, from the requests for dates submitted, those where they feel the problem is particularly interesting or that accelerator techniques have a particular role to play, possibly because of the small sample available.

2.6 Applications

Conventional C–14 dating is well established as a means of dating sites from the past 50,000 years when historical dating is not possible, so many C–14 dates are quoted in articles as evidence for the date of a site without further discussion. One of the first achievements of C–14 dating was to provide a chronological framework for the Neolithic and to show that the spread of framing occurred earlier and over a longer period than had been assumed previously. Recent examples of the use of conventional C–14 dating include the dating of various features at the Bronze Age settlement at Knight's Farm, Burghfield, Berkshire.[16] The dates obtained ranged from 1680 ± 50 bc for charcoal from an oven to 290 ± 120 bc for charcoal associated with angular finger-decorated pottery, though the majority of the dates lay between 1245 ± 95 bc and 565 ± 250 bc. The authors discuss the dates and suggest that the date for the oven is early because mature oak was used to produce the charcoal. They also consider the date of 290 ± 120 bc rather later than expected.

Otlet et al.[17] dated 20 samples from the Iron Age hillfort at Hascombe in Surrey, including 11 from a single pit containing both grain and charcoal. Five grain samples from this pit had a mean age of 2088±25 bp, while 3 samples of charcoal from the same pit had a mean age of 2010±51 bp. They also dated charcoal from features expected to be contemporary with the pit and found that combining all the charcoal dates for this period gave a mean age of 2020±29 bp. Thus, surprisingly, the charcoal appears to be younger than the grain, which the authors suggest is evidence for short-term fluctuations in the rate of ^{14}C production. However, as they point out, this evidence is not conclusive because the two sets of dates overlap at the 2σ level and so one cannot say with certainty that the two materials have produced different dates. They also draw attention to the current problems of calibrating C–14 dates, because the date of 2020±29 bp becomes AD 107±57 or 100 BC – AD 10 or 38±55 BC, depending on the calibration system used. Coin evidence suggested that the main period of occupation of the site was about 60–65 BC. In another case, 16 radiocarbon dates ranging from 3430±90 to 2640±70 bp were obtained for the structures excavated at Shaugh Moor.[18] The excavators used these to confirm ideas on the order in which the structures were built. They also compared dates on charcoal from post holes and hearths within the same house and argue that several of the houses were occupied for 500–600 years, though in view of the error limits on the dates the occupation period could have been shorter than this. Finally, the British Museum is engaged in dating material from the British Bronze Age in order to show how the different stages developed and overlap in various areas, and have already published enough dates to enable them to draw tentative conclusions about the development of the British Bronze Age.[19]

Other, more experimental, uses include several attempts to date a variety of shells. Shells suffer from two disadvantages compared to other materials. Firstly, normally the only part of the shell which contains sufficient carbon for dating is the calcium carbonate component. This is prone to recrystallisation and hence introduction of modern carbon. Fortunately, recrystallised calcium carbonate always forms calcite while many shells are made of aragonite. These two forms can easily be distinguished by the use of X-ray diffraction measurements (see Chapter 8) so by selecting only aragonite for dating it is possible to avoid the problem of recrystallisation. The second problem is that many molluscs use calcite from dissolved limestone (a source of 'dead' carbon) to build their shells; this can introduce up to 50 per cent 'dead' carbon into the living shell and can lead to the shells' C–14 age being too old by up to 2,500 years. Recent attempts to date shells have included measurements on modern shells of a similar species and from the same source to estimate the size of this 'hard-water' error, because it appears to depend on either the source or type of shell being studied.

Studies[20] on Margariitfera auricularia (Spengler), a freshwater mollusc from the Thames, and a similar modern species, suggested that for this species the hard-water effect was neglible. Thus the dates on the ancient shells of 4860 ± 40 bp, 4340 ± 45 bp and 4140 ± 50 bp needed no correction and showed that Margariitfera auricularia (Spengler) did survive the last glaciation and was present in Britain during the Neolithic. However, another study[21] in which charcoal and associated snail shells were dated found the dates for the shells to be approximately 500 years earlier than the date for the charcoal. This was in agreement with studies on modern snail shells from the site which gave ages roughly 500 years earlier than expected. In a final study[22] measurements on modern shells suggested the 'hard-water' effect produced an error of about 2,500 years in the age of shells from a site in the Isle of Wight. Applying this correction to the original date of 1990 ± 65 bc gave the expected Romano–British date for the site. These studies suggest that while it is possible to date mollusc shells, care has to be taken in correcting for the 'hard-water' effect and hence such dates are likely to be less accurate than dates on other materials. Burleigh and Kerney[23] suggest that the errors on shells are likely to be 5–10 per cent of the age. The alternative approach would be to remember that the dates on shells can be in error by up to 2,500 years, because the older the samples the less important such an error is.

New applications have also arisen from the use of accelerator mass spectrometry for dating small samples. This technique is still in its infancy and so the possibilities it offers are still being explored. Gillespie et al.[24] gives examples of some possible uses in a recent paper. These included dating amino acids from the collagen in an ivory gouge from Chile, charcoal in slag from Cyprus and soot encrustations on pottery. All the dates obtained agreed with the expected dates. They were also able to date directly a date stone found at Wadi Kubbaniya in Egypt. The stone had been used as evidence of early farming activities on the basis of a conventional C–14 date on some associated charcoal. On accelerator dating this charcoal gave a date of 17,150±300 bp in agreement with the conventional date but two separate fractions from the stone gave dates of 101.5 bp±2.5 per cent modern standard and 350±200 bp respectively showing that the stone was recent and hence not evidence for early farming.

Work has also been done on the development of horticulture in the United States.[25] A selection of plant remains were dated by accelerator mass spectrometry and compared with the dates obtained on associated charcoal by conventional β decay methods. They found that squash was being used 7,000 years ago as suggested by the conventional dates and that annuals were being cultivated 4,000 years ago, but that the evidence for the early introduction of maize was due to more recent maize finding its way into earlier layers. In particular, maize found in a layer dated by β decay methods to 7,920±150 bp was found to have a date of only 250±300 bp, showing that it was modern contaminant. Similarly the dates for maize found on several sites dated by β decay to around 2,000 bp range from 600±400 to 0±300 bp suggesting that in these cases the maize is also a modern contaminant. The one possible exception is Crane where β decay dates ranged from 2,050±70 to 1,710±70 bp, while the date for the maize was 1,450±350 bp. This leaves it unclear as to whether the maize really is ancient or is a modern contaminant, in which case the age was expected to be less than 1,200 bp.

Finally accelerator dating has been used to help resolve the dispute as to when man first reached America. The calciche coating one of the bones of a skeleton found buried in the Yaha desert, California had given a β decay date of 21,500±1,000 bp. This agreed with an amino acid racemisation date of 23,600±2,600 BP, but these dates were disputed as being incompatible with the cultural evidence. To resolve this dispute accelerator dating was therefore carried out using most of the remaining bone (a large part of it had been stolen earlier).[26] Both organic and inorganic fractions were measured and all gave ages of less than 4,000 bp in agreement with the cultural evidence. Measurements on two calciche fragments associated with the site gave dates of 28,700±2,000 bp and 3,050±250 bp. Work at the Radiocarbon Accelerator Unit at Oxford[27] also suggests that several of the skeletons in North America that were thought to date from before the last glaciation on the basis of acid racemisation dates calibrated using a single conventional carbon date (see Chapter 5), do not, instead they date from between 5,000 and 6,000 years ago. Thus accelerator C–14 dating has reduced the evidence for man's early arrival in North America.

Notes and Further Reading

C–14 dates for British sites are summarised in 'Archaeological site index to radiocarbon dates for Great Britain and Ireland', British Archaeological Abstracts Supplement, Council for British Archaeology. *Radiocarbon* is a journal devoted to C–14 dating and is the main place where dating laboratories publish C–14 dates and other articles on C–14 dating. It is published by the American Chemical Society.

1. Richard Gillespie, *Radiocarbon User's Handbook* (Oxford University, Committee for Archaeology, Monograph no. 3, 1984), pp. 18–24.

2. International Study Group, 'An inter-laboratory comparison of radiocarbon measurements in tree rings', *Nature*, vol. 298 (1982), pp. 619–23.

3. Gillespie, *Radiocarbon User's Handbook*, pp. 30–2.

4. J.A. Campbell, M.S. Baxter and Leslie Alcock, 'Radiocarbon dates for the Cadbury massacre', *Antiquity*, vol. 53 (1979), pp. 31–8.

5. Gordon W. Pearson, 'High precision radiocarbon dating by liquid scintillation counting applied to radiocarbon time-scale calibration', *Radiocarbon*, vol. 22 (1980), pp. 337–45. J.R. Pilcher, M.G.L. Baillie, B. Schmidt and B. Becker, 'A 7,272 year tree-ring chronology for western Europe', *Nature*, vol. 312 (1984), pp. 150–2.

6. A definitive calibration for the past 4,500 years is due to be published in a special 'Calibration' issue of *Radiocarbon* in 1986.

7. Jeffrey Klein, J.C. Lerman, P.E. Damon and E.K. Ralph, 'Calibration of radiocarbon dates: tables based on the consensus data of the workshop on calibrating the radiocarbon time scale', *Radiocarbon*, vol. 24 (1982), pp. 103–50. G.W. Pearson and M.G.L. Baillie, 'High-precision ^{14}C measurement of Irish oaks to show the natural atmospheric ^{14}C variations of the AD time period', *Radiocarbon*, vol. 25 (1983), pp. 187–96. G.W. Pearson, J.R. Pilcher and M.G.L. Baillie, 'High-precision ^{14}C measurement of Irish oaks to show the natural ^{14}C variations from 200 BC to 4000 BC', *Radiocarbon*, vol. 25 (1983), pp. 179–86.

8. A.A. Burchuladze, S.V. Pagava, P. Povinec, G.I. Togonidze and S. Usaïev, 'Radiocarbon variations with the 11 year solar cycle during the last century', *Nature*, vol. 287 (1980), pp. 320–2. P.P. Tans, A.F.M. de Jong and W.G. Mook, 'Natural atmospheric ^{14}C variation and the Suess effect', *Nature*, vol. 280 (1979), pp. 320–2. C.P. Sonnett and H.E. Suess, 'Correlation of bristlecone pine ring widths with atmospheric ^{14}C: a climate–sun relation', *Nature*, vol. 307 (1984), pp. 141–3.

9. B.S. Ottaway (ed.), *Archaeology, dendrochronology and absolute chronology* (Department of Archaeology, University of Edinburgh, 1983).

10. Gordon W. Pearson, 'Precise ^{14}C measurement by liquid scintillation counting', *Radiocarbon*, vol. 21 (1979), pp. 1–21. P.P. Tans and W.G. Mook, 'Design, construction and calibration of a high accuracy carbon–14 counting set up', *Radiocarbon*, vol. 21 (1979), pp. 22–40.

11. Pearson, 'High precision radiocarbon dating by liquid scintillation counting applied to radiocarbon time-scale calibration', pp. 337–45.

12. G.H. Harbottle, E.V. Sayre and R.W. Stonner, 'Carbon–14 dating of small

samples by proportional counting', *Science*, vol. 206 (1979), pp. 683–5. R.L. Otlet, G. Huxtable, G.V. Evans, G.D. Humphreys, T.D. Short and S.J. Conchie, 'Development and applications of the Harwell small counter facility for the measurement of ^{14}C in very small samples', *Radiocarbon*, vol. 25 (1983), pp. 565–75.

13. R.E.M. Hedges, 'Radiocarbon dating with an accelerator: review and preview', *Archaeometry*, vol. 23 (1981), pp. 1–18. E.T. Hall and Richard Burleigh, 'Accelerator dating (AMS)', *Antiquity*, vol. 58 (1984), pp. 205–6.

14. J.O. Wand, R. Gillespie and R.E.M. Hedges, 'Sample preparation for accelerator-based radiocarbon dating', *Journal of Archaeological Science*, vol. 11 (1984), pp. 159–63.

15. R. Gillespie, J.A.J. Gowlett, E.T. Hall, R.E.M. Hedges and C. Perry, 'Radiocarbon dates from the Oxford AMS system: Archaeometry datelist 2', *Archaeometry*, vol. 27 (1985), pp. 237–46.

16. Richard Bradley, Sue Lobb, Julian Richards and Mark Robinson, 'Two Late Bronze Age settlements on the Kennet Gravels: excavations at Aldermaston Wharf and Knight's Farm, Burghfield, Berkshire', *Proceedings of the Prehistoric Society*, vol. 46 (1980), pp. 217–95, especially p. 283.

17. F.H. Thompson, 'Three Surrey Hillforts: Excavations at Anstiebury, Holmbury and Hascombe 1972–1977', *Antiquaries Journal*, vol. 59, no. 2 (1979), pp. 245–318, especially pp. 305–9.

18. G.S. Wainwright and K. Smith, 'The Shaugh Moor project: second report — the enclosure', *Proceedings of the Prehistoric Society*, vol. 46 (1980), pp. 65–122 especially pp. 117–21.

19. R. Burleigh, K. Matthews, J. Ambers and I. Kinnes, 'British Museum natural radiocarbon measurements XII', *Radiocarbon*, vol. 23 (1981), pp. 14–23.

20. R.C. Preece, R. Burleigh, M.P. Kerney and E.A. Jarzembowski, 'Radiocarbon age determination of fossil Margaritifera auricularia (Spengler) from the River Thames in West London', *Journal of Archaeological Science*, vol. 10 (1983), pp. 249–58.

21. R. Burleigh and M.P. Kerney, 'Some chronological implications of a fossil molluscan assemblage from a Neolithic site at Brook, Kent, England', *Journal of Archaeological Science*, vol. 9 (1982), pp. 29–38.

22. R.C. Preece, 'The biostratigraphy and dating of a postglacial slope deposit at Gore Cliff near Blackgang, Isle of Wight', *Journal of Archaeological Science*, vol. 7 (1980), pp. 255–65.

23. Burleigh and Kerney, 'Some chronological implications of a fossil molluscan assemblage from a Neolithic site at Brook, Kent, England'.

24. R. Gillespie, J.A.J. Gowlett, E.T. Hall and R.E.M. Hedges, 'Radiocarbon measurement by accelerator mass spectroscopy: an early selection of dates', *Archaeometry*, vol. 26 (1984), pp. 15–20.

25. N. Conrad, D.L. Asch, N.B. Asch, D. Elmore, H. Gove, M. Rubin, J.A. Brown, M.D. Wiant, K.B. Farnsworth and T.G. Cook, 'Accelerator radiocarbon dating of evidence for prehistoric horticulture in Illinois', *Nature*, vol. 308 (1984), pp. 443–50.

26. T.W. Stafford Jr., A.J.T. Jull, T.H. Zabel, D.J. Donahue, R.C. Duhamel, K. Brendel, C.V. Haynes Jr., J.L. Bishoff, L.A. Payen and R.E. Taylor, 'Holocene age of the Yaha burial: direct radiocarbon determinations by accelerator mass spectometry', *Nature*, vol. 308 (1984), pp. 446–7.

27. J.L. Bada, R. Gillespie, J.A.J. Gowlett and R.E.M. Hedges, 'Accelerator mass spectrometry radiocarbon ages of amino acid extract from California paleoindian skeletons', *Nature*, vol. 312 (1984), pp. 442–4.

3 THERMOLUMINESCENCE DATING AND RELATED TOPICS

3.1 Introduction

Thermoluminescence (or TL) is the light emitted by certain minerals when they are heated. Because the amount of light emitted increases as the sample ages, it forms the basis of the dating technique known as thermoluminescence (or TL) dating. This technique is possibly best known for its use in distinguishing modern fakes from ancient ceramics in the art world, but it has also been used to date pottery and other heated materials including burnt flint and the remains of sand cores from cast metal statues. Recently, it has also been used to date calcite and loess.

For the archaeologist, TL dating has several important strengths. Firstly, it is an absolute technique so it is not necessary to calibrate the dates using measurements on samples of known ages. Secondly, it covers a wide age range since, given suitable material, it can be used to date samples from 50 to 500,000 years old, making it one of the few techniques that can provide absolute dates for early Paleolithic sites. Finally, the material being dated is normally directly associated with human activity so there are unlikely to be problems, such as re-use, which can arise with other techniques when dating large timbers. Its main drawback is that, for maximum accuracy, the burial conditions of the sample, including the water content of the soil, need to be known. This means that samples for TL dating cannot be selected once an excavation is finished. Given favourable conditions, dates can be determined to better than ±10 per cent.

Recently ESR (electron spin resonance) dating, which is based on similar basic ideas to TL dating, has been applied to materials of archaeological interest, in particular calcite. It has also been used for work where TL dating cannot be used, such as determining the temperature to which various materials (including ivory and cereal grains) have been heated in the past, and determining the provenance of marble.

36

3.2 Basic Principles

3.2.1 Origins of Thermoluminescence

Many solids consist of atoms of two elements, one of which has lost one or more electrons and so is positively charged while the atoms of the other element have one or more extra electrons. These charged atoms are known as ions and arrange themselves in regular patterns to produce an electrically neutral solid (see Figure 3.1a). Such structures are known as ionic or crystal lattices and are very rigid, because each ion can be thought of as being confined within a limited volume. Occasionally, however, this regular pattern is spoilt by a lattice defect, many types of which are known. One simple example is when an atom is replaced by a different atom which, being of the wrong size or charge, will distort the lattice near it (see Figure 3.1b). Alternatively part of a row of atoms may be missing so, again, the lattice becomes distorted in an attempt to fill the gap. Such faults in the lattice structure are known as lattice defects and play a crucial role in the production of thermoluminescence.

If this lattice is then bombarded by high energy particles such as are produced in radioactive decay, some of the electrons will be hit so hard that they will leave the atoms they are normally associated with and move through the lattice. Eventually most of them will either return to the atom they originally came from or join another atom that has also just lost an electron, but a few of them will become trapped by lattice defects. This results in some of the ions becoming more positively charged and some of the lattice defects more negatively charged (Figure 3.1c).

In many instances the electrons remain trapped for millions of years but, if given sufficient energy, they can escape from the traps and combine with a positive charge within the lattice. This recombination is often brought about by heating the sample and can result in the emission of a small flash of light — the phenomenon known as thermoluminescence. The amount of energy required to release an electron from a trap depends on the type of trap involved so different traps are said to have different depths. Deep traps require more energy for the electrons to be released from them than shallow ones. If, when the sample is heated, the light output is plotted against temperature a series of peaks will be observed (a glow curve). These peaks correspond to the common trap depths within the sample and their height is a measure of the number of trapped electrons (see Figure 3.2).

Figure 3.1 Crystal lattices and the production of TL

(a)

(b)

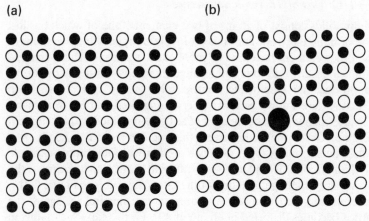

A perfect crystal lattice: all the ions are arranged in regular rows and columns

A crystal lattice containing a lattice defect caused by an impurity ion. Because the impurity ion is larger than the other ions, the lattice near it is distorted so that the ions near the impurity are not in regular rows and columns

(c)

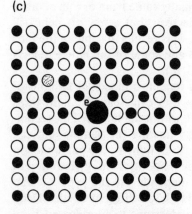

A situation in which TL may be produced. An electron has been trapped by the impurity ion and on returning to its original position will emit a flash of light

● positive ion
○ negative ion
◉ neutral atom
⬤ impurity ion
e electron

Figure 3.2 A typical glow curve

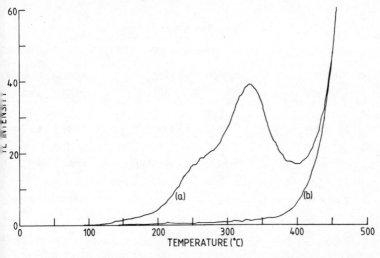

Curve *a* is the light output due to the TL stored in the pottery and curve *b* the blackbody radiation due to the sample being hot. (Courtesy Dr M.J. Aitken)

3.2.2 Properties of Radioactive Particles

Before thermoluminescence can be used to date materials it is necessary to know how it increases with time in a crystal. One of the main factors affecting this is the type and energy of the radioactive particles hitting the crystal and producing the trapped electrons. In the archaeological context the material being dated is frequently quartz crystals extracted from pottery which has been buried in soil for thousands of years. The radioactive particles producing the trapped electrons thus come from the decay of nuclei in both the soil and the pottery (but not the quartz) and are produced mainly by four sources. These start with the decay of uranium 238, uranium 235, thorium 232 and potassium 40. U–238, U–235 and Th–232 all decay into unstable daughters (i.e. products which undergo further decays) before finally producing stable nuclides (see Figure 3.3). Such a sequence of decays is known as a decay chain. The decay of K–40, however, produces stable daughters. Eighty-nine per cent of its nuclei undergo β decay to produce calcium 40 but in 11 per cent of decays the K–40 nucleus captures an electron and emits a γ ray to become argon 40. This electron capture process forms the basis of potassium–argon

Figure 3.3 The decay chains of most importance in TL dating

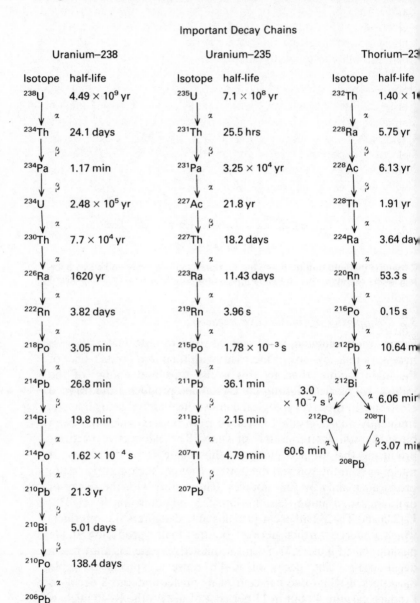

Important Decay Chains

Uranium–238		Uranium–235		Thorium–23	
Isotope	half-life	Isotope	half-life	Isotope	half-life
^{238}U	4.49×10^9 yr	^{235}U	7.1×10^8 yr	^{232}Th	1.40×1
^{234}Th	24.1 days	^{231}Th	25.5 hrs	^{228}Ra	5.75 yr
^{234}Pa	1.17 min	^{231}Pa	3.25×10^4 yr	^{228}Ac	6.13 yr
^{234}U	2.48×10^5 yr	^{227}Ac	21.8 yr	^{228}Th	1.91 yr
^{230}Th	7.7×10^4 yr	^{227}Th	18.2 days	^{224}Ra	3.64 day
^{226}Ra	1620 yr	^{223}Ra	11.43 days	^{220}Rn	53.3 s
^{222}Rn	3.82 days	^{219}Rn	3.96 s	^{216}Po	0.15 s
^{218}Po	3.05 min	^{215}Po	1.78×10^{-3} s	^{212}Pb	10.64 m
^{214}Pb	26.8 min	^{211}Pb	36.1 min	^{212}Bi	
^{214}Bi	19.8 min	^{211}Bi	2.15 min	^{212}Po ^{208}Tl	3.0×10^{-7} s / 6.06 min
^{214}Po	1.62×10^{-4} s	^{207}Tl	4.79 min	^{208}Pb	60.6 min / 3.07 min
^{210}Pb	21.3 yr	^{207}Pb			
^{210}Bi	5.01 days				
^{210}Po	138.4 days				
^{206}Pb					

The α and β indicate the particles emitted in the decays dating (see Chapter 5). These radioactive decays thus provide α, β and γ rays of a variety of energies which may produce trapped electrons within the quartz crystals. The half-lives of the parent nuclei are so long that their concentration in the soil and pottery can normally be taken to be constant.

However, not all of these particles can travel equally far in soil or pottery, because some are stopped by much less material than others. Most α particles can be stopped by a sheet of paper and have an average range in pottery of $25\mu m$ (micrometres or 10^{-6} metres). Thus α particles from the soil are unimportant in producing trapped electrons in pottery and even those in the pottery itself only affect the outer surface of the quartz crystals. β particles have a greater range, with most only being stopped by a thinnish metal sheet and having a range in pottery of a few millimetres. Thus provided thick (greater than 0.5cm) sherds are used only β particles from the pottery itself will be important in producing trapped electrons and these may not reach the centre of large quartz crystals. Finally γ-rays are much more penetrating, requiring several centimetres of lead (a substance which is very efficient at stopping radiation) to stop most of them. In pottery their average range is 30cm, so γ-rays from the soil as well as from the pottery are important in producing trapped electrons in the quartz.

Thus, when determining the rate at which trapped electrons are produced in a crystal, it is necessary to consider the type of particles likely to be hitting the crystals as well as their number.

3.2.3 The Basis of TL Dating

For the growth of TL to provide a useful dating technique for the archaeologist, it must be possible to relate the start of the growth of the sample's TL to the archaeological event of interest. In pottery this is provided by the firing, because it heats the clay to a sufficiently high temperature to empty or drain the traps of any electrons which entered them in geological times. Then the traps slowly start to fill as the crystals within the pottery are bombarded by the radiation produced by the decay of the radionuclides present in the pottery. Once the pottery is buried, radionuclides in the surrounding soil also contribute to the bombardment of the crystals. Thus, as time passes, the number of electrons trapped slowly increases and by measuring the number of electrons trapped (e.g. by producing a glow curve) the age of the sample can be found. This is the basis of TL dating.

In practice, the procedures involved are rather more complicated than this suggests, because the number of electrons trapped does not depend just on the age of the sample. It also depends on the radiation dose received: that is on the number and type of particles bombarding the sample. It is thus necessary to measure both the radiation produced by the pottery itself and also that produced by the soil in which it was buried, and then to calculate the amount of this radiation which will actually contribute to the production of TL. In addition, it is also necessary to measure the number of traps within the sample, because the more traps there are the more TL that will be produced in a given time.

Apart from pottery other heated materials which can be dated using this method include stones, heated flint, lavas and some types of slag. TL dating has also been applied to materials which have not been heated in the past. When crystals form their electron traps are empty, but the traps slowly fill over time as with pottery. Thus TL dating has been applied to crystalline materials such as calcite, whose date of formation can be of interest to archaeologists. Alternatively, with wind-blown soil like loess, the exposure to sunlight while it is in the air may empty the electron traps. The date of its deposition as a sediment can then be found by measuring the TL which has built up since that event.

3.3 Standard TL Dating

3.3.1 Sample Requirements

Whenever possible the site to be dated should be discussed with the scientist who will make the measurements, because selecting the most suitable samples can be difficult. In addition, it is desirable that the radiation dose received by each sample from the soil (the environmental dose) be measured as accurately as possible. This will require the scientist to visit the site on one or more occasions, because it is best done using a technique known as TL dosimetry, in which metal capsules containing a substance which is affected by radiation in a similar way to pottery but much more quickly, are buried at the place from which the samples are to be taken. The capsules are left in place for between several months and a year, before being taken to the laboratory where the radiation dose they have received will be measured and the average radiation dose during the year found. If it would not be possible to recover the capsules at a later date (for instance in a rescue dig on a building site) then the radiation dose from the soil can be determined in a few minutes using a scintillation counter. This technique, though less accurate than TL dosimetry, is sufficiently accurate for most purposes. The detector of the counter is placed in a hole 10cm wide and at least 30cm deep in the soil surrounding the sample.

If the scientist is visiting the site to measure the environmental dose, then he will be able to advise on the most suitable samples and ensure that they are collected properly. If not, then the following procedures should be followed. For heated materials such as pottery, burnt clay and flint, 6 to 12 samples which have been heated to at least 450°C are required from each feature to be dated. In all cases the outer layer of the sample is discarded in the laboratory because its TL may have been affected by exposure to sunlight. For flint the laboratory needs to be able to remove the outer 2mm of the sample to leave a disc at least ½cm by 3cm. Thus the flints submitted must be at least 1cm by 3½cm. Irregular shaped flints are no use unless they will produce a disc this size or bigger. For pottery and other heated materials the samples should weigh at least 10g and be at least 6mm thick. In all cases larger samples are better. If possible a variety of fabric types or materials should be submitted in case some prove unsuitable for dating. The samples themselves should have been buried to a depth of at least 30cm for at least two-thirds of their age, otherwise the environmental dose will be difficult to estimate. In addition, if possible, the samples should be at least 30cm from any boundary such as the edge of a pit or a change of soil type and also from large stones as, again, such factors make the estimate of the environmental dose less accurate.

In order that the TL carried by the samples is preserved intact, they should be placed in opaque plastic bags within a few minutes of being removed from the soil. In addition, exposure to high temperatures (above 100°C), direct sunlight, ultra-violet, infra-red, x-rays, β-rays and γ-rays should be avoided. One of the factors affecting the radiation dose received by the samples is their water content, and that of the surrounding soil, because a high water content will reduce the amount of radiation reaching the crystals which can carry TL. Therefore, the samples should not be washed and the bags they are placed in should be tightly tied, so that the water content of the samples can be estimated in the laboratory. If washing is essential, then no detergents or other additives should be used and the samples should not be dried. In addition, the laboratory should be told whether or not the samples have been washed.

Because the radiation dose from the soil is important when calculating the age of the sample, detailed information about the burial conditions of the sample should accompany it. This should take two forms: firstly, samples of the different soil types and other material within 30cm of the sample should be placed in individual plastic bags and tightly tied, so that their moisture content can be measured in the laboratory. Small stones should be present in their original proportions. For ceramic samples only a small handful of each soil is required, but for flints ½kg of soil should be submitted as the environmental dose is relatively more important in producing TL in flint than in pottery. Because only the moisture content and radionuclides present in these samples are going to be measured and not their ancient TL, exposure to sunlight and other forms of radiation does not matter once they have been bagged. Secondly, detailed diagrams and photographs, showing from where the samples were taken and the soil types and other deposits for 30cm around the sampling points, should be submitted at the same time. It is important that any large stones or rocks present are accurately marked because they will affect the radiation dose received by the samples. In addition, as much information as possible about how typical the water content of the soil samples submitted is and how it varies between contexts should be included. If the water table has ever been near the sampling site, any information about changes in its level are also important. Finally, any information about short- or long-term changes in rainfall is also useful.

For loess the basic sampling procedures are similar. At present only wind-blown sediments can be dated, so sediments containing a non-wind-blown component should be avoided. In addition, sediments which have a high carbonate or organic component are also unsuitable for dating. When obtaining the sample it must not be exposed to direct sunlight and exposure to daylight or fluorescent light should be kept to less than 10 minutes. The best samples come from the centre of a layer at least 60cm thick. For each date two samples of loess, each weighing about ½kg, are required. The first centimetre of the exposed loess should be removed. Then the samples should be collected and placed in opaque, moisture-tight containers, which should then be placed in black plastic bags. The whole operation should be carried out as quickly as possible, so that the samples are exposed to light for the minimum practical length of time. In addition, if the environmental dose is not being determined by on-site measurements, a further ½ to 1 kg of loess is needed for this. The container for this sample does not need to be opaque or moisture-tight. Finally, any information about the likely water content of the loess during its burial should be included with the samples.

For some types of material it is essential that the scientist visits the site and determines the environmental dose by on-site measurements. With calcite the environmental dose from the surrounding sediment is likely to be more important than the radioactive minerals within the calcite itself in producing the trapped electrons responsible for TL. In addition, the irregular shape of many calcite deposits makes calculating the environmental dose difficult. Hence, on-site measurement of the environmental dose is essential. Stalagmitic floors, stalagmites, stalactites and fragments of calcite buried in thick layers of sediment can all be dated, providing a sample at least a few centimetres across can be obtained. Again, if burnt stones are being sampled, the environmental dose needs to be determined by on-site measurements before the structure is disturbed. In other cases, if it appears that there might be problems in determining the environmental dose (e.g. if dating pot sherds from a rock-cut ditch) then the scientist who will do the dating should be consulted before the samples are removed, so that the environmental dose can be measured on-site, if this is thought to be desirable.

From the above account, it will be seen that the decision to collect samples for TL dating is best made before an excavation is started, so that when suitable samples are located they can be bagged immediately. If it is possible that samples for TL dating might be required once an excavation is finished, then areas of the site should be left undisturbed, so that samples can be obtained from them later on.

3.3.2 Laboratory Procedures

Several different techniques are used by TL laboratories to obtain dates, though the two basic steps involved are the same, because in all cases the date is found using the equation:

$$\text{age} = \frac{\text{archaeodose}}{\text{dose-rate}}$$

Thus one first has to determine the archaeodose, i.e. the total amount of radiation absorbed by the material being dated since the event of interest. One then measures the dose-rate, i.e. the amount of radiation per year produced by both the environment and the sample itself which contribute to the archaeodose.

Two main techniques are in use: the quartz-inclusion technique and the fine-grain technique. For both techniques the first step in the laboratory is the same, namely the extraction from the sample submitted of crystal grains of a suitable size and material for the TL dating technique being used. In the quartz-inclusion technique mineral grains 100μm in diameter or larger are extracted from the crushed sample and treated with hydrofluoric acid. The treatment is designed to remove the outer surface of quartz grains, which have absorbed the α particles emitted by the sample and completely dissolve the other mineral grains present. Because the quartz grains themselves are almost non-radioactive, the centres of such grains have been affected only by the environmental dose and the dose from the rest of the sample. Thus the difficulties in measuring the proportion of the dose-rate due to α particles are avoided. In addition quartz is unaffected by some of the problems which afflict the other materials, such as felspars, used in TL dating. In the fine-grain technique only grains less than 10μm are used so α particles contribute to the dose-rate as well as β particles and γ-rays.

In a third technique, the felspar-inclusion technique, alkali felspar grains are separated from the other minerals present in the sample, by using the fact that the felspars are less dense than the other minerals and will float in suitable liquids while the rest of the material sinks. The felspar grains are then divided into groups according to size and a date obtained for each size range.

Dating felspar has several advantages over dating quartz. They produce a stronger TL signal and can also be used to date earlier samples (up to 500,000 years old) because they saturate more slowly (see section 3.3). In addition, if large grains (above 1mm in diameter) are dated, the main contribution to the dose-rate is from the potassium that forms part of the felspar, so the uncertainties in the measurement of the dose-rate from the environment and the rest of the sample become less important. The main disadvantage of using felspars is that some of them suffer from anomalous fading (see section 3.3).

Once grains of a suitable size and mineral have been selected equal numbers of them are deposited on a series of discs, which are used in the determination of the age of the sample. The first step is to measure the TL carried by the grains on one of the discs. This is done by heating it quickly to 500°C and using a photo-multiplier to measure the light output. A plot of the light output against temperature is made (i.e. a glow curve is produced) which can be used to calculate the amount of TL carried by the grains. Unfortunately, grains from different samples acquire different amounts of TL when subjected to the same amount of radiation. Hence it is necessary to determine the sensitivity of the sample, i.e. the amount of TL acquired by the sample when subjected to a known quantity of radiation. This is done by subjecting several of the discs to known amounts of radiation and obtaining glow curves from them. By making the amount of radiation given similar to the expected archaeodose it is possible to compare the amount of TL emitted by the unirradiated disc with that emitted by the irradiated discs and hence calculate the archaeodose. In the quartz-inclusion technique the discs need only be subjected to β radiation because the sensitivity to γ-radiation is similar to that for β radiation; but when using fine grains some of the discs must also be subjected to α radiation because the sensitivity of the grains to this may be different.

For recent samples (medieval and later) the light output above 300°C due to TL may be so weak that it cannot be distinguished from the background light level. (All materials, when heated to sufficiently high temperatures, emit light: this is why coals in a fire glow. The TL output of a crystal, therefore, needs to be sufficiently strong that it can be distinguished from this background light, known as blackbody radiation.) This means that the quartz-inclusion and fine-grain techniques cannot be used for recent samples. Instead the pre-dose technique is suitable. This uses the change in sensitivity of the peak at 110°C in the quartz glow curve which occurs when the sample is heated after being subjected to a small dose of radiation. The size of the change provides a measure of the archaeodose and hence the age of the sample. The pre-dose technique can only be used for samples less than about 1,000 years old because when the archaeodose is large no change in sensitivity occurs.

The annual dose-rate can be measured while the archaeodose is being determined because it involves measurements on all the minerals present in the sample rather than on selected grains. The first step is to measure the ability of the sample to take up water because this affects the fraction of the α and β particles emitted by the sample which will produce TL in the grains being dated. The sample is then dried, powdered and the number of β particles emitted measured so that their contribution to the dose-rate can be found. This is often done by measuring the TL produced by the β particles in a TL phosphor (a material which is very sensitive to TL). If the α dose-rate is important, the α particles emitted by the sample are also counted and their contribution to the dose-rate calculated. In addition, when using the felspar inclusion technique, the potassium content of the felspar grains is measured using a standard analytical technique such as atomic absorption spectroscopy (see Chapter 7) so that the contribution of the potassium to the dose-rate can also be calculated.

Finally, if the environmental dose-rate was not measured at the site, this is done by measuring the radiation from the soil submitted along with the sample. Assumptions are then made about the relative importance of α, β and environmental radiation in producing the TL in the sample being studied so that they can be combined to give the total dose-rate. The age of the sample can then be calculated. The steps involved in dating a sample are discussed in more detail by Fleming and by Aitken.[1]

3.3.3 Problems

The problems which can arise in the laboratory with TL dating fall into two groups: those which arise when trying to determine the annual dose-rate and those which arise because the TL of the sample does not behave as predicted by simple theories and hence lead to problems in determining the archaeodose. Probably the main limitation in determining the annual dose-rate is set by variations in the water content of the sample and surrounding soil while it was buried. Ages differing by 40 per cent can be produced, depending on whether it is assumed a sample is completely dry or saturated with water. While such extreme cases should not arise, the effect of long-term climatic changes (TL dating can be used on samples from before the last ice age) can lead to uncertainties in age of up to ±4 per cent. In addition water may transport soluble uranium or thorium salts to or from the sample and its surroundings and thus the annual dose-rate, as determined today, will not reflect the average annual dose-rate experienced in the past by the sample.

Figure 3.4 Non-ideal relationships between amount of TL emitted and radiation dose absorbed

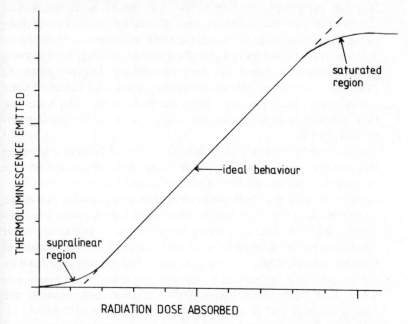

The central portion of the curve shows the ideal, i.e. amount of TL increasing linearly with radiation dose. The lower portion of the curve shows supralinearity and the upper portion saturation

Another complication in determining the annual dose-rate is that radon (one of the elements in the decay chains for both uranium and thorium) is a gas. It can thus diffuse out of the pottery, resulting in the annual dose-rate decreasing from the time of burial to the present. If this problem were overlooked, the age of the sample could be overestimated by up to 20 per cent. Fortunately, the rate of escape of radon from the sample can be measured in the laboratory and corrected for.

Non-ideal behaviour of the sample's TL occurs in several forms. The first two arise because the assumption that TL increases linearly with radiation dose does not hold for all radiation doses. In supralinearity, which occurs in samples which have only experienced small radiation doses, the TL increases more slowly than does the radiation dose. A correction for this effect can be calculated from the measurements made in the laboratory. By contrast, saturation occurs in samples which have absorbed large quantities of radiation so the growth of TL with radiation dose becomes sublinear (see Figure 3.4): i.e. the TL increases more slowly than does the radiation dose. Saturation arises when most of the electron traps in the sample are full, and hence, any electron knocked out of place by radiation becomes more likely to combine with a positive charge within the crystal than to fall into an electron trap. Saturated samples cannot be dated, and hence, if the annual dose-rate is low, TL dating can be used for older samples than when it is high. Saturation can be detected by laboratory measurements.

A further form of non-ideal behaviour is that heating a sample may change its TL sensitivity. This means that the amount of TL produced in the sample by a fixed radiation dose will depend on whether or not the sample has been heated. In particular, consider a sample which has been heated to produce a glow curve from its ancient TL and has then been subjected to a radiation dose equivalent to that which produced the ancient TL. If this sample is then heated to obtain a second glow curve and the two glow curves compared it may appear that they were produced from a sample which had been given two different, rather than equivalent, radiation doses and so the sample's age would be calculated incorrectly. This problem can be eliminated by suitable laboratory procedures.

Spurious TL can also cause problems because, if its presence is not recognised, it may lead to an overestimate of the sample age. It is the name given to any TL not produced by radiation from the radioactive decay of nuclides in the sample and its environment. It can be caused by chemical reactions, friction or light exposure, but its effects can be minimised by heating the samples in an inert atmosphere (normally nitrogen or argon).

A final problem is fading. This is the name given to the process whereby some of the electrons trapped in antiquity (which should contribute to the TL of the sample when it is measured in the laboratory) escape from the traps while the sample is buried. This results in a reduction in the amount of TL carried by the sample and so an underestimate of the sample's age. Hence, only the TL produced by electrons from deep traps (above 300°C in the glow curve) is used for dating because such electrons are expected to remain trapped for 10^5 years or more. Unfortunately, in some minerals, particularly felspars, it is found that a large proportion of

he electrons which, on the basis of simple theory, are in traps
leep enough for them to remain for a long time, may escape
within a few days of being trapped. This behaviour is known as
anomalous fading and can be detected by comparing the glow
curve produced by a recently irradiated sample with one produced
by a sample irradiated several months ago.

Figure 3.5 A typical plateau test

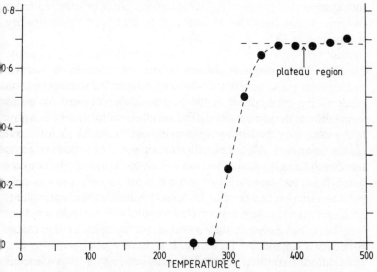

N is the natural TL (i.e. the TL acquired in antiquity) and N + β the TL after the
sample has been irradiated in the laboratory. Only the temperature interval
corresponding to the horizontal portion of the curve can normally be used for
dating purposes (drawn from glow curves in M.J. Aitken, *Physics and
Archaeology*, 2nd edn. Clarendon Press, Oxford, 1974)

A test commonly used to check that samples are suitable for TL
dating is the plateau test. It is a plot of the ratio of the ancient TL
carried by a sample at a given temperature to the TL produced in
the same sample by a laboratory irradiation at the same temperature (see Figure 3.5). If there were no problems with TL dating the
ratio would be constant, but in practice it is found that on heating
the sample from room temperature to 500°C the ratio increases
and only becomes constant at about 300°C. This is because on an
archaeological timescale electrons in the low temperature traps
can escape although they will remain trapped during the laboratory
experiments. If no plateau is present there may be problems due to

spurious TL or fading so, unless the effect can be corrected for, the sample is not suitable for TL dating.

3.3.4 Presentation of Results and Accuracy

The standard form for TL dates is:

date ($\pm$ error p, $\pm$ error a, sample reference);

for example

2010 BC $\pm$130, $\pm$320   Y240c

The date 2010 BC needs no comment because it is in calendar years and hence directly comparable with dates from historical sources and most other dating methods. It is the average date obtained for all the samples from the same context. The sample reference number is given to the sample by the laboratory carrying out the dating: Y is the code for the laboratory, 240 the project number and c the context reference number. The only unusual feature, which could usefully be copied in other dating techniques, is that two errors are quoted. The first error, p, is the experimental error and is found by studying the range of dates obtained from measurements on the samples from a single context. If it is large this suggests that some of the samples used were not particularly suitable for TL dating. It is useful when comparing dates from different contexts but similar conditions, either from one site or several. The second error, a, is an estimate of the total likely error and takes account of all the quantifiable sources of error such as uncertainties in the calculation of the annual dose-rate. It is the error which should be used when comparing TL dates from disparate sites (e.g. desert sites with water-logged sites) and also when comparing TL dates with dates from other methods such as C–14 dating. Sometimes in practice only the error a is quoted.

Both errors are quoted at the 1 σ level (i.e. the 68 per cent confidence level) so to be 95 per cent certain that the date of the sample lies in the range considered one needs to use the 2 σ error limit. For the example quoted the date should lie between 2650 and 1370 BC. Both the errors are normally a constant percentage of the sample's age irrespective of its age. Typical values are 3 per cent for p and 8 per cent for a.

3.4 Recent Developments

3.4.1 Introduction

Recent developments in TL dating have taken place on various fronts. Firstly, attempts have been made to reduce the errors associated with the standard dating techniques. In particular, some of the factors which affect the build-up of TL in the grains, such as the distance β particles can penetrate into the grains, have been investigated.[2] Also alternative techniques, such as γ-ray spectroscopy, have been studied in attempts to find more accurate ways of measuring the annual dose-rate.[3]

3.4.2 Applications to New Materials

Of more immediate interest to the archaeologist is the extension of TL dating to materials other than pottery. The use of flint, loess and calcite has already been mentioned (Section 3.1). Initial attempts to date flint suggested that thin slices would have to be used, even though this made the measurement process more complicated, because crushing the samples in order to extract grains of known size resulted in the production of spurious TL. Recent work,[4] however, has shown that washing the grains with dilute acid after extraction removes the spurious TL and enables normal techniques to be used. Several flints from Longmoor Inclosure, a Mesolithic site in East Hampshire, were dated and they gave ages in agreement with those expected from the type of microlithic assemblage. More recently the technique has been applied to flints from two sites at Hengistbury Head in Dorset[5] and dates of 9750 ± 950 years BP for Powell Mesolithic site and $12,500 \pm 1150$ BP for Hengistbury Upper Paleolithic site were obtained.

Various groups have developed techniques for dating loess and other sediments in which the geological TL is removed by sunlight immediately prior to the deposition of the sediment. Wintle[6] obtained TL ages ranging from 14.5 to 18.8kyr for loess in Southern England in agreement with the expected late Devensian age. Late Pleistocene loess and soils developed on loess from Normandy[7] have also been dated and gave mean ages ranging from 13kyr for the most recent period of deposition to 115 ± 10kyr for soil from the last interglacial. All the dates agree with the ages expected on geological grounds. Work has also been carried out on marine sediments in which TL dating techniques gave ages in agreement with those obtained by other means.[8]

Encouraging results have also been obtained in preliminary attempts to date the vitrified material from Scottish vitrified forts.[9] In particular seven samples from Craig Phadrig, Inverness gave dates ranging from 1870 ± 110 to 1653 ± 100 BP which are not only self-consistent but also in agreement with the C–14 dates for the site. A small number of samples from four other sites have also been dated. The material from both Dun Lagaidh and Langwell Dun appeared to be similar in age to that from Craig Phadrig, while that from Knockfaril and Tap O'Noth appeared to date from about the middle of the second millennium BC. The dates from Tap O'Noth, however, were rather scattered. This work, thus, offers the possibility of establishing whether the vitrification was produced deliberately during the construction of the forts or accidentally during their destruction and also when the first hillforts were built in Scotland.

Finally progress has also been made with the TL dating of calcite. Debenham and Aitken[10] discuss the problems of dating calcite and describe the technique they use. They also report TL dates for Pont Newydd in North Wales and Caune de l'Arago in France and compare them with uranium series dates. Most of the TL dates are in agreement with the uranium series dates, but there are some discrepancies. They suggest these could be due to a variety of problems, including radon loss or fading, which could explain why some of the TL dates from Caune de l'Arago were later than the associated uranium series dates.

3.4.3 New Techniques

The heating of samples, which is necessary in conventional TL dating techniques to enable the number of trapped electrons to be measured, can cause problems such as the production of spurious TL. Recently several alternative techniques have been developed, which enable the trapped electron population of the sample to be determined, but which do not involve heating the sample. ESR (electron spin resonance) spectroscopy has found application in archaeology not only as a dating technique, but also for detecting whether various materials had been heated in antiquity and for provenance studies. It is currently being used for a variety of applications and is discussed further in section 3.6.

More recently an alternative technique in which a laser is used to eject trapped electrons has been developed.[11] Once freed, the electrons combine with luminescence centres to produce flashes of light which are observed and counted by photomultipliers as in TL dating. This new technique of optical dating has been tested on quartz from a variety of sediments of known age and most samples gave ages in agreement with the expected ages. However, two recent samples gave ages which were older than expected. At present it is not clear whether this is due to problems with the method or just to the samples not being of the age expected. Further work is needed before it becomes a routine archaeological technique.

3.5 Applications

Applications of TL dating fall into two main groups, namely authenticity testing and the dating of archaeological sites.

3.5.1 Authenticity Testing

The large sums of money that are often paid for authentic ancient ceramics and bronzes of artistic merit have led to many modern forgeries being produced. Sometimes the forgeries can be detected on stylistic grounds, but many are so good that this is not possible. As one solution to this problem, TL dating has been widely used to determine the maximum age of objects whose authenticity has been questioned. Because only a maximum age is required, the measuring technique is simplified and only a very small sample is required: normally about 20mg is drilled from an inconspicuous part of the object (with bronzes the remains of the sand casting core are sampled). Furthermore, the burial conditions will normally be unknown, so the environmental dose can only be estimated. In most cases, the forgeries are likely to be less than 100 years old, while the genuine object will be considerably older (five hundred to several thousand years). Thus, even if there is a large uncertainty in the age obtained, it can still be decided whether or not an object is a fake. There are however certain exceptions: for example, authenticity testing will only tell whether a supposed Greek vase was made in the nineteenth century and will not normally exclude the possibility that it was a Roman copy. In addition, it has been suggested that modern forgers have found ways of irradiating their products to produce an artificially high number of trapped electrons. Then, when authenticity testing is carried out, the TL signal will be sufficiently strong to suggest the object is ancient rather than modern. However, no proof that this has been done successfully has yet been found and it seems likely that to fake the ancient TL convincingly would be so expensive that the forgers would instead produce works of art, such as stone sculptures, which cannot be tested by TL studies.

Recent examples of the use of TL dating to check the authenticity of ceramic objects include work on five Samian poinçons of Central Gaulish type from the British Museum.[12] TL dating of other similar poinçons had shown that some of them were fakes, so it was decided to check whether those in the British Museum were genuine. Small samples were taken from five of the poinçons of interest and their maximum age determined using the fine-grain method. This gave ages ranging from 360 to 140 years, showing that the poinçons were nineteenth-century forgeries; if they were genuine they would have been about 1,800 years old. By contrast TL dating of an unusual pot- lid from Spong Hill, North Elmham, Norfolk, gave a possible age range of AD 1090 to AD 460 (95 per cent confidence level) showing that it was Anglo-Saxon and not a nineteenth-century fake.[13]

3.5.2 Dating of Archaeological Sites

At present not many TL dates have been published. This may be partly because many of the laboratories which do TL dating are more interested in research than providing a service to archaeologists, so that once a particular problem has been overcome they move onto a different one. However, this may change as Durham University has recently set up a dating service for archaeological ceramics; the purpose is to provide dates for archaeological sites and not to carry out independent research.[14] They offer a two-tier service with the first tier being survey dating, which aims to date samples with an overall accuracy of ±20 per cent within one month of sample submission. If greater accuracy is required and the survey dating suggests that the samples are suitable, then a dating programme can be undertaken after discussion between the laboratory and the archaeologist. This programme would aim to provide dates with an overall accuracy of ±5 to ±10 per cent and would require a minimum of 10 sherds which cover the range of occupation at the site. In addition, it would be necessary to bury radiation monitors on the site for several months. No samples should be submitted until the laboratory has been consulted. Costs are available on request.

Vyner[15] used the service to date the burning of the mortuary structure which occurred before the completion of the Neolithic funerary cairn at Street House, Loftus. He obtained a date of 3575 BC (±830) and comments that the errors are large because the material was not particularly suitable for TL dating.

The ESF booklet on thermoluminescence dating[16] includes several examples of the recent use of TL dating for archaeological sites. Wagner dated pottery wasters and burnt clay from a medieval kiln at Lubeck in Germany using both the fine-grain and the quartz-inclusion techniques. He obtained a date for the abandonment of the kiln of AD 1244 (±26 years, ±60 years). Two Viking sites in Denmark have also been dated. Sherds from the early Viking layers at Ribe gave a date of AD 700 (±20 years, ±80 years) in agreement with the archaeological estimate of AD 700–800 and a dendrochronological date of AD 710. Burnt stones and sherds from two Viking houses at Lejre gave a date of AD 1040 (±30 years, ±60 years) in agreement with the date expected on archaeological grounds of AD 950–1050. Finally, Wagner and Weiner dated sherds from the Early Bronze Age settlement at Demirichüyük in Turkey using the fine-grain and quartz-inclusion techniques. Unfortunately, although 41 sherds were obtained from 13 layers covering the whole of the Early Bronze Age, only 10 ultimately proved suitable for dating. The dates obtained reflected the stratigraphic sequence at the site and range from 3075 BC (±190 years, ±410 years) to 1980 BC (±130 years, ±270 years). These dates are in agreement with the calibrated C–14 dates for the site and suggest the Early Bronze Age began in north-western Anatolia about 3000 BC.

3.6 Electron Spin Resonance Spectroscopy

Whenever possible electrons combine to form pairs. For example, when atoms combine to form molecules they normally do so in such a way that the molecule has an even number of electrons and hence no unpaired electrons. Occasionally, however, atoms occur in which there are unpaired electrons. Electron spin resonance spectroscopy (ESR) is a means of detecting these electrons. It does this by establishing whether there are any electrons present capable of absorbing energy of a particular wavelength when a sample is placed in a magnetic field of known strength. By looking at such factors as the amount of energy absorbed and the range of wavelengths over which this absorption occurs it is then possible to draw conclusions about some of the electrons present and their surroundings. The technique has been used to help solve a variety of archaeological problems. It has the advantages that it can be carried out non-destructively and that only small samples are needed, but the disadvantage that at present it is less readily available than conventional TL dating.

The main role for ESR studies in archaeology may well be as an alternative to TL for dating bone and calcite, because it enables the trapped electron population of the sample, and hence the archaeodose, to be determined without having to heat the sample. Less than 1g of material is required for each sample. Hennig et al.[17] have described its use for dating the fossil hominid cranium from Petralona Cave in Greece. The find has been a source of much controversy with suggested dates ranging from 70,000 to 700,000 years BP. They obtained an age of $198,000 \pm 40,000$ years for the calcite on the bone and $127,000 \pm 35,000$ for the bone itself. They suggest that the age of the bone is low because re-crystallisation, which would free trapped electrons, had occurred in it after it was buried and hence the age of the site is about 200,000 years. At present ESR spectroscopy provides the only absolute method for dating bones which are too old or too small to be dated by the C–14 method.

Another use of ESR spectroscopy has been to determine the temperature to which a variety of materials have been heated in antiquity. Heating certain materials produces species, such as carbon radicals and manganese II (atoms in which there are unpaired electrons), which can be detected by ESR spectroscopy. Because the exact form of the signal obtained during ESR spectroscopy depends on the temperature to which the material has been heated, the maximum temperature to which the material had been subjected can be determined. Hillman et al.[18] studied the changes in ESR signal produced by heating modern grain and used this information to help understand the ESR signals from ancient grain. In particular, they concluded that the maximum temperature to which uncharred grain from King Zoser's Pyramid had been heated was 100°C, but that charred grain from a level at Mycenae, which had been destroyed by fire, had been heated to a maximum temperature of 250°C. Finally they looked at grain from Wadi Kubbaniya which appeared charred and was associated with 18,000 year old charcoal. They showed that the grain had only been heated to about 150°C and, therefore, was probably a modern contaminant. Studies have also shown that ESR spectroscopy can be used to determine the maximum temperature to which flint[19] and ivory[20] have been heated.

ESR is also known as electron paramagnetic resonance (EPR) and under this name was used by Schreurs et al.[21] in a study of the effect of iron, sulphur and manganese on the colour of ancient glass.

A final example of the use of ESR spectroscopy has been in determining the origin of marbles. Cordischi et al.[22] analysed marble samples both from quarries in the Mediterranean area and also from a variety of marble objects. In most cases they were able to draw conclusions about the origins of the marbles, though in many cases they were left with several quarries as possible sources of the marble. Lloyd et al.[23] studied marble from a variety of American quarries and also concluded that ESR spectroscopy is a useful way of distinguishing between different marble sources.

Thus ESR spectroscopy is currently being used to solve a variety of archaeological problems.

Notes and Further Reading

For a more detailed and technical account of both the principles and techniques involved in TL dating readers should consult *Thermoluminescence Techniques in Archaeology* by S.J. Fleming (Oxford University Press, 1979). The European Science Foundation has also published a handbook for archaeologists on *Thermoluminescence Dating* by G.A. Wagner (European Science Foundation, 1983). It provides a brief outline of TL dating techniques, examples of its use and details of sample requirements. The range of materials which can be dated by the TL method is discussed by A.G. Wintle in 'Thermoluminescence dating: a review of recent applications to non-pottery materials', *Archaeometry*, vol. 22, no. 2 (1980), pp. 113–22.

1. S.J. Fleming, *Thermoluminescence Techniques in Archaeology* (Oxford University Press, 1979); M.J. Aitken, *Thermoluminescence Dating* (Academic Press, 1985).
2. V. Mejdahl, 'Thermoluminescence dating: beta-dose attenuation in quartz grains', *Archaeometry*, vol. 21, no. 1 (1979), pp. 61–72.
3. R.L. Meakins, B.L. Dickinson and J.C. Kelly, 'Gamma ray analysis of K, U and Th for dose-rate estimation in thermoluminescence dating', *Archaeometry*, vol. 21, no. 1 (1979), pp. 79–86.
4. J. Huxtable and R.M. Jacobi, 'Thermoluminescence dating of burned flints from a British Mesolithic site: Longmoor Inclosure, East Hampshire', *Archaeometry*, vol. 24, no. 2 (1982), pp. 164–9.
5. R.N.E. Barton and J. Huxtable, 'New dates for Hengistbury Head, Dorset', *Antiquity*, vol. 57 (1983), pp. 133–5.

6. A.G. Wintle, 'Thermoluminescence dating of late Devensian loesses in southern England', *Nature*, vol. 289 (1981), pp. 479–80.

7. A.G. Wintle, N.J. Shackleton and J.P. Lautridou, 'Thermoluminescence dating of periods of loess deposition and soil formation in Normandy', *Nature*, vol. 310 (1984), pp. 491–3.

8. A.G. Wintle and D.J. Huntley, 'Thermoluminescence dating of a deep sea sediment core', *Nature*, vol. 279 (1979), pp. 710–12.

9. D.C.W. Sanderson, F. Placido and J.O. Tate, 'Scottish vitrified forts: background and potential for TL dating', presented to the 4th specialist Seminar of TL and ESR dating, Worms, September 1984, and published in *Nuclear Tracks* (vol. 10, nos. 4-6 (1985), pp. 799–809). My thanks to Dr Sanderson for permission to quote the dates for the forts.

10. N.C. Debenham and M.J. Aitken, 'Thermoluminescence dating of stalagmitic calcite', *Archaeometry*, vol. 26, no. 2 (1984), pp. 155–70.

11. D.J. Huntley, D.I. Godfrey-Smith and M.L.W. Thewalt, 'Optical dating of sediments', *Nature*, vol. 313 (1985), pp. 105–7.

12. Donald M. Bailey and Sheridan G.E. Bowman, 'Thermoluminescence examination of five Samian poinçons of Central Gaulish type', *Antiquaries Journal*, vol. 61, no. 2 (1981), pp. 352–6.

13. Catherine Hills, 'Anglo–Saxon chairperson', *Antiquity*, vol. 54 (1984), p. 52.

14. Ian Bailiff and Iain Watson, 'TL dating service' (University of Durham).

15. G.W. Wagner, in collaboration with M.J. Aitken and V. Mejdahl, 'Thermoluminescence dating', *Handbooks for Archaeologists*, no. 1 (European Science Foundation, 1983).

16. B.E. Vyner, 'Neolithic Cairn at Street House Loftus', *Proceedings of the Prehistoric Society*, vol. 50 (1984), pp. 151–95.

17. G.J. Henning, W. Herr, E. Weber and N.I. Xirotiris, 'ESR-dating of the fossil hominid cranium from Petralona Cave, Greece', *Nature*, vol. 292 (1981), pp. 533–6. The problems of dating the cranium are also discussed by A.G. Wintle and J.A. Jacobs, 'A critical review of the dating evidence for Petralona Cave', *Journal of Archaeological Science*, vol. 9 (1982), pp. 39–47.

18. G.C. Hillman, G.V. Robins, D. Oduwole, K.D. Sales and D.A.C. NcNeil, 'The use of electron spin resonance spectroscopy to determine the thermal histories of cereal grains', *Journal of Archaeological Science*, vol. 12 (1985), pp. 49–58.

19. G.V. Robins, N.J. Seeley, M.C.R. Symons and D.A.C. McNeil, 'Manganese (II) as an indicator of ancient heat treatment in flint', *Archaeometry*, vol. 23, no. 1 (1981), pp. 103–7.

20. G.V. Robins, C. del Re, N.J. Seeley, A.G. Davis and J.A.-A. Havario, 'A spectroscopic study of the Nimrud Ivories', *Journal of Archaeological Science*, vol. 10 (1983), pp. 385–95.

21. J.W.H. Schreurs and R.H. Brill, 'Iron and sulphur related colours in ancient glasses', *Archaeometry*, vol. 26, no. 2 (1984), pp. 199–209.

22. D. Cordischi, D. Monna and A.L. Segre, 'ESR analysis of marble samples from Mediterranean quarries of archaeological interest', *Archaeometry*, vol. 25, no. 1 (1983), pp. 68–76.

23. R.V. Lloyd, P.W. Smith and H.W. Haskell, 'Evaluation of the manganese ESR method of marble characterisation', *Archaeometry*, vol. 27, no. 1 (1985), pp. 108–16.

4 ARCHAEOMAGNETISM

4.1 Introduction

Archaeomagnetism is the study of the history of the Earth's magnetic field as recorded by archaeological material such as pottery and kilns. It is part of the wider study of paleomagnetism which uses information from rocks and other geological material to extend the picture back as close as possible to the formation of the Earth. For historical reasons, associated with the development of the science, the terms archaeomagnetism and paleomagnetism are often used to refer specifically to the study of directional changes of the field, with the term archaeointensity being used for studies of the changes in intensity or strength of the field.

For the archaeologist, the chief use of archaeomagnetism has been for dating archaeological sites, although it has also been used for a variety of technological studies. Suitable samples can be obtained from two main sources. These are, firstly, fired or heated material such as pottery, hearths, kilns and volcanic lavas; and secondly, sediments from lakes and caves. The periods in which dating is possible fall into two groups. Initially, the main use of archaeomagnetism was in dating fairly recent sites with ages ranging from the present to a maximum of around 10,000 years where under favourable conditions an accuracy of ±20 years can be obtained. Recently long-term changes in the field have been used to date Early Man sites in the period before about 0.5 million years. Here the possible accuracy is much less being, at best, thousands of years and often much less.

Archaeomagnetic dating differs significantly from most of the other scientific dating methods such as C–14 and TL because of the way the Earth's magnetic field varied in the past. The difference arises because the changes in the direction and intensity of the field are random so that sometimes the intensity increases and sometimes decreases. Similarly, changes in direction are not always in the same direction. This has two important consequences. Firstly, any given direction or intensity is likely to have occurred on more than one occasion in the past. Thus, if

61

archaeomagnetism is to provide a unique date for a sample, a rough estimate of the sample age is needed, possibly provided by TL dating. Secondly, as it is impossible to predict the past direction and intensity of the Earth's magnetic field, calibration curves of past direction and intensity have to be built up using information derived from samples of known age.

4.2 The Basis of Archaeomagnetism

4.2.1 The Structure of the Earth's Field

Observatories around the world have studied and kept records of the behaviour of the Earth's magnetic field for approximately the past 400 years. At first, the field was thought to be like that which would be produced by a bar magnet situated at the centre of the Earth. Such a field has well-defined north and south magnetic poles and is known as a dipole field (see Figure 4.1). The dipole (i.e. bar magnet) producing the field is at present inclined at an angle of about 10° to the geographic or rotation axis of the Earth and changes slowly in size, being currently 20 per cent weaker than it was 2,000 years ago, though bigger changes have been observed on a geological timescale. The angle between the dipole and rotation axis presumably also changes slowly, because, when all the available information is considered, its average position lies within 5° of the rotation axis. These changes are too slow to be of use in dating archaeological material.

As records became more detailed, it was found that this simple picture of a single dipole producing the field was an over-simplification. Instead, when the shape of the field due to a single dipole was compared with the known shape of the Earth's field, it was found that only about 80 per cent of it could be explained by a single dipole. The remaining 20 per cent is known as the non-dipole field and can be thought of as being due to further small dipoles (about eight at present) situated roughly half way between the centre and surface of the Earth. The non-dipole field can, thus, be split into a series of distinct features, each of which affects an area 1,000 kilometres or so across. The size and position of these non-dipole features change quite rapidly with features having a lifetime of roughly a thousand years. It is the changes in these features which are of most use in dating archaeological objects because they produce easily measurable

Figure 4.1 The Earth's magnetic field

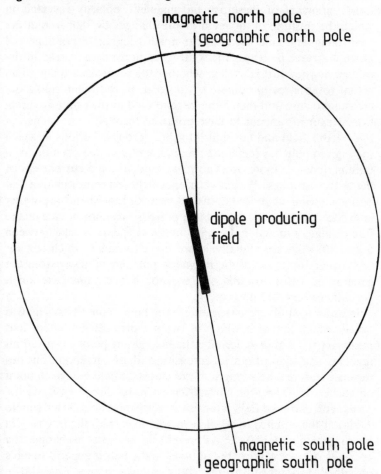

Figure shows the position of the main dipole and magnetic poles relative to the rotation axis and geographic poles of the Earth

changes in the direction and strength of the total magnetic field at an archaeological site. The changes in the field due to the non-dipole features are often referred to as secular variation to distinguish them from long-term changes in the field. At present the non-dipole field is moving slowly westward at a rate of 0.2 degrees per year: a phenomenon known as 'westward drift'.

As well as the above short-term changes in the field there are also longer-term changes due to changes in the main dipole. The most important of these are the magnetic polarity reversals in which the position of the main dipole changes by 180° so that the south magnetic pole lies near the north geographic pole and the north magnetic pole near the south geographic pole instead of the other way round. It is unclear whether the reversals are due to an actual rotation of the dipole or, instead, to the main dipole decreasing to zero and then being regenerated in the opposite direction. Reversals appear to have occurred throughout existence of the Earth's field and are split into three groups. Periods in which the main dipole has remained predominantly in one position for a million years or more are known as 'epochs': the current epoch being the Brunhes. Within each epoch there are normally a few periods lasting a hundred thousand years or less when the polarity is in the opposite direction. Such periods are known as 'events'. The change of direction during a reversal appears to take between 5 and 10,000 years. Finally, there are excursions which last for 1,000 years or so when the magnetic poles move away from the geographic poles towards the equator but do not take up a permanent reversed position.

In order to study the changes with the time of the Earth's field in detail, which has to be done before samples can be dated, it is necessary to be able to describe the field at any point exactly. This involves specifying both its intensity and its direction. The intensity measures the strength of the magnetic field at a given point on the Earth. The unit normally used today for intensity is the Tesla: currently the field intensity varies from about 30 μT (micro Tesla) at the equator to 60 μT near the poles with the intensity in Britain being about 50 μT. At present the intensity is changing by about 2½ μT per century but at times in the past it appears to have remained constant for several centuries and at others it has shown much more rapid changes: in France between 0 and 200 AD the intensity doubled, rising from 50 to 100 μT.

The direction is specified by the use of two quantities: declination and inclination. Declination is the angle between geographic and magnetic north and can be found by measuring the angle between a compass needle free to move in a horizontal plane and geographic north. Its current value and rate of change can be found from Ordnance Survey maps. At present (1985) the declination in Britain is about 9° west and is decreasing by about ½° in three years. This is close to the maximum observed rate of change of 5° in 20 years, but at times, for example between 1500 and 1600 AD, the declination has remained almost constant. The declination can take any value between 0 and 360° though degrees east and west are also used. In Britain over the past 2,000 years it has remained between 30° west and 30° east. The inclination (or dip) is the angle between the field and the horizontal and can be found using a compass needle pointing to magnetic north and free to move in a vertical direction. The current value of the inclination in Britain is about 66° and it has remained approximately constant since 1900 AD, though in the past, it has changed by 10° per century. It can take any value in the range 0±90°, though in Britain over the past 2,000 years it has varied between +50 and +80°.

4.2.2 Plotting of Field Variations

One problem when trying to compare the changes with time of the field at different points on the Earth is that, even if the field were due to a single dipole, its measured direction and intensity would depend on the place where the measurements were made. Because of this, the direction and intensity, as measured at some particular place, are not normally plotted directly, but instead are converted into a form which can be easily compared with measurements from other places. For directional studies two methods are used. The first is applied when all the directions are from the same region and involves converting the values of declination and inclination measured at individual sites into the values they would have if measured at a central point in the region. For Britain Mancetter is often used. When comparing results from different parts of the world virtual pole positions are commonly used. A virtual pole is obtained by calculating the latitude and longitude of the north pole of a single dipole at the centre of the Earth that would produce the observed field direction at the site. This has the advantage that, if non-dipole features did not exist, virtual pole positions from all over the world would be the same at any one time. Whichever correction is used the plot of direction against time will take the same form. Because the field direction is a vector (i.e. its direction as well as its magnitude is important), it is often plotted on a stereographic projection in which declination of the field or longitude of a virtual pole is plotted around the circumference of the circle and inclination or latitude is plotted

Figure 4.2 Virtual pole positions for England (solid line) and Japan (dotted line) for the past 1,500 years

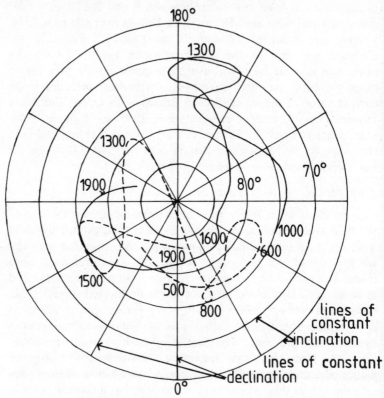

Source: After M.J. Aitken, *Physics and Archaeology*, 2nd edn, Clarendon Press, Oxford, 1974

along a radius from 0° at the outside to 90° at the centre. Figure 4.2 shows secular variation curves for England and Japan plotted in this way. If the variations in direction are small then a normal Cartesian plot can be used with declination along the horizontal and inclination along the vertical axes (see Figure 4.3). Such plots are often referred to as Bauer plots. Alternatively declination and inclination can be plotted separately against time. This is frequently done with measurements from sediments where depth rather than time in years can be plotted on the vertical axis (see Figure 4.4).

Intensity values are also corrected for the effect of geographic

Figure 4.3 The magnetic direction curve used by the Ancient Monuments Laboratory for dating sites in Britain

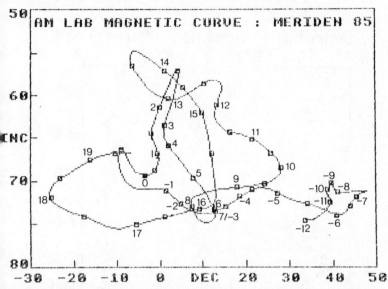

The markers are at 50 year intervals; positive and negative numbers indicate hundreds of years AD and BC respectively. The curve is based upon measurements on features whose dates have been established by other means and the measurement of lake sediment cores (Courtesy Dr A.J. Clark and the Ancient Monuments Laboratory)

position in one of two ways. The first is to calculate the ratio of the ancient field intensity to that of the present day intensity at each individual site. The alternative is to calculate the ratio of the intensity of the ancient field to the intensity of the field that would be produced at the site by a dipole of stated size and position (such as an axial geocentric dipole of 8×10^{22} Am^2 (Amperes metre^2)). Either of these ratios can then be plotted against time on a normal graph (see Figure 4.5) to show how the intensity has changed with time.

4.2.3 Basic Principles of Rock Magnetism

In order to understand the principles behind magnetic dating, it is necessary to know why and how rocks and pottery can be magnetised. This section considers this and defines some of the terms used. In it 'rock' is taken to include materials of archaeological importance suitable for magnetic dating such as pottery and other objects made out of clay and sediments. Rocks

Figure 4.4 Plots of inclination and declination for sediment cores from Lake Windermere

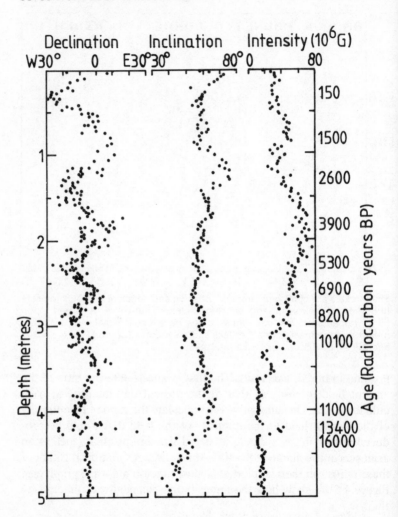

The intensity value is the intensity of the magnetisation of the samples and not the intensity of the Earth's magnetic field. Hence it cannot be used for dating. The declination values are relative and have been put in to make measuring changes in declination easier. The scale could just as easily run from 0 to 60°E (or W)

Source: After R. Thompson, 'Paleomagnetism and paleoliminology', *Nature*, vol. 242, 1973

Figure 4.5 Intensity of the Earth's magnetic field in Egypt and Mesopotamia between 2300 and 500 BC

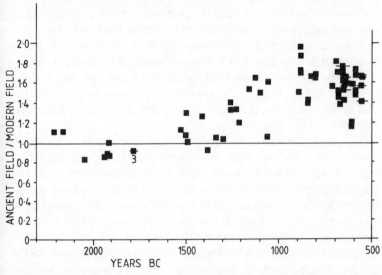

Obtained from measurements on archaeological samples of known age. The intensity is plotted as the ratio of the ancient field at the site to the field due to an axial geocentric dipole of strength 8×10^{22} Am^2 (the present day dipole strength)

Source: After M.J. Aitken, P.A. Alcock, G.D. Bussell and C.J. Shaw, 'Paleointensity studies on archaeological material from the Near East', in *Geomagnetism of Baked Clays and Recent Sediments*, edited by K.M. Creer, P. Tuckolka and C.E. Barton, Elsevier, 1983

contain a few per cent of small (roughly 100nm (nanometres or 10^{-9}m) in diameter) iron oxide particles or grains which are permanently magnetised like tiny bar magnets. Many of these grains are needle-shaped and so normally the magnetisation or magnetic moment of the grain is fixed parallel to the long axis of the grain. In unfired clay and similar materials these grains and their magnetic moments are randomly distributed throughout the material (see Figure 4.6a) so that the clay has no measurable magnetic moment. If later energy is supplied to the clay in a suitable form, such as heat, the individual grain moments become free to rotate and flip very rapidly between the two alignments parallel to the long axis of the grain. If an external magnetic field is present then, at any instant, more of the moments will be aligned in the direction of the field than against it. Then, when the energy supply is removed (e.g. the sample is allowed to cool down) this alignment becomes fixed and so the rock acquires a magnetisation in the direction of the external field. For a given set of conditions, the stronger the external field the greater the number of individual moments which will align themselves with the field and so the rock will record the intensity of the magnetic field as well as its direction (see Figures 4.6a and 4.6b). For sediments the magnetisation is due to the rotation of the whole grain during the formation of the sediment rather than just rotation of its magnetic moment, but the end result is still that the sediment acquires a magnetisation in the direction of any external field.

The energy required to produce alignment can be supplied in several ways. The two most commonly found in archaeomagnetism are heat and alternating magnetic fields (as are used to magnetise magnetic tapes). Different grains require different amounts of energy to enable them to align. This has important consequences for archaeomagnetism because it enables samples to be demagnetised in stages, thus providing checks on the reliability of the information obtained. Consider first what happens when a sample is heated. As the temperature is increased, more and more of the magnetic moments become free to change direction and align themselves with any external field. For any particular grain the temperature above which its magnetic moment can change direction is fixed because it depends on the size and mineral nature of the grain. The temperature at which this movement becomes possible is known as the blocking temperature because below it the magnetic moment is blocked and unable to change direction. If a grain then cools from above its blocking temperature to below it in the presence of an external magnetic field the direction of its magnetic moment becomes blocked or 'frozen' in a direction aligned with the external field. When this happens to a large number of grains the rock acquires a stable magnetic moment in the direction of the external magnetic field.

Another important property of magnetic grains is their Curie temperature. This is the temperature above which a magnetic grain loses its permanent magnetisation and so ceases to behave like a bar magnet. Its value depends solely upon the mineral involved and is 578°C for magnetite and 680°C for haematite, the magnetic minerals most commonly encountered in archaeomagnetism. Thus, only those grains whose blocking temperature is less than the Curie point for that particular mineral can contribute to the magnetisation of the rock.

Figure 4.6 The acquisition of a permanent magnetisation by a sample

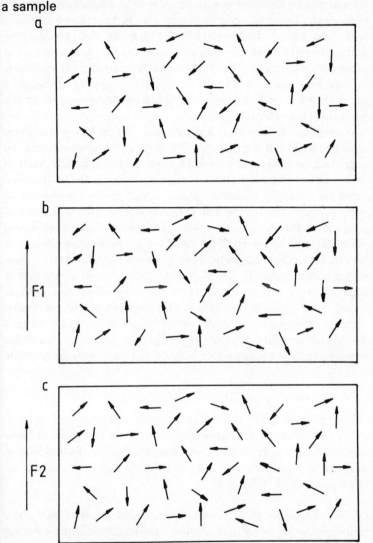

(a) Before magnetisation, e.g. in unfired clay, the grain moments are randomly arranged.

(b) After firing in a weak magnetic field, F1, some of the moments have realigned in the direction of the field to produce a small magnetisation in the field direction.

(c) After firing in a stronger field, F2, more of the moments have realigned in the direction of the field to produce a stronger moment in the field direction.

The final important property of magnetic grains is their coercivity. This determines whether or not the magnetic moment of a grain can change direction when it is in an alternating magnetic field. The higher the coercivity of the grain, the stronger the alternating field required to make its moment change direction. If a direct external magnetic field is present when an alternating field is reduced from above to below the coercivity of a group of magnetic grains then the rock acquires a long-lasting magnetisation in the direction of the external field.

In the above discussion it was assumed that each magnetic grain could be thought of as consisting of a single bar magnet and that the magnetic grains were surrounded by non-magnetic material and so were unaffected by the other magnetic grains in the rock. Such grains are called single domain grains. Large grains, however, tend to be divided into several bar magnets whose moments point in different directions. These grains are known as multi-domain grains and samples containing them are generally considered unsuitable for archaeomagnetic work because the behaviour of their magnetisation is usually less stable and more complex than that of single domain grains. In between come pseudo-single domain grains, which are intermediate in size between single and multi-domains, having only a small number of domains. Such samples show behaviour like that of single domain grains and so these pseudo-single domain samples may be used for archaeomagnetic work.

4.2.4 Different Types of Remanent Magnetisation

This section describes the different types of remanent (or long-lasting) magnetisation of importance in archaeomagnetism and how they are acquired by samples. Because the names of the different types are so long, they are normally referred to first by their initial letters, e.g. NRM, TRM, etc.

4.2.4a NRM or Natural Remanent Magnetisation. Normally, for a sample to be of interest in archaeomagnetism, it must have an NRM. This is the magnetisation produced in the sample in antiquity and will be made up of one or more different types of remanent magnetisation, commonly a TRM and a VRM.

4.2.4b TRM or Thermo-Remanent Magnetisation. A TRM is the magnetisation produced in a sample by heating it and allowing it to cool in a magnetic field. It is the remanent magnetisation of most use in archaeomagnetism, because it is found in fired pottery and other heated clay such as hearths and kilns, as well as in lavas and other heated rocks. Furthermore, it is easy to produce TRMs under controlled conditions in the laboratory.

If the temperature to which the sample is heated is less than its Curie point then a PTRM (Partial Thermo-Remanent Magnetisation) is produced, so in some samples the NRM contains two or more PTRMs.

4.2.4c DRM or Depositional (or Detrital) Remanent Magnetisation. A DRM is the magnetisation produced in a sediment during its deposition by the rotation of the magnetic grains so that their magnetic moments align themselves with any field present. The consolidation of the sediment may take several hundred years, during which time some of the grains may continue to be affected by changes in the Earth's magnetic field. The magnetisation then represents an average of the field over that time period, and hence, strictly speaking is a PDRM (Post-Depositional Remanent Magnetisation). Stable DRMs and PDRMs are found in both lake and cave sediments and studies have also suggested that the silt from the bottom of ditches and pits carries a stable DRM.[1] DRMs and PDRMs have been widely used to study the directional changes of the Earth's magnetic field, but, so far, they have not been used to study intensity changes, because no-one has yet successfully reproduced a DRM in the laboratory.

4.2.4d SRM or Shear Remanent Magnetisation. This is the final type of NRM of use to archaeologists. It is produced in mud when it is thrown into wooden moulds to make bricks, and has been used to study intensity changes as recorded by adobe bricks from Egypt and Peru.

4.2.4e VRM or Viscous Remanent Magnetisation. The other types of magnetisation that may be encountered in an NRM are normally a hindrance rather than a help to the archaeomagnetist. That most frequently encountered is the VRM, and refers to the change in the NRM caused by changes in the Earth's field after the initial acquisition of the remanence, whether a TRM, DRM or PDRM. In general, the older the sample, the larger the fraction of the NRM due to the VRM. Fortunately, for samples of archaeological interest VRMs only affect grains with low coercivities or low blocking temperatures, and so any VRM in a sample can easily be removed by the use of either a small alternating field (10 mT, say), or by heating the sample to a moderate temperature (around 200°C) and allowing it to cool in the absence of a magnetic field.

4.2.4f IRM or Isothermal Remanent Magnetisation. IRM's can be produced in rocks and other materials by lightning strikes. They appear to be rare in archaeological samples, and can easily be removed by use of a small alternating field.

4.2.4g CRM or Chemical Remanent Magnetisation. The worst problems are caused by CRMs: the magnetisation produced if chemical changes in the sample, after the initial acquisition of the NRM, produce magnetic minerals whose moments are aligned with the Earth's field. This is because the behaviour of a CRM, when the sample is heated or placed in an alternating field, can be indistinguishable from that of a TRM.[2] The possibility of CRMs causing problems can be reduced by selecting material which has been heated to a high temperature and shows no sign of weathering, because such samples are less likely to acquire CRMs. As a further check, the samples from a site should, whenever possible, include a range of materials, e.g. two different fabric types for pottery, because the size of any CRM produced is affected by the material of which the sample is made. Thus, if two samples of the same age and from the same place, but made of different material, record the same field direction or intensity, then they are unlikely to be affected by a CRM. The fact that archaeomagnetism has achieved the results it has, suggests that CRMs do not normally cause serious problems in archaeological samples.

4.2.4h ARM or Anhysteretic Remanent Magnetisation. Finally, two types of magnetisation are frequently used in laboratory experiments. The first is the ARM, which is produced by reducing the alternating field applied to a sample to zero while the sample is also in a direct magnetic field. The behaviour of ARMs is very similar to that of TRMs, but they can be produced much more quickly in the laboratory (in minutes instead of hours). They can, therefore, be used to check that any information about the Earth's field recovered from a sample is likely to be accurate.

4.2.4i SIRM or Saturation Isothermal Remanent Magnetisation.
The other magnetisation is the SIRM, which is the magnetisation
acquired by a sample when it is placed in a very strong magnetic
field (about 10T) at room temperature. By studying how the
magnetisation of the sample increases as the field is increased to
this value, information is obtained about the nature and quantity
of magnetic minerals that the sample contains.

4.2.5 Metals

So far the discussion has considered the magnetic properties of
single domain samples such as pottery and rocks. However, iron
is well known for its magnetic properties so the obvious question
is: are iron objects suitable for archaeomagnetic work? The
answer is no, because any magnetisation in iron will be multi-
domain, and so iron objects do not accurately record information
about the Earth's magnetic field in the past. A further complication is that iron distorts any magnetic field in which it is
placed, tending to channel the field through itself, because of its
high magnetic permeability. Hence samples cannot even be
obtained from kilns (or other structures) which contained iron
objects when they were last fired, because the direction or
intensity experienced by such samples would be different from
the mean magnetic field in the area at that time.

Some metal objects such as brass coins can, however, be used
in archaeomagnetic work. This is because they contain iron only
as an impurity in a non-magnetic matrix. It is, thus, in a single-
domain state and so able to carry a stable magnetisation, which
can provide useful information about the object.

4.3 Directional Dating

4.3.1 Introduction: Circumstances in which Directional Dating can be Useful

In order for directional dating to be possible, both suitable
samples and a calibration curve for the place and period of interest
must exist. Normally, a single calibration curve can be used for an
area up to about 1,000 kilometres across, so a single curve is used
for the whole of Britain. Curves also exist for Japan, several parts
of the United States and Eastern Europe, amongst other places
(see Creer et al.[3] for a recent selection). The calibration curve for

Britain is shown in Figure 4.3 (see above). From about 1600 onwards observatory records were used to produce the plot, but the earlier points were obtained from measurements on samples of fired clay from archaeological sites of known ages. Lake sediments extend the record of directional changes back to about 11,000 BP in Britain (see Figure 4.4 above) and similarly for other parts of the world, though, because they tend to record the average field direction for several hundred years, their record is kept separate from that obtained from sources which record the instantaneous field direction. Furthermore, because the samples are obtained as long cores with the youngest sediment at the top, declination and inclination are often both plotted against depth on separate graphs, as in Figure 4.4. By making assumptions about the speed at which the sediment was deposited, the different parts of the core can then be dated.

Before collecting samples for directional dating, the calibration curve for the region in question should be examined, preferably in consultation with the person who will make the measurements, in order to decide whether directional measurements will provide useful information. Figure 4.3 shows some of the problems. Firstly, the direction has been the same (or nearly so) on several occasions in the past, for example, the direction was the same at 1400 and 1200 AD. This means that in order to obtain a unique date, an approximate age must be known for the sample being dated. Secondly, measurements of the field direction from samples are only accurate to about 1° at best. Thus with Roman samples it is necessary to know whether they are older or younger than 200 AD in order to avoid an uncertainty of up to 400 years in the date. Finally, the likely error on any date can only be determined by finding the dates included in a circle of radius 1° placed at the likely date of the sample. If the direction is changing rapidly this error will be ±20 years, but if slowly will be greater and so other dating techniques may offer a more accurate date.

Once it has been established that directional measurements might give useful dates, the next requirement is to find suitable samples. A major restriction is that any material sampled must be in exactly the position it was in when it acquired its magnetisation. Thus for heated materials, samples of archaeological interest are obtained mainly from kilns and hearths. Burnt soil and other clay-based material (e.g. bricks) from destruction levels in buildings may also provide samples if they have been heated to at least

00°C and it is certain that they have not been disturbed since they were at that temperature. Lavas and other rocks heated by volcanic eruptions are another source of useful samples if they are associated with an archaeological event. Sediments from lakes and caves can also be used for directional dating and attempts have been made to use the sediments deposited in the bottoms of ditches and other archaeological features.

.3.2 Sampling Techniques and Measurement Procedures for Heated Samples

The sampling techniques for and laboratory measurements on heated materials and sediments are different, though in both cases the person who will make the measurements should visit the archaeological site to collect the samples to ensure that he knows their precise initial orientation. For heated materials the samples are normally obtained by removing part of the structure being sampled, so that only a set of stumps about 10cm by 10cm is left in their original position. Wooden frames are then placed round these stumps and filled with plaster of Paris. This plaster is carefully levelled, because it will provide a reference surface when the inclination is measured. When the plaster is dry, a theodolite is used to mark the position of the Sun at a known time, so that the position of geographic north can be found and used as a reference for the declination. Next, a compass is used to mark the position of magnetic north. This position is compared with the expected modern position, to check that the magnetic field near the samples is not distorted by large masses of igneous rocks or the presence of iron, because if it is the magnetic direction obtained from such samples will not provide a reliable date. Finally, the prepared samples are cut away from the ground and taken to the laboratory to be measured. For each date a minimum of five samples is required, though more are useful. When dating kilns about 20 samples may be required, because it has been found that the direction recorded by the sample depends on its position within the kiln.[4] Thus, only by taking a large number of samples and using the average direction obtained, can an accurate estimate of the ancient direction be obtained. Several causes of this scatter have been suggested but none fully explains the observations.[5]

Once in the laboratory the stumps are cut into several smaller specimens of a size suitable for the equipment which will determine the ancient direction, normally cubes or cylinders 1 cubic inch in volume. The minimum sample size is determined by two factors: firstly, the sample's magnetisation must be strong enough for the direction to be measured accurately; and secondly, the surface area must be large enough for the orientation marks to be transferred accurately. Tests are then carried out to ensure that the magnetisation carried by the samples records the direction at the time of interest and not later changes in the field. These tests normally consist of demagnetising a representative selection of samples in a series of steps and measuring the direction after each demagnetisation. The direction should remain the same throughout the demagnetisation process, or at least, after a few demagnetisation steps become steady. Any samples where the direction changes throughout the demagnetisation process must be discarded. If the final heating of the sample in antiquity was insufficient totally to remagnetise the sample, two portions of the demagnetisation may show a steady direction, and so it will be necessary to decide which direction corresponds to the event of interest. The demagnetisation can be carried out in two different ways. The first is thermally, by heating at an interval of 50°C, to successively higher temperatures between about 100 and 700°C and allowing the sample to cool in the absence of a magnetic field. This is the best way of treating TRMs, because it is the most reliable way of separating the components of magnetisation due to ancient reheating of the samples. However, it has the disadvantage of being slow, because at higher temperatures the specimens normally need to cool overnight before the direction of magnetisation is remeasured, though it is possible to heat up to about a dozen specimens at one time. The alternative is to use an alternating magnetic field (af) to reduce the magnetisation to around 10 per cent of its initial value by increasing the demagnetising field in steps of 10 mT up to about 100 mT. This has the advantage of speed, because a set of demagnetisations and measurements can be completed in under an hour and is better than thermal demagnetisation at detecting and removing IRMs due to lightning strikes, but there is a greater danger that the specimens will acquire an unwanted magnetisation during the process, making it difficult to determine the true ancient direction. During the demagnetisation process, the magnetic field at the sample is reduced to a minimum, either by using shielding to prevent the Earth's magnetic field reaching the sample, or by using an electric current to produce a magnetic field which will exactly ancel the original magnetic field where the demagnetisation is performed.

Several different types of magnetometer are used to measure the direction and strength of the magnetisation of the samples. The first group includes the parastatic and astatic magnetometers which contain one or more magnets free to rotate about one axis. When the sample is moved into the measuring position the magnets rotate, and by measuring the size of the rotation the direction and strength of the sample's magnetisation can be found. The next group is the spinner magnetometers in which the sample is rotated at speeds of up to 400 Hz. This produces an alternating voltage in a fluxgate system or other pick-up coil. By measuring this voltage the direction and strength of the sample magnetisation can then be found. Finally, cryogenic (or SQUID) magnetometers have recently begun to be widely used, because they are more sensitive than other magnetometers and enable measurements to be done more quickly. In them the direction and strength of the sample magnetisation is found by measuring the changes in the current flowing in a superconducting ring produced by moving the sample. The equipment and techniques used for measuring the ancient direction are described in more detail in Collinson.[7]

Once it has been established that the samples carry a stable magnetisation, it is not essential to carry out the full demagnetisation process, though, if possible, all the samples should be fully demagnetised in case their behaviour is different to that of the first samples. Instead, if it is necessary to save time, the other specimens from the same site can be demagnetised using the minimum temperature or alternating field required to produce a stable direction in the first samples studied. Some demagnetisation will always be required to remove any VRMs acquired by the samples.

After measurements have been carried out on every sample, all the acceptable values are combined together to give both an average value for the direction and an estimate of the likely error in it. Because errors may arise in both declination and inclination, this error produces a circle of confidence which encloses an area within which the true direction from the sample has a 95 per cent probability of lying. This circle of confidence fulfils a similar role to the error a in TL dating, though it corresponds to the $2\,\sigma$ level. An alternative name is α_{95} where the $_{95}$ indicates that the circle has been drawn to enclose the area corresponding to the 95 per cent confidence limit. α_{99} or α_{90} can also be used.

4.3.3 Sediments

The techniques for sampling sediments depend on whether or no
they are under water. For those from lake bottoms, specia
equipment is used to extract cores up to 20m in length and 55cm i
diameter. If the sediment is on dry land, for example in a cave
then the samples may also be obtained by pushing sample-sizec
boxes into the sediment at regular intervals, so that samples are
obtained from the complete age range covered by the sediment
As with heated samples, it is essential that the original orientatio
of the sediment is marked on the container before the sample i
removed from the sediment. After removal the samples are
wrapped in plastic to prevent the sediment starting to dry out
because this may result in distortion of the magnetic record i
carries.

Single samples from sediments are unlikely to be useful fo
dating, because the process of magnetising the sediments tends to
smooth out extremes of declination and inclination. Hence, in
stead of finding where a single direction occurs on the calibratio
curves as is done with heated materials, it is necessary to match
periods of increasing or decreasing inclination and declination and
assume that the maximum and minimum values for the declinatio
(or inclination) occurred at the same time in both the sediment and
the calibration curve.

Once back in the laboratory the cores are normally split into
smaller samples and the ancient direction determined as for heatec
samples. The main difference is that only af demagnetisation ca
be used to check the stability of the magnetisation, because
heating the samples would be liable to lead to changes in the
sediment. It is also possible to af demagnetise and measure the
direction of magnetisation along a core without first splitting it into
smaller samples, though special equipment is needed. As a further
check, when using long cores, that the sediment has reliably re
corded changes in the magnetic field and that a core has not shifted
position while being removed, several cores should be taken and
their records compared.

Once the inclination and declination have been plotted agains
depth for each core or set of samples, master plots for the site are
then made by combining these separate declination and inclinatio
records and the standard deviation on the measurements i
estimated. These site declination and inclination plots are the
compared with the calibration plots for the region and attempt

made to match the maxima and minima of inclination and declination in the two cases. If this can be done satisfactorily a date can be obtained for the site, though due to uncertainties as to when the magnetisation was acquired, there may be an uncertainty of several hundred years in the result.

4.4 Intensity Dating

4.4.1 Introduction

The use of changes in the intensity of the Earth's magnetic field for dating archaeological material has both advantages and disadvantages over directional dating. Its major advantage is that samples are normally easier to obtain because changes in the position of the sample after it has been magnetised are unimportant. Thus pottery sherds can be dated. The disadvantage is that the measurement procedure involves remagnetising the sample in conditions as close as possible to those in which the sample was originally magnetised. This is time consuming and the chances of success are less than in directional work. Furthermore, sediments cannot be used for samples because, at present, DRMs cannot be reproduced in the laboratory. In the past this has resulted in far more directional work than intensity work being carried out, but currently the position is changing for several reasons. Firstly, a new measurement technique has been developed which has cut the time needed for a measurement from several weeks to less than a day and also produces results from samples which previously had been unsatisfactory. Secondly, the development of new, more sensitive equipment enables smaller samples to be used. This provides an alternative way of reducing the time for a complete intensity determination to a few hours, and also means that a mircoprocessor can be used to control the steps in the measurement process, thus freeing people for other work.

Apart from its potential as a dating technique, a knowledge of the past changes in intensity of the Earth's magnetic field is also of interest to those geophysicists who study the Earth's magnetic field and try to discover how it is produced. Short-term changes are of particular interest to them, so the archaeologist may well find himself approached by the scientist for samples of known date which will enable him to investigate these changes, rather than the archaeologist asking the scientist for a date.

To turn first to the requirements which must be satisfactorily fulfilled before intensity dating can help the archaeologist in his work. These are similar to those for directional dating. First a calibration curve must exist for the time and place of interest because, as in directional dating, the changes in intensity that are of most use in dating are due to non-dipole features and hence are different in different parts of the world. Figure 4.5 (above), shows the changes in intensity that have occurred in Egypt and Mesopotamia between 2300 and 500 BC and was built up from measurements on archaeological samples. Examination of it shows that at certain times the intensity changes are faster than at others, and that only at some periods are the changes in intensity at a suitable rate to be of use in dating. Between 2300 and 1500 BC there appears to be practically no change, so the uncertainty in date for samples from such a period would be large. Hence another dating technique would probably be more suitable. Then between 1000 and 500 BC the changes are so rapid that the same intensity would be obtained for several dates. Thus it would be impossible to decide which was the true date, and so a large uncertainty in date would result. Hence another dating technique should be used. Only between 1500 and 1000 BC would dates likely to be of use be obtained. Even then an approximate idea of the age of the sample is required, because the intensity has been the same on many occasions in the past. Thus, before submitting samples for dating, the problem should be discussed with the person who will do the dating to ensure that useful results can be obtained.

Currently, there are two sources of suitable samples for dating. The major one is heated material of which the best type is probably well-fired pottery, though hearths, kilns, burnt earth, lavas and heated rocks may also be suitable provided they have been heated to at least 700°C. The other source is adobe or sun-dried mud bricks, formed by throwing mud into a wooden mould, such as have been found in both Egypt and Peru. While the orientation of the samples is unimportant, the place of manufacture of pottery needs to be known, because this could affect the calibration curve that needs to be used, or at least, corrections for the dependence of intensity on latitude. Thus locally made ware is probably best, though imported ware could be used provided it is made clear where it was manufactured. For each date a minimum of six sherds or other samples will be needed to enable the uncertainty in the late to be estimated. When possible a variety of pottery fabrics should be submitted in case not all fabrics prove suitable for dating. The size of the individual samples will depend on the laboratory performing the measurements, because some have equipment specially designed for use with archaeological samples and so can use pottery cylinders only 3mm in diameter and 3mm in height.[8] Most laboratories require larger samples — often either 1 cm or 1inch discs.

Once in the laboratory, suitable samples will be cut or drilled from the material submitted taking care to use equipment which will not affect the samples' magnetisation. The ancient magnetic intensity as recorded by the sample is then measured. In principle, this is a simple process since what is done is to compare the original magnetisation of the sample with that produced by remagnetising it in a magnetic field of known strength, using conditions as close as possible to those under which it was initially magnetised. It is then an easy matter to calculate the ancient intensity, because the ratio of the initial magnetisation (the NRM) to the new magnetisation (which will normally be a TRM) should be the same as the ratio of the ancient field (F^A) to the laboratory (F^L); or, put mathematically:

$$\frac{F^A}{F^L} = \frac{NRM}{TRM}$$

4.4.2 Measurement Techniques

In practice, the requirement that the conditions for the remagnetisation be as close as possible to those under which the sample was magnetised initially are not always easy to fulfil. Consider first the problems which arise when the initial remanence is a TRM. In order to remagnetise the sample in the laboratory it is necessary to heat it to a temperature of about 700°C. Such a high temperature is very likely to lead to chemical alteration of the magnetic minerals present in the sample, for example the original firing may have been in a reducing atmosphere, but the laboratory firing in an oxidising atmosphere, and hence the above relationship will not hold. In addition, the NRM between room temperature and about 200°C may have become a VRM, rather than being the original TRM, so again the relationship will not hold. Finally, the sample may have been reheated at some point, so that the original PTRM below say 350°C was destroyed and replaced by a PTRM produced in a different magnetic field to that which produced the original TRM. Even if the two magnetic fields were of the same intensity, the new magnetisation of the sample is unlikely to be in the same direction as the original magnetisation. This will result in the new magnetic moment of the sample being less than the original because magnetic moments are vector quantities.

A vector quantity is one in which its direction, as well as its magnitude, is important, and so when two vectors are added together the result can be any value between the difference between the two quantities and the sum of the two. For example, if two men each push the same box with a force of 10 Newtons, the direction in which the box moves will depend on whether or not they both push in the same direction. If they do, then the box will move in the direction in which they are pushing, but if they push in opposite directions, then it will stay still. If however, they push on adjacent sides, then it will move diagonally (see Figure 4.7). Thus if one is to predict the final position of the box, one needs to know not only the forces with which it is pushed, but also the directions in which they are applied. Similarly, with magnetic moments, in order to calculate the size of a magnetic moment produced by combining two individual moments, one needs to know their directions as well as their sizes.

These problems mean that intensity values calculated by measuring the strength of the NRM of a sample and then remagnetising it in a single step in a known magnetic field and measuring the strength of the TRM acquired are unlikely to be accurate. Instead various techniques have been developed to overcome these problems. The two best established are the Thellier technique and the Shaw technique. Both make use of the fact that for any grain there is a fixed minimum temperature or alternating field which will demagnetise or remagnetise it. Thus, by demagnetising the sample in steps and then remagnetising it using the same steps, it is possible to find a temperature range or coercive force range which should give an accurate intensity value. In the Thellier[9] technique the sample is heated to a certain temperature ($T1$) and allowed to cool in zero field which removes the NRM below $T1$. It is then reheated to the same temperature, $T1$, but allowed to cool in the laboratory field so the sample acquires a PTRM below $T1$. These two steps are then repeated at successively higher temperatures until the original NRM has been totally

Figure 4.7 Vector addition

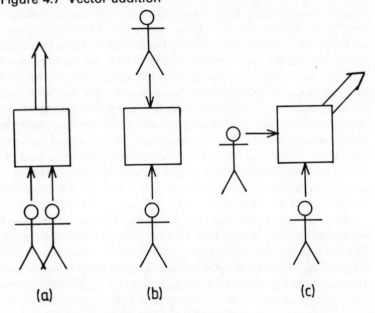

$\longrightarrow$ direction of individual forces

$\Longrightarrow$ direction of movement of box

(a) Both men push in the same direction so the box moves in the direction of the force.
(b) The men push in opposite directions so the resultant force is zero and the box stays still.
(c) The men push at right angles to each other so the box moves diagonally.

destroyed and replaced by a TRM produced in the laboratory field. The magnetisation of the sample at room temperature is measured after each heating. This procedure has the advantage that it is possible to identify the temperature at which the magnetic minerals in the sample start to change.

In the Shaw[10] technique an alternating magnetic field is used for all the demagnetisation steps. First of all, the NRM is demagnetised in a series of steps. The sample is then heated to above its Curie point and allowed to cool in a magnetic field of known intensity. The TRM produced by this is then demagnetised using the same steps as were used to demagnetise the NRM. The magnetic moment remaining is measured after every demagnetisation.

Because the TRM is produced in a single heating, it is difficult to identify the coercive force range (i.e. alternating field range) which is unaffected by the heating. Therefore, two further stages are included to enable this region to be identified. These consist of giving the sample two further ARMs, which are demagnetised using the same steps as were used to demagnetise the NRM. The first is given and demagnetised immediately after the NRM has been demagnetised, while the second is given and demagnetised once the TRM has been demagnetised. Thus the first ARM is demagnetised before the sample has been heated in the laboratory, while the second is given after it has been heated. Hence by comparing the two ARM demagnetisation curves it is possible to find any coercive force regions which are unaffected by the heating of the sample.

Once the measurements are complete, the values are then plotted so that the ancient field intensity can be calculated. In the Thellier technique it is normal to plot the NRM remaining at each temperature against the TRM produced at the same temperature. This produces a plot known as an Arai plot (see Figure 4.8). In the Shaw technique the NRM remaining after a given demagnetisation step is plotted against the TRM remaining at the same step and the first ARM plotted against the second in the same way. For the perfect sample these plots will be straight lines, though in practice the low temperature or coercivity points will normally lie off the line because the NRMs are affected by VRMs, while the high temperature or coercivity points will lie off the line because they are affected by mineral alteration. The ancient field value can then be found using the slope of the linear part of the plot, because this slope should be equal to the ratio NRM/TRM. When using the Shaw technique the ARM plot is also examined, because if no mineral alteration has occurred it should be a straight line of slope 1. Any coercive force range where this is not the case should not normally be used when calculating the ancient field value from the NRM/TRM plot. It has been suggested that, providing the ARM plot is linear, the value of its slope can be used to correct for mineral changes that have taken place.[11] However, any values obtained in this way should be treated with caution, because there is no guarantee that the change in an ARM on heating is exactly proportional to the change in a TRM. In both techniques any changes in the slope of the plots due to partial refiring of the samples in antiquity can be identified by checking whether or not the direction of the sample's NRM remains constant during the demagnetisation process.

Both techniques have their advantages and their disadvantages. Originally the Thellier technique was very slow because it took about three weeks to obtain an intensity value from one sample. Today, however, some laboratories use cryogenic or SQUID (Super-conducting QUantum Interference Device) magnetometers which are very sensitive and allow samples as small as 3mm in diameter to be measured.[12] This enables the time required to heat and cool a sample to be reduced from overnight to a few minutes. An intensity determination using the Thellier technique can, therefore, be completed in three hours. The recent machines designed to measure small samples are also now microprocessor controlled, so that the carrying out of a complete intensity determination (using either the Thellier or Shaw technique) from the measuring of the sample's initial magnetisation to the final plotting of the results can be carried out when no-one is present. The microprocessor can also calculate the ancient field intensity once it has been told which temperature interval or coercive force range to use. The Shaw technique was originally developed to enable intensity determinations to be completed much more quickly than was possible at that time using the Thellier technique. Because the sample only had to be heated once, an intensity determination could be completed in a maximum of two days, though in some apparatus the complete determination can be done in four hours. Today, the main advantage of the Thellier technique is probably that, because it uses thermal demagnetisation, it is better than the Shaw technique at separating the different components of magnetisation of a sample that has been reheated. The Shaw technique is, however, the only technique which can be used for intensity determinations on sun-dried mud bricks.[13] For such samples the magnetisation given in the laboratory is an SRM, not a TRM, but otherwise the technique is the same as for fired materials. For heated samples it is not possible to say in advance which technique will produce the better results.

The increase in the number of intensity determinations being carried out has, as is frequently the case in science, resulted in new problems, which can produce inaccurate results, being discovered. The first of these is that the size of the magnetic moment acquired by a sample in a given field depends on the rate at which the sample is cooled.[14] In particular, if rapid sample cooling (i.e. a few

Figure 4.8 Arai plot for the Thellier technique

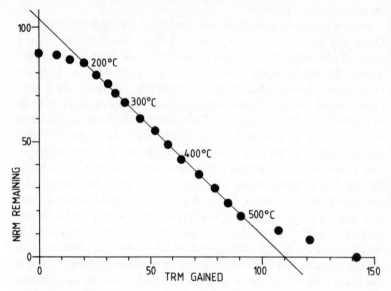

The points below 200°C are affected by a VRM while those above 500° are affected by mineral changes so only the temperature interval 200–500°C can be used to calculate the ancient field intensity

minutes) is used in the laboratory, the ancient field intensity is likely to be underestimated by, on average, 11 per cent because, when originally fired, the samples would probably have taken over a day to cool. The size of the error can be estimated by re-magnetising the sample in a laboratory field but using an oven in which the sample will cool slowly. An intensity determination using fast cooling is then carried out on the sample and the intensity value obtained compared with the intensity of the field used to remagnetise the sample during the slow cool.

Another recently discovered problem is that some pottery is more easily magnetised by a field parallel to its surface than by one perpendicular to it: an effect known as anisotropy.[15] The moment acquired from a field parallel to the original surface of the sample can be twice that acquired in a field perpendicular to this surface. This means that, when remagnetising samples in the laboratory, it is necessary to apply the laboratory field in the same direction as the field in which the NRM was acquired or large errors in intensity values may occur. This is not as simple as it sounds, because a further consequence of this anisotropy is that the direction of the sample's NRM is not necessarily the same as the direction of the field producing it, but can differ from it over 10°. This effect can be overcome by adjusting the direction of the remagnetising field until it produces a moment in the same direction as the NRM.[16]

Recently, another method for determining intensities has been published[17] which involves observing the changes in a sample's magnetisation that occur when it is held at a high temperature (200°C for example) first in the absence of a magnetic field and secondly in a known magnetic field. It is claimed that this method can overcome some of the problems of alteration encountered in the other methods, but so far too little work has been done with it to say whether it will prove of great use.

Under favourable circumstances, determination of intensity values should enable samples to be dated to within ±25 years of the time of heating. This requires that the likely error in the intensity value is less than 5 per cent, which is a considerably smaller error than is acceptable to many geophysicists. They have, therefore, devised a variety of other methods for measuring the magnetic field intensities from ancient materials which are not capable of the precision of the Thellier or Shaw techniques when they are used carefully. These methods are thus not suitable for dating archaeological material.

4.5 Magnetic Reversals

So far the methods considered have been suitable for dating samples from the recent past (up to about 10,000 years old). Magnetic reversals are primarily used for dating geological samples and showing whether two rock formations are of the same age. However, they have also been used to date Early Man sites in various parts of the world. Figure 4.9 shows the reversals which are of interest to the archaeologist. Reversals can be used for dating sites in one of two ways. The simpler is to establish whether the find is associated with a normal or reversed magnetic field. This limits the possible ages: in particular any sample associated with a reversed polarity must be older than 0.73 million years, though the converse is not true. Alternatively, if the magnetic epoch from which the sample comes can be established then a more precise dating may be possible. This is only possible if the sample is either buried under sediment that has been deposited continuously to the present day or else is associated with a series of lava flows which provide a continuous record of field polarity from the time of the sample to the present day. The magnetic reversals recorded by the overlying material can then be counted, enabling the polarity interval associated with the sample to be found. The danger is that the record is incomplete with one or more reversal missing, either because there were times when no sediment was deposited, or else because the lava flows were too infrequent to record all the reversals, and so the sample will be given too recent a date. In practice, dates derived in this way are probably of more use as a check that dates obtained by other methods e.g. potassium/argon are reasonable.

Suitable samples and sample treatment are similar to those for directional dating, because magnetic reversals are just extreme changes of direction and so details are not repeated here. One complication which affects polarity dating, but not ordinary directional dating, is that occasionally samples acquire their magnetisation anti-parallel rather than parallel to the Earth's magnetic field. In sediments this can be caused by movement or other physical disturbance, so any sediments which are sampled should be as undisturbed as possible. With rocks the causes are more complicated, though in some cases the problem can be detected by remagnetising the sample in the laboratory and checking that the magnetisation is in the expected direction. The best solution to the problem is to show that different rock types or both rocks and sediments show the same pattern of reversals. If only one rock type is suitable for sampling it should show both normal and reversed directions of magnetisation.

4.6 Applications

4.6.1 Changes in the Earth's Magnetic Field and their Relevance to C–14 Dating

In the wider scientific field, one of the more important uses of archaeomagnetism is the information it provides about changes in the direction and intensity of the magnetic field. Because archaeological material can often be dated to within a few years, it enables the short-term changes in the Earth's field to be studied

Figure 4.9 The main magnetic reversals over the past 5 million years

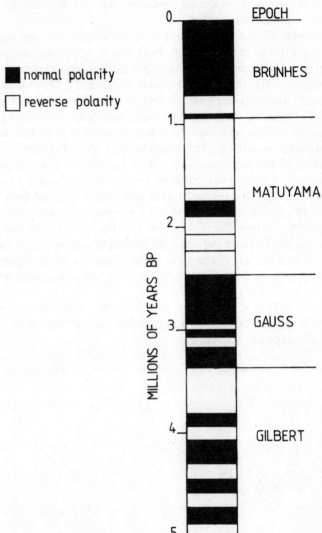

Some disputed Events have been omitted
Source: After D.H. Tarling, *Paleomagnetism-applications in geology, geophysics and archaeology*, Chapman and Hall, 1983

and provides information on how fast changes can occur. This is particularly important to those who are attempting to explain how the Earth's field is produced, because fast changes are more difficult to explain than slow.

Knowledge of the changes in the Earth's field also has more direct applications in archaeology, both as a direct dating method, examples of which are given in the next section, and also because the strength of the Earth's field affects the rate of ^{14}C production and hence influences C–14 dating. One of the original assumptions behind C–14 dating was, that the rate of production of ^{14}C in the atmosphere was constant, but this is now known not to be the case. Instead, changes in the Earth's magnetic field affect the rate of ^{14}C production in the following way. ^{14}C is produced in the Earth's atmosphere by cosmic ray particles coming in from outer space. However, the Earth's magnetic field acts as a shield and deflects many of the particles away from the atmosphere, so they do not produce ^{14}C. When the field is strong (i.e. when the dipole moment is large) more particles are deflected so less ^{14}C is produced. Similarly, when the field is weak more ^{14}C is formed. Figure 4.10 shows both the change in the Earth's magnetic field

Figure 4.10 The relationship between the intensity of the Earth's magnetic field (curve *a*) and the concentration of ^{14}C in the atmosphere (curve *b*)

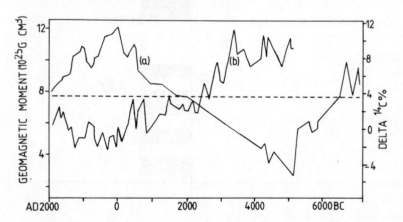

Source: After V. Bucha, 'The influence of the Earth's magnetic field on radiocarbon dating', in *Radiocarbon variations and absolute chronology*, edited by I.V. Olsson, Almqvist and Wiksell, Stockholm, 1970

and changes in the initial ^{14}C content of wood as deduced from tree ring studies for the past five millennia. As is to be expected, the two plots are almost 180° out of phase, with the maximum in the field occurring slightly before the minimum in the ^{14}C plot. Thus ultimately, it may be possible to use the changes in the Earth's magnetic field intensity to correct C–14 dates for changes in the rate of ^{14}C production in those periods where tree ring calibration is not possible. A word of warning is necessary here. It is the worldwide average of the magnetic field which is important when considering the effect of changes in the field on the rate of ^{14}C production, and not the local field value such as is used for intensity dating. Thus to correct C–14 dates, intensity measurements from all over the world are needed, so that they can be combined to give an average. One current problem is the lack of information from the Pacific when compared to Europe. This is particularly important because at present the field in the Pacific is affected by large non-dipole features and it is not known how far back in time they existed.

4.6.2 Dating

The earlier discussion of both forms of magnetic dating assumed that only absolute dates were of interest, which required the existence of the necessary calibration curves. However, even when calibration curves do not exist, magnetic work may still provide relative dating: in particular it may help determine whether two events or structures were contemporary, but, unlike other forms of relative dating, it cannot determine which was the earlier event unless other information is available. A recent example of the use of relative magnetic dating is the work by Downey and Tarling[18] on the end of the Minoan civilisation. They collected samples both from the various materials produced by the eruption of Santorini, and also from some of the buildings in Crete and Santorini which had been destroyed by fire in the final stages of the Minoan civilisation. They measured the magnetic direction and intensity recorded by as many of the samples as possible, and found the measurements fell into two distinct groups, with the first group containing ash from the earliest stages of the Santorini eruption and sites in Central Crete, and the second, later material from Santorini and sites in Eastern Crete. By examining the difference in direction and intensity and considering the normal rates of change of the magnetic field, they argue that there were two eruptions about 20 years apart, and that the earthquakes associated with these eruptions were responsible for the destruction levels. Central Crete never recovered from the effects of the first eruption, while Eastern Crete continued until the second eruption led to the destruction of buildings weakened in the earlier eruption. By using magnetic dating they were thus able to show a much closer connection in time between the collapse of Minoan civilisation and the eruption of Santorini than had been shown previously.

So far as absolute dating is concerned, most work recently seems to have involved the use of magnetic reversal stratigraphy to date Early Man sites in Europe and Africa. Several groups have used magnetic reversal dates to confirm the results of K/Ar (potassium/argon) dates. One group,[19] working at a site in central Italy, found that the sediments associated with human activity were all reversibly magnetised, showing that they must be older than 0.73 Myr when the last reversal occurred. Such a date was consistent with the K/Ar date of 0.73 ± 0.04 Myr for the material immediately overlying the site and thus provides evidence of early human activity in Europe. Similar work has also been done at sites in France and Ethiopia.[20]

Work on more recent sites include measurements of the magnetic direction of a series of cave sediments from the Late Upper Paleolithic site at Kirkhead Cave in Britain.[21] The change in direction with time was compared with the changes observed in sediments from Lake Windermere and found to give a date of between 11 and 10.5 kyr bp, which was in agreement with the dates provided by pollen and mollusc studies. On the basis of this date, the authors suggest that the recolonisation of Britain after the last glaciation occurred later than previously thought, at least in marginal areas.

Two more recent sites where magnetic dating was carried out are the hillforts of Hascombe and Holmbury in Surrey.[22] Multiple samples were taken from the silt at the bottom of ditches excavated at the two sites. In addition, at Hascombe it was also possible to sample burnt rock associated with a pit. The mean direction obtained from the Holmbury silt was declination $9.6W \pm 3.4°$, inclination $64.8 \pm 1.4°$, while at Hascombe the burnt rock gave a direction of declination $8.6W \pm 4.6°$, inclination $65.3 \pm 1.9°$ and the silt a direction of declination $7.9W \pm 7.9°$, inclination $66.1 \pm 3.2°$. The samples from one feature sampled were too scattered to be of use, while the large scatter on the direction on the silt from Hascombe is thought to be due to post-depositional disturbance. These directions correspond with a date of 70–0 BC, which is in agreement with the coin evidence from the site and suggest that, at least in some circumstances, the silt from pits and ditches can be used to date archaeological sites.

A final example of dating shows the importance of using a sufficiently detailed calibration curve. In an attempt to resolve the controversy as to whether the inscribed tablets from Glozel were modern fakes or not, various scientific studies were carried out on them. TL work gave a date of between 350 BC and AD 250 suggesting that, while not modern, they were at least much more recent than the Early Neolithic date originally suggested. To confirm this, magnetic intensity work was carried out on several samples[23] and an intensity value of $47 \pm 7 \mu T$ obtained. In the original work, this value was compared with a calibration curve derived using widely spaced measurements from Eastern Europe, which showed that between 1500 BC and AD 1500 the intensity never dropped below about $60 \mu T$, so the samples could not have come from this time interval; a result in direct conflict with the TL date. However, $47 \mu T$ is very close to the current field strength in France confirming the idea that the samples were modern fakes. Since the original work, evidence for much more rapid changes in intensity of the field than originally thought possible has been found. In particular measurements on Roman pottery from France[24] have shown that between AD 0 and 200 the intensity increased from 50 to $100 \mu T$, a change that the original calibration curve was too coarse to show, so the tablets could have been made around AD 0; a result in agreement with the TL date.

4.6.3 Other Applications

Although studies of the magnetic properties of materials are primarily used by archaeologists as a dating tool, they have also been used for a variety of other purposes including provenance studies and determination of firing temperatures. Probably the most important use is determining whether material has been heated, and if so, what was the highest temperature reached. This can be done quite simply, either by heating the sample slowly in the absence of a magnetic field and observing how the magnetisation changes as the sample is heated, or else by heating it to successively higher temperatures in the absence of a magnetic field and measuring the magnetisation remaining after each heating at room temperature. Then, providing the past heating was to less than the Curie temperature of the sample, the temperature at which the magnetisation disappears is the temperature to which the sample had been heated. Studies of the magnetisation of burnt clay from an early hominid site in Africa[25] have been used to argue that the temperature reached by the clay (400°C) is such that the burning was caused by a deliberate use of fire rather than occurring accidentally. This technique has also been used to determine the temperature of ashes and other material from volcanic eruptions when they bury archaeological remains. Material from Herculaneum was found to have been heated to 400°C when Vesuvius erupted in AD 79,[26] while the temperature of the ash at Santorini ranged from over 500°C near the vent to 300°C at Akrotiri.[27] Finally, such studies can be used to determine the firing temperature of pottery if it is suspected that only a low temperature was used (below 700°C). In most cases the firing of pottery uses temperatures greater than the Curie temperature of the minerals in the pottery and so magnetic studies only provide a minimum firing temperature.

Several groups have also studied the magnetic properties of copper and brass coins in which iron is present only as an impurity. They have found that many coins carry a stable remanence, though the directions were too scattered to be of use for dating. They did, however, reach various conclusions about how the coins were made. In particular, it was shown that Roman coins were always struck with the emperor's head downwards and that silvering was carried out by holding the coins vertically in a hot solution.[28] By studying the production of SIRMs in the coins, another group was able to distinguish between cast and struck coins.[29]

A final use of the magnetic properties of archaeological objects is in provenance studies, because most of the materials used by man (metals, clay, rocks) contain iron as a minor or trace element. The strength of magnetisation acquired by a sample in a given field and how the magnetisation changes when the field is changed depend on the amount of iron present and the mineral form in which it is present. These properties can be investigated cheaply and non-destructively in the laboratory and the technique has been applied to European obsidians. By measuring the magnetisation acquired in a field of 0.35 T, it was found that most though not all the obsidian sources could be distinguished from each other.[30] It has also been suggested that such studies could be used to distinguish coins made from different ore sources.[31]

Notes and Further Reading

There are various books on paleomagnetism available which provide more detailed accounts of how and why rocks and other materials acquire remanent magnetisation, and how this magnetisation is investigated in the laboratory, though their approach involves more mathematics and physics than used here, and any applications discussed are mostly in geophysics and geology rather than archaeology. In particular, D.W. Collinson, *Methods in Rock Magnetism and Paleomagnetism* (Chapman and Hall, 1983) gives detailed descriptions of the instruments and experimental techniques used in paleomagnetism; D. Tarling, *Paleomagnetism — applications in geology, geophysics and archaeology* (Chapman and Hall, 1983) has a very small section devoted specifically to the archaeological applications of paleomagnetism, and finally K.M. Creer, P. Tucholka and C.E. Barton (eds), *Geomagnetism of baked clays and recent sediments* (Elsevier, 1983) summarises recent work on samples from throughout the world in the period of archaeological interest, and list some of the laboratories which carry out such work.

1. F.H. Thompson, 'Three Surrey hillforts: Excavations at Anstiebury. Holmbury and Hascombe 1972–1977', *Antiquaries Journal*, vol. 59, no. 2 (1979), pp. 245–318.

2. G. Haigh, 'The process of magnetisation by chemical change', *Philosophical Magazine*, vol. 3 (1958), pp. 267–86.

3. K.M. Creer, P. Tucholka and C.E. Barton (eds), *Geomagnetism of baked clays and recent sediments* (Elsevier, 1983).

4. M.J. Aitken and H.N. Hawley, 'Archaeomagnetism: evidence for magnetic refraction in kiln structures', *Archaeometry*, vol. 13 (1971), pp. 83–5.

5. G.S. Hoye, 'A magnetic investigation of kiln wall distortion', *Archaeometry*, vol. 24 (1982), pp. 80–4.

6. A. Stephenson, 'Gyroremanent magnetisation in a weakly anisotropic rock sample', *Physics of Earth and Planetary Interiors*, vol. 25 (1981), pp. 163–6; R.L. Wilson and R. Lomax, 'Magnetic remanence related to slow rotation of ferromagnetic material in alternating magnetic fields', *Geophysical Journal of the Royal Astronomical Society*, vol. 30 (1972), pp. 295–303.

7. D.W. Collinson, *Methods in rock magnetism and paleomagnetism*, (Chapman and Hall, 1983).

8. D. Walton, 'Archaeomagnetic intensity measurements using a SQUID magnetometer', *Archaeometry*, vol. 19 (1977), pp. 192–200.

9. E. Thellier and O. Thellier, 'Sur l'intensite du champ magnetique terrestre dans le passe historique et geologique', *Annales Geophysics*, vol. 15 (1959), pp. 285–376; M.J. Aitken, 'Basic techniques for archaeointensity determination', in K.M. Creer, P. Tucholka and C.E. Barton (eds), *Geomagnetism of baked clays and recent sediments*, pp. 79–83.

10. J. Shaw, 'A new method of determining the magnitude of the paleomagnetic field. Application to five historic and five archaeological samples', *Geophysical Journal of the Royal Astronomical Society*, vol. 39 (1974), pp. 133–41.

11. M. Kono, 'Reliability of paleointensity methods using alternating field demagnetisation and anhysteretic remanence', *Geophysical Journal of the Royal Astronomical Society*, vol. 54 (1978), pp. 241–61.

12. M.J. Aitken, P.A. Alcock, G.D. Bussell and C.J. Shaw, 'Archaeomagnetic determination of the past geomagnetic intensity using ancient ceramics: allowance for anisotropy', *Archaeometry*, vol. 23 (1981), pp. 53–64.

13. K.P. Games, 'The magnitude of the paleomagnetic field: a new non-thermal, non-detrital method using sun-dried bricks', *Geophysical Journal of the Royal Astronomical Society*, vol. 48 (1977), pp. 315–29; N.M. Gunn, and A.S.

Murray, 'Geomagnetic field magnitude variations in Peru derived from archaeological ceramics dated by thermoluminescence', *Geophysical Journal of the Royal Astronomical Society*, vol. 62 (1980), pp. 345–68.

14. J.M.W. Fox and M.J. Aitken, 'Cooling rate dependence of thermoremanent magnetisation', *Nature*, vol. 283 (1980), pp. 462–3.

15. J. Rogers, J.M.W. Fox and M.J. Aitken, 'Magnetic anisotropy in ancient pottery', *Nature*, vol. 277 (1979), pp. 644–6.

16. M.J. Aitken et al., 'Archaeomagnetic determination of the past geomagnetic intensity using ancient ceramics', pp. 53–64.

17. D. Walton, 'Re-evaluation of Greek archaeomagnitudes', *Nature*, vol. 310 (1984), pp. 740–3.

18. W.S. Downey and D.H. Tarling, 'Archaeomagnetic dating of Santorini volcanic eruptions and fired destruction levels of late Minoan civilization', *Nature*, vol. 309 (1984), pp. 519–23; Bill Downey and Don Tarling, 'The end of the Minoan civilization', *New Scientist*, no. 1421 (13 September, 1984), pp. 48–52.

19. M. Coltori, M. Cremashchi, M.C. Delitala, D. Esu, M. Fornaseri, A. McPherson, M. Nicoletti, R. van Otterloo, C. Peretto, B. Sala, U. Schmidt and J. Sevink, 'Reversed magnetic polarity at an early Lower Paleolithic site in Central Italy', *Nature*, vol. 300 (1982), pp. 173–6.

20. N. Thouveny and E. Bonifay, 'New chronological data on European Plio-Pleistocene faunas and hominid occupation sites', *Nature*, vol. 308 (1984), pp. 355–8; A.J. Schmitt and A.E.M. Nairn, 'Interpretations of the magnetostratigraphy of the Hadar hominid site, Ethiopia', *Nature*, vol. 309 (1984), pp. 704–6.

21. S.J. Gale, C.O. Hunt and G.A. Southgate, 'Kirkhead Cave: biostratigraphy and magnetostratigraphy', *Archaeometry*, vol. 26 (1984), pp. 192–8.

22. F.H. Thompson, 'Three Surrey hillforts', pp. 245–318, especially pp. 309–11.

23. M.F. Barbetti, 'Archaeomagnetic analyses of six Glozelian ceramic artefacts', *Journal of Archaeological Science*, vol. 3 (1976), pp. 137–51.

24. J. Shaw, 'Rapid changes in the magnitude of the archaeomagnetic field', *Geophysical Journal of the Royal Astronomical Society*, vol. 58 (1979), pp. 107–16.

25. J.A.J. Gowlett, J.W.K. Harris, D. Walton and B.A. Wood, 'Early archaeological sites, hominid remains and traces of fire from Chesowanja, Kenya', *Nature*, vol. 294 (1981), pp. 125–9.

26. D.V. Kent, Dragoslav Ninkovich, Tullio Pescatore and Stephen R.J. Sparks, 'Paleomagnetic determination of emplacement temperature of Vesuvius AD 79 pyroclastic deposits', *Nature*, vol. 290 (1981), pp. 393–6.

27. W.S. Downey and D.H. Tarling, 'Archaeomagnetic dating of Santorini volcanic eruptions and fired destruction levels of late Minoan civilization', pp. 519–23; 'The end of Minoan civilization', pp. 48–52.

28. D.H. Tarling, 'Archaeomagnetic properties of coins', *Archaeometry*, vol. 24 (1982), pp. 76–9.

29. G.S. Hoye, 'Magnetic properties of ancient coins', *Journal of Archaeological Science*, vol. 10 (1983), pp. 43–9.

30. J.M. McDougall, D.H. Tarling and S.E. Warren, 'The magnetic sourcing of obsidian samples from Mediterranean and Near Eastern sources', *Journal of Archaeological Science*, vol. 10 (1983), pp. 441–52.

31. B.K. Tanner, D.W. Macdowall, I.B. Maccormack and R.C. Smith, 'Ferromagnetism in ancient copper-based coinage', *Nature*, vol. 280 (1979), pp. 46–8.

5 OTHER DATING TECHNIQUES

5.1 Introduction

This chapter provides brief accounts of various dating techniques which have been used by archaeologists, but which are unlikely to be as widely used as those described in detail above. This is for a variety of reasons: some, such as potassium-argon dating, can only be used to date Early Man and their main use lies in dating geological samples which pre-date man. Others, such as amino acid racemisation dating, can only provide relative dates and have to be calibrated using measurements on samples of known age. In addition, amino acid racemisation dating was originally developed to date bone samples which were either too old or too small for conventional radiocarbon dating, and so the development of accelerator C–14 dating and ESR dating of bone may soon replace it. There are also a variety of scientific principles behind the techniques. Uranium series and potassium-argon dating are both based on the radioactive decay of specific nuclides, while obsidian hydration and acid racemisation dating use the physical or chemical changes which occur in materials while they are buried.

The techniques described in this chapter are likely to prove less accurate than those described in the earlier chapters, and the archaeologist should bear their limitations in mind when considering dates obtained using them. In particular, with some of the techniques the association between the sample dated and the object of archaeological interest is frequently indirect, and so thought needs to be given to what the association implies about the date of the archaeological feature. Secondly, several of the techniques require a knowledge of the burial temperature of the object: while this can be estimated, its exact value will always be uncertain, particularly for objects dating from before the end of the last ice age. Finally, some of the techniques have to be calibrated using samples which have been dated using another technique. This is frequently done using C–14 dates from one or two samples. In such cases it must be remembered that 1 in 20 C–14 dates lie more than two standard deviations away from the true date and so there will always be some doubts about the accuracy of sets of dates calibrated in this way, particularly when the number of calibration dates is small.

5.2 Uranium Series Dating

5.2.1 Introduction

For the archaeologist, uranium series dating is probably the most important technique to be discussed in this chapter because, until satisfactory techniques for the TL dating of calcite had been developed, it was the only technique which could provide absolute dates in the period 30,000 to 100,000 years BP when neither conventional C–14 nor potassium-argon dating are possible. In practice, it has been used to date sites ranging in age from 12,000 to 350,000 years. Compared to potassium-argon dating, it has the advantage that the material dated (calcium carbonate such as calcite) is much more likely to be associated directly with human activity than are the volcanic rocks needed for potassium-argon dating. It may also be possible to apply it directly to bones and shells.

5.2.2 Principles of Uranium Series Dating

Uranium series dating is based on the fact that when calcite (or other forms of calcium carbonate) are formed they normally contain uranium but no thorium, because of the different chemical properties of these two elements. However, as time passes, the uranium undergoes radioactive decay producing thorium (see Figure 5.1) so old calcite does contain thorium. Thus, if one knows the concentration of uranium in the newly formed calcite, one can work out how old the calcite is by measuring the amount of thorium present today. The technique is thus, in some ways, the reverse of C–14 dating, since in it one measures the amount of the daughter nuclide that has been produced rather than the amount of the parent that remains.

In practice, uranium series dating can be more complicated than C–14 dating because all the isotopes of uranium are radioactive and produce radioactive daughters. However, to obtain satisfactory dates, it is necessary to work with parent nuclides which are reasonably common and have half-lives of very roughly the same length as the age of the site being dated, so that there will be

Figure 5.1 The radioactive decays of importance in uranium series dating

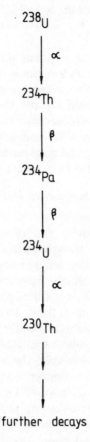

further decays

measurable amounts of the daughters present in the sample. In addition, the half-life of the daughter being studied should be roughly the same length as, or longer than, the age of the site being dated because if the half-life were only a few seconds the daughter would decay almost as fast as it was produced, and so its concentration would be too low to be easily measured. For these reasons the nuclide most commonly used is ^{234}U and its decay product ^{230}Th. Their ratio is determined in the laboratory by dissolving the carbonate in acid and then chemically separating the thorium from the uranium. The α particles emitted by both elements are then studied and used to determine the ratio

^{230}Th/^{234}U. The ratio ^{238}U/^{234}U is determined at the same time, because ^{234}U is produced by the decay of ^{238}U and so the concentration of ^{238}U in the sample will affect the ^{230}Th/^{234}U ratio of the sample. The age of the sample can then be calculated from these measurements.

Protactinium behaves in a similar way to thorium and it too is not present in calcite at its formation. The ^{231}Pa/^{230}Th ratio can, therefore, also be used to determine the sample's age, though because ^{231}Pa is produced by the decay of ^{235}U, this is not normally possible with archaeological samples. This is because ^{235}U is less common than ^{238}U, and so the concentration of ^{231}Pa will not be high enough to be measured accurately. The technique is described in more detail by Schwarz.[1]

5.2.3 Accuracy of Uranium Series Dating and Likely Sources of Problems

Uranium series dating can be used for samples ranging in age from 5,000 to 500,000 years, though for recent samples other dating techniques such as C–14 are often preferable, because they can be more directly related to man's activities. This range is largely set by the precision with which the isotope ratio can be determined, since for more recent samples the ^{230}Th concentration is too low to be measured easily, while for older samples the ^{230}Th concentration changes so slowly that any date obtained would cover a wide range. For very old samples the rate of production of ^{230}Th equals the rate at which it decays, so the concentrations remain constant, i.e. the production of ^{230}Th is in equilibrium with its decay. Thus uranium series dating is also known as radioactive disequilibrium dating. Within the age range stated, the theoretical accuracy of the method is better than ± 10 per cent (1 σ level). Thus, under favourable conditions, the uncertainty in age ranges from $\pm 12,000$ years for a 150,000 year old sample to $\pm 25,000$ years for a 400,000 year old sample. In practice, the errors are likely to be bigger than this, because this sort of accuracy is only obtainable for samples containing a high concentration of uranium. In addition, the half-lives of the nuclides involved are not known very accurately (cf. the problems with the C–14 half-life). Finally, the measurements in the laboratory are not normally done with the maximum possible accuracy.

Other problems arise because it is necessary to select the most suitable samples. The first requirement is that the calcite or travertine (another form of calcium carbonate) must be related as closely as possible to the object of archaeological interest. Ideally the object should be embedded in the calcite, because then it would be rather older than the date of formation of the calcite. This situation is rare, and a more likely one is that the objects of archaeological interest will be in a layer of sediment lying between two layers of calcite. Dating these layers will then give upper and lower limits for the age of the objects. Alternatively, the archaeologically important sediment may contain lumps of calcite which have broken off stalagmites or stalactites. Dating these fragments will provide a maximum age for the sediment, since the calcite must have formed before the sediment. Finally, calcite may form in hollow bones or cracks between rocks or stones, so again it can be used to provide a minimum age for the bone or other object, because they must be older than the calcite.

The other requirement is that the calcite should be free from impurities and still contain all its original uranium. The most likely sources of impurities in calcite are wind- and water-borne material from the nearby soil and bone fragments. Both of these are likely to contain thorium, resulting in newly formed calcite having a non-zero age. Hence, dating contaminated samples will result in too old an age being obtained for the calcite. In addition, if the calcite is porous, water may get into it and leach out uranium. This will again result in the age of the sample being overestimated, because when measurements are made in the laboratory the thorium content of the sample will be unchanged, while the uranium content will be lower than it should be. While it is possible to correct for such effects, doing so will increase the uncertainty in the age, so whenever possible the samples chosen should be non-porous (to reduce leaching) and as far as possible free from detrital material like bone fragments and sediment. Recrystallisation can also cause problems, because when it occurs, uranium and thorium will be free to move within the calcite. If secondary overgrowths are produced at the same time, they will contain no thorium and so the age of the sample will be too young.

Bone has also been used for uranium series dating.[2] Here there is a further source of error, because new bone contains no uranium, so the first step is for uranium from the ground water to be deposited in the bone. The thorium content of the bone will then also start to increase. However, unless the period over which uranium is deposited in the bone is short compared to the age of the bone (for example if the bone is rapidly sealed in an impermeable layer) the age of the sample will be underestimated, because the concentration of uranium measured in the laboratory will be greater than the average content during the burial of the bone. Measuring the uranium content of ancient bones is a well-known technique for determining their relative ages (see section 5.7), so many bones will be unsuitable for uranium series dating.

One important way of reducing the chance of inaccurate results is to have several samples from each site, and preferably several from each layer dated. It is then possible to check that all samples from the same layer give the same age, and that the youngest layers give the youngest dates etc. If they do not, there is a problem somewhere and the dates must be treated with caution. As a further check, the dates obtained by uranium series dating should agree with the dates obtained by some other method such as TL for the same layer.

Approximately 100 g of calcite are required from each sample to be dated.

5.2.4 Applications

A range of Paleolithic sites throughout Europe has been dated by the uranium series method. Gascoyne et al.[3] obtained ages ranging from 135 ± 8 to 114 ± 5 kyr BP for the calcite encrusting bone from the Victoria Cave in North England. The bones came from a typical 'hippotamus fauna', so they concluded that the Ipswichian interglacial corresponds to substage 5e of the marine isotope record (see Chapter 6.2). One problem they found was that calcite from close to the bone gave too young an age, presumably because uranium had migrated from the bone to the calcite.

Uranium series dating has also been used to date several layers in the Middle Pleistocene hominid site at Pont Newydd cave in Wales.[4] The most recent stalagmitic floor had a maximum age of 20 kyr, while the Lower Breccia which contained the bulk of the archaeological finds, had a minimum age of 170 kyr. This was consistent with an age of 180 ± 20 kyr for derived stalagmite from the Lower Breccia and a TL date of 200 ± 25 kyr for a burnt flint from immediately below the Lower Breccia.

Blackwell et al.[5] studied 50 samples from the cave system of La Chaise-de-Vouthon (Charente) in France which contained large tool assemblages and some hominid remains. The ages obtained ranged from 9 ± 2 kyr for the youngest travertines to

$245 ^{+42}_{-28}$ kyr for the oldest, and agreed with the pollen dates for the system. However, the uranium series dates enable more detailed conclusions to be drawn about the ages of the various deposits and showed that the transition from an Acheulian to a Mousterian industry occurred about 100,000 years ago.

In addition sites at Nahal Zin, Israel;[6] Vertesszöllös, Hungary;[7] Pech de l'Aze, France;[8] and Bilzingleben, East Germany[9] have been dated by this method. Further dates are summarised by Schwarz.[10]

5.3 Potassium-Argon Dating

5.3.1 Introduction

The main application of potassium-argon dating has been by geologists to date rock samples which pre-date man, but since it can be used to date samples as young as 100,000 years, it has also been used by archaeologists to date Early Man sites, particularly in Africa. Its main disadvantage from the archaeological viewpoint is that the material dated is volcanic lava and so, if archaeological sites are to be dated, it must be possible to connect them with the eruption of a volcano. Unfortunately for the archaeologist, sites buried by volcanic eruptions are rare, so it is necessary to use geological considerations to relate archaeological sites to distant volcanic eruptions. Potassium-argon dating has also been used to fix the dates of the reversals of the Earth's magnetic field which can then be used to date archaeological sites (see Chapter 4). Finally, potassium-argon dating has been used to determine the provenance of honestones.

5.3.2 Principles of Potassium-Argon Dating (K-Ar dating)

The principle behind potassium-argon dating is similar to that behind uranium series dating, since it is another technique in which the growth of a decay product is used to date the formation of the sample. Potassium is very common in the Earth's crust and is present in most rocks and minerals. It has two common isotopes, ^{39}K which is stable and ^{40}K which is radioactive and is present as a constant fraction of the total potassium (0.012 per cent). Eighty-nine per cent of ^{40}K decays, via β particle emission, to calcium 40 which is stable and is the most common isotope of calcium. However, the majority of ^{40}Ca in rocks is not radiogenic (produced by radioactive decay). Thus the production of ^{40}Ca cannot be used to date rocks. However, approximately 11 per cent of ^{40}K decays by electron capture to argon 40 which is also stable. Argon is a highly unreactive gas and so, when rocks are molten as in volcanic eruptions, any argon present in the rocks escapes. As a result newly solidified volcanic rocks contain no argon. Subsequently as the ^{40}K decays, ^{40}Ar is produced and the argon content of the rocks increases. In many minerals this argon remains trapped for millions of years, so by measuring both the potassium and argon contents of the rock it is possible to determine the time of formation of the rocks. Because the half-life of ^{40}K is approximately 1 billion (1×10^9) years, only samples older than about 100,000 years contain sufficient argon for their age to be measured accurately.

Two different techniques are commonly used to determine potassium-argon dates. In the original technique, the potassium and argon contents of the rock are determined separately. The potassium content is measured using a standard chemical technique such as atomic absorption spectroscopy (see Chapter 7) and the ^{40}K content found by assuming it is a constant fraction of the total potassium content. (The ^{40}K decays so slowly that on an archaeological timescale the ^{40}K content of the rocks will remain approximately constant.) The rock is then melted in a vacuum in order to drive off the trapped argon. A known quantity of ^{38}Ar, referred to as a spike, is added to the argon from the rock and the isotopic composition of the gas measured using a mass spectrometer. The relative concentration of three isotopes are of particular interest: ^{36}Ar, ^{38}Ar and ^{40}Ar. The ^{40}Ar/^{38}Ar ratio enables the amount of ^{40}Ar present in the original rock to be calculated. ^{36}Ar is present in atmospheric argon as a constant fraction (0.34 per cent of total argon) and is not radiogenic. Thus if any ^{36}Ar is present in the sample it shows that the sample has absorbed argon from the atmosphere after its formation. Hence some of the ^{40}Ar in the sample may have come from the atmosphere and not from the decay of ^{40}K. By measuring the amount of ^{36}Ar present, it is possible to correct the ^{40}Ar value for the effects of absorption. Unless this is done the age of the sample will be overestimated. The contamination of samples by atmospheric argon is one reason why samples younger than about 100,000 years cannot be dated, since it is not possible then to correct the dates for the effects of atmospheric argon satisfactorily.

More recently, the ^{40}Ar/^{39}Ar method has been developed; it has several advantages over the earlier technique. In it the rock sample is bombarded with energetic neutrons which produce ^{39}Ar from ^{39}K. The sample is then heated and the argon thus released is collected and its isotopic composition determined using a mass spectrometer. In this case no spike is needed, since to calculate the age of the sample only the relative concentrations of ^{40}Ar and ^{40}K are needed. The relative concentration of ^{40}Ar is measured directly, while the ^{40}K relative concentration can be found from the ^{39}Ar concentration, since it is really a measure of the ^{39}K concentration. The ^{36}Ar concentration can again be used to correct for the effects of contamination by atmospheric argon. The advantages of this method are that no ^{38}Ar spike is needed, that the weight of the sample need not be known accurately and that inhomogeneities in the distribution of potassium within the sample are less important.

5.3.3 Accuracy and Problems

Given good samples, potassium-argon dates can be determined with an accuracy of ± 10 per cent, but in less favourable conditions the accuracy may only be ± 50 per cent. The main limitations on accuracy arise because it is necessary to ensure that the ^{40}Ar in the sample comes only from radioactive decay since the sample's formation and that none of the ^{40}Ar produced in the sample has escaped. If the sample contains excess ^{40}Ar its age will be over-estimated, while if some of the ^{40}Ar has escaped the age will be too young. In addition, if the potassium concentration of the sample has changed since its formation the age will also be inaccurate.

The correction of ages for the effects of excess ^{40}Ar due to contamination by atmospheric argon have already been discussed. Excess ^{40}Ar may also be present in the sample if some of the ^{40}Ar that was formed before the event being dated remained trapped, so that when the sample re-solidified it already contained some ^{40}Ar. This results in the sample having a finite rather than zero age at its time of formation. The use of the ^{40}Ar/^{39}Ar method often enables this excess argon to be detected, because the argon trapped in the sample can be released in stages by heating the sample to successively higher temperatures. An age can then be calculated for each temperature interval. If there are no problems then all the ages will be the same (curve *a*, Figure 5.2). If, how-ever, excess argon is present, then in many cases, it will be re-leased either more or less readily than the radiogenic ^{40}Ar of

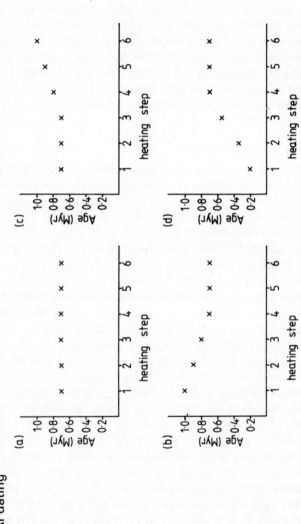

Figure 5.2 Possible behaviour of different samples on heating to different temperatures in the course of K/Ar dating

(a) Well-behaved sample: all heating steps give the same age; (b) Excess argon strongly bound: heating steps 1–3 may give the correct age; (c) Excess argon weakly bound: heating steps 4–6 may give the correct age; (d) Some radiogenic argon has escaped from the sample: heating steps 4–6 may give correct age

nterest and so high ages will be obtained for some temperature
ntervals. Curve *b* shows the case where the excess argon is weakly
ound (i.e. escapes at low temperatures), while curve *c* shows the
trongly bound case.

The problems of escaping argon can be reduced by a careful
election of samples. Firstly, avoid any sample which may have
een reheated in antiquity, because this will have made it easier
or argon to escape. Then, argon can escape more easily from
ome minerals than others. Minerals which are particularly
uitable for potassium-argon dating include high temperature
otassium felspars such as sanidine, and sodium-calcium felspars
uch as plagioclase as well as pumice, biotite, hornblende,
nuscovite and nepheline, because they all have to be heated to at
east 150°C before argon is likely to escape. In contrast, the com-
non potassium felspars such as orthoclase and microline can lose
rgon even at room temperature, and so are unsuitable for
otassium-argon dating. The $^{40}Ar/^{39}Ar$ method can detect the
ccurrence of argon loss, because the ages for the low temperature
ntervals will be too low, and only those for the high temperature
ntervals will be constant (see curve *d*). If there are problems in
electing the most suitable minerals for potassium-argon dating, an
xpert should be consulted.

A further way of ensuring that accurate dates are obtained is to
ave several different minerals dated for each event of interest,
ecause if they all give the same age, it is likely to be correct.

Approximately 10g of rock are needed for each sample, though
he exact amount will depend on the potassium content of the
ninerals present. Potassium-argon dating is discussed further by
Curtis.[11]

.3.4 Applications

Recently the potassium-argon dating of archaeological sites seems
o have been plagued by problems, with the result that the original
lates for several sites have been revised after fresh measurements
n samples from the sites. Part of the reason for this was that the
alues for the rates at which ^{40}K undergoes electron capture and β
lecay were revised in 1978, as was the expected ratio of ^{40}K to
otal potassium in rocks. Thus dates published before 1978, using
he old constants, will be 2.67 per cent less than those which use
he new constants. A more worrying reason for some of the
evisions is that the earlier dates were wrong because equipment

was incorrectly calibrated, and so measurements of the volume of argon or weight of potassium from the samples were wrong in some laboratories. Such errors make it impossible to compare the dates from different laboratories but now that these problems have been noticed it is to be hoped that they will not occur again, and that potassium-argon dating will, in future, provide reliable dates for the archaeologist.

In particular, there were problems with the original potassium argon dates for both the KBS tuff from the East Turkana region of Kenya, where many stone tool and hominid remains have been found, and also with those for the volcanic material associated with the Hadar hominid site in Ethiopia. The original work on the KBS tuff by various workers produced ages ranging from 0.53 ± 0.33 Myr to 2.64 ± 0.29 Myr. Drake et al.,[12] when publishing revised dates for the site, reported that their original dates were wrong because the balance that they used when measuring the potassium content of the samples was incorrectly calibrated. McDougall et al.,[13] when reporting fresh dates for the tuff, concluded that among the reasons for the wide range of dates obtained originally were contamination of the samples by material from earlier eruptions and failure in the laboratory to extract all the argon from the samples. In addition, Walter and Aronson[14] have published revised dates for the Hadar site, partly because the argon content of the rocks had been measured incorrectly, leading to the sample ages being underestimated by up to 20 per cent.

However, the recent work on the KBS tuff suggests that the problems of using potassium-argon dating have now been overcome since different workers using a variety of techniques have all produced ages which cluster around 1.89 Myr. Drake et al.[15] used the $^{40}K/^{40}Ar$ method to obtain an age of 1.8 ± 0.1 Myr, while McDougall et al.[16] using the same method produced ages ranging from 1.88 to 1.92 Myr with a mean of 1.89 ± 0.01 Myr. These dates are also in agreement with a fission track age of 1.87 ± 0.04 Myr, which is further confirmation that the problems of potassium-argon dating have been solved. The fresh work[17] on the Hadar site in Ethiopia produced ages of 2.93 ± 0.11 Myr for the BKT–2 tephra and 3.60 ± 0.15 Myr for the Kada Moumou basalt. The hominid remains lie below the BKT–2 tephra and so are older than 2.9 Myr.

Other recently published potassium-argon dates include a date of 1.42 Myr for the layer overlying some australopithecine fossils from Chesowanja in North Kenya[18] and a date of 233 ± 3 kyr for the basalt overlying an Acheulian site in Israel.[19]

Thus it seems that, providing potassium-argon dating is carried out carefully, it can be the main dating technique for use on sites older than about 300,000 years.

5.3.5 Potassium-Argon Dating and Provenance Studies

Mitchell et al.[20] used potassium-argon dates on schist honestones from Viking sites in Denmark, Norway, West Germany and Poland to find likely sources of the raw materials. They conclude that a possible source for the dark grey schist which is Caledonian in age, with potassium-argon dates ranging from 403 ± 10 to 446 ± 7 Myr, is west Norway. A possible source for the light grey schist which is Cambrian in age (potassium-argon dates from 920 ± 30 to 950 ± 15 Myr) is Telemark in south Norway. Thus the honestones were made from imported rather than local material.

5.4 Fission Track Dating

5.4.1 Introduction

Fission track dating has similarities with TL dating, in that it also uses the damage produced in crystal lattices by the decay of atomic nuclei in order to date the formation of the material. Its main use has been for dating volcanic glasses like pumice and obsidian, but it can also be used to date some man-made glass and minerals extracted from pottery. It has been used on objects ranging in age from 20 years to 1 billion years. Normally, however, for samples from the recent past, the laboratory time required to obtain an accurate age is too great for fission track dating to be a satisfactory method. Today for recent sites, TL dating would probably be a more suitable dating method, but fission track dating is still used for Early Man sites, especially where potassium-argon dating cannot be applied.

5.4.2 Principles of Fission Track Dating

As well as undergoing normal radioactive decay, nuclei of uranium 238 occasionally undergo a much more violent process: spontaneous fission. In this process the nucleus splits into two roughly equal halves, both with mass numbers in the range 70 to 160. These two halves fly apart with tremendous force and so do great damage to the nearby crystal lattice. This damage is not visible to the naked eye, but if the glass or crystal is placed in a suitable etching agent (hydrofluoric acid for glass) the damaged areas are attacked more readily than the rest of the surface, so that the fission tracks are enlarged sufficiently to be visible under an optical microscope. In many glasses and minerals, the tracks can survive at room temperature for millions of years and are only destroyed by heating to temperatures above 500°C. Thus the melting associated with the production of glass and the firing of pottery destroys any tracks which were present before these events. After the heating the number of tracks then starts to increase steadily with time, and so, by counting the number of tracks per unit area, it is possible to determine the age of the sample.

In practice, it is also necessary to determine the concentration of ^{238}U within the sample, since this can range from a few per cent in certain types of nineteenth-century glass where uranium was added as a colourant, to less than 1 part per million in volcanic glasses. This is done by irradiating the sample with slow (low energy) neutrons from a nuclear reactor, in order to induce fission in nuclei of uranium 235. (This is the process used in nuclear reactors to produce electricity.) The sample is then re-etched and the number of fission tracks produced calculated. Because the number of neutrons hitting the sample and the rate at which they produce fission are both known, the concentration of ^{235}U in the sample can be calculated. It is then assumed that the ratio $^{235}U:^{238}U$ is constant and approximately 1:138 so that the concentration of ^{238}U can be calculated. Since the rate at which ^{238}U undergoes spontaneous fission is known, it is then possible to calculate the age of the sample.

5.4.3 Accuracy and Problems

The main limitation on the accuracy of fission track dating is ensuring that a large enough area of the sample is examined, so that enough ancient tracks are counted to enable an accurate estimate of the sample age to be made (cf. the problems of counting sufficient decays in C–14 dating). To obtain an accuracy of ± 10 per cent (1 standard deviation) it is necessary to count a least 100 tracks. This may not sound many, but it takes about an hour to scan a surface area of $1 \, cm^2$ using a suitable microscope to detect the fission track etch pits. Furthermore, as most material only contain a few parts per million of uranium, and less than 1 in a million nuclei of ^{238}U undergo spontaneous fission (most undergo normal radioactive decay) fission tracks are comparatively rare except in very old samples. For example, a 10,000 year old volcanic glass containing 3 ppm of uranium would only have a track density of 10 tracks per cm². Thus it would take 10 hours to count sufficient tracks to enable the object to be dated to the 1 σ level. This would be very tedious for the person doing the counting, and hence fission track dating is only really suitable for very old samples or those with a very high uranium concentration. For example, if a sample contains 1 ppm of uranium it will only be possible to count sufficient tracks to date it in under an hour if it is over 300,000 years old. For more recent samples TL or some other dating method should be used. Hence fission track dating is not normally applicable to pottery. The one exception is if the pottery contains minerals which have a high concentration of uranium, because then the track density may be sufficiently great for the counting to be completed in a reasonable length of time. For example, zircons contain 0.1 to 1 per cent of uranium, so fission track dating could be used on zircons from pottery as young as 300 years old. The problems of fission track dating are discussed further by Fleischer.[21]

5.4.4 Applications

A recent application of fission track dating has been in helping to resolve the controversy over the potassium-argon dates for the KBS tuff and associated hominid remains in northern Kenya (see section 3.4). Gleadow[22] discusses the problems he encountered when applying the fission track method to zircons from the KBS tuff. In particular, the zircons had only a low track density. He also found that the rate of etching depended on the orientation of the tracks, resulting in some tracks becoming visible more quickly than others. From his measurements on the zircons, he concluded that the age of the tuff is 1.87 ± 0.04 Myr, in agreement with the revised potassium-argon dates for the tuff.

The fission track method has also been used to date several Early Paleolithic sites in Japan.[23]

5.5 Obsidian Hydration Dating

5.5.1 Introduction

Obsidian hydration dating is a method for obtaining dates from worked pieces of obsidian. Although attempts have been made to obtain absolute dates using it, it is probably best used only as a relative dating technique because any dates obtained depend both on the burial conditions and on the obsidian's precise source. Its main advantage is that it is cheap and quick to do, so a large number of obsidian hydration dates can be obtained for the cost of a single C–14 date. Thus it is possible to build up a detailed picture of how the obsidian from a site was used, and in particular, whether it was all worked at the same time or whether some types of object were made earlier than others. Its other advantage is that the actual production of the object of interest is dated rather than material above or below it, so that the dates obtained are directly related to the archaeological problem. Objects ranging in age from 500 to 100,000 years have been dated, though the actual age range which can be dated will vary from site to site.

5.5.2 Principles of Obsidian Hydration Dating

When a fresh surface is formed on a piece of obsidian, it very slowly absorbs water from its surroundings and a hydration layer is formed on the exposed surface. The water slowly penetrates into the obsidian, so as time passes the hydration layer becomes thicker. This is similar to, though very much slower than, the way water will travel up a piece of blotting paper when only part of it is dipped in water. The thickness of the hydration layer can easily be found by looking at a thin slice of obsidian removed from the artefact under a microscope, because the hydration layer will appear different to the main body of the obsidian. Hydration layers vary in thickness from less than $1\mu m$ to about $20\mu m$ and they can be measured with an accuracy of about $\pm0.2\mu m$. Thus by measuring the thickness of the hydration layers on a selection of obsidian objects, it is possible to determine whether the objects are of the same or different ages, providing they are all made from obsidian of the same chemical composition.

5.5.3 Problems

If absolute ages (i.e. ages in calendar years) are to be obtained using obsidian hydration dating, it is necessary to know the rate at which the hydration layer grows. This is where the problems arise. The growth of the hydration layer is normally thought to obey the following equation:

$$D^2 = kt$$

where D is the thickness of the hydration layer and t the length of time for which the surface of the obsidian has been exposed; k is a constant which must be determined for each site and set of samples. The first important point about the equation is that the age of the sample is proportional to the square of the thickness of the hydration layer. Thus the thicker the layer the more slowly it grows (see Figure 5.3).

Figure 5.3 The variation of the thickness of an obsidian hydration layer with time

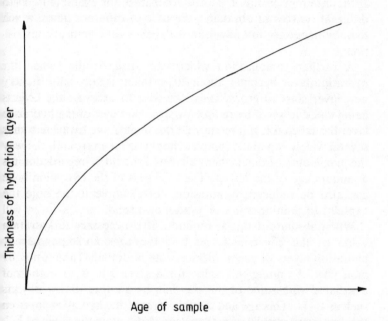

If only relative dates are required (i.e. if the samples are only to be arranged in order of age), the value of the constant k need not be known, as long as those factors which affect its value are the same for all the samples considered. It has been found that both the burial temperature and the precise chemical composition of the obsidian affect the rate at which the hydration layer grows and hence the value of k. However, the water content of the environment is unimportant, because under natural conditions the surface of the obsidian is always saturated with water. For relative dating, providing all the samples are from the same site so that it can be assumed that they will all have experienced the same climatic changes, a knowledge of the burial temperature is not required.

Differences in chemical composition between the objects pose more serious problems, because even if all the obsidian comes from a single source, chemical variations within the source may be sufficient to lead to different values of k for different objects.[24] Thus before relative ages can be established for the objects, it is first necessary to group them according to their chemical composition, so that only the objects within a single group are compared. If the different groups are to be compared, for example to see if different sources of obsidian were used at different times, it will then be necessary to know how k depends on chemical composition.

A further complication which can arise, is that when the hydration layer becomes about 20µm thick, it may fall off and a new layer start to grow. Thus it is wise to examine the objects being dated to see if there are any signs that part of the hydration layer has fallen off. If it seems that this might have happened, then several widely separated samples should be taken from the object, the maximum age that is then calculated should be regarded as the minimum age of the object. The thickness of the hydration layer can also be reduced by abrasion, for example if the object is exposed to running water or wind-blown sand.

When absolute dating is required, it is necessary to know the value of the constant k, so that the ages corresponding to hydration layers of given thickness can be found. The most common way of finding this value for a given site is to date finds associated with some of the obsidian by another dating method such as C–14. This age and the thickness of the hydration layer on the associated obsidian are then used to calculate the value of k. If more than one type of obsidian is present, then it will be necessary to calculate the value of k for each type of obsidian. When using this method to obtain absolute dates care must be taken to ensure that the age used when calculating the value of k really is the age of the manufacture of the artefact. If it is not, then all the dates obtained for that site by obsidian hydration dating will be wrong. The other problem with this method of calculating k is that the value obtained represents the average value since the burial of the object used for calibration. Thus it may not be a realistic average value for all the obsidian objects from the site. In particular if the objects cover a long time span, during which there was a marked climatic change such as the end of the last glaciation, then the value of k obtained by this method will only apply to some of the objects dated. For example k can increase by a factor of 10 from $0.4\mu m^2/$thousand years to $4.5\mu m^2/$thousand years when the effective environmental temperature increases from 1°C to 20°C. In one case,[25] when the hydration rate was determined for obsidian artefacts from six sites in Japan, which had been dated by the C–14 method and ranged in age from 1,000 to 15,000 years, it was found that the hydration rate was 25 per cent higher over the past 4,000 years than previously.

5.5.4 Applications

At present obsidian hydration dating seems to have been mainly used in Central and North America, but recently Michels et al.[26] used the technique to provide a large number of absolute dates for Prospect Farm Site in Kenya. They were unable to date phase 1 of the Middle Stone Age; the artefacts from phase 2 had heavily damaged surfaces and gave ages which were obviously too young (less than 90,000 years). The obsidian artefacts from the later layers, however, all gave acceptable dates ranging from $119,646 \pm 1668$ BP for phase 3 to $2,562 \pm 129$ BP for the Pastoral Neolithic. At some periods two types of obsidian, which hydrated at different rates, were in use, and so by dating both types, it was possible to obtain two sets of dates for these periods which agreed with each other. In addition, for the later phases (after about 10,000 BP) the dates obtained using obsidian hydration dating agreed with those obtained on associated material using the C–14 method. These comparisons are tabulated in Michels el al.,[27] which also describes the method used for calculating k. This involved measuring the size of the hydration rim produced in the laboratory when the obsidian was held at 200°C for varying lengths of time. It was then possible to calculate the value of k from these measurements and so obtain obsidian hydration dates which were independent of any other dating technique, though the burial temperature will still have to be estimated if absolute dates are to be obtained.

5.6 Amino Acid Racemisation Dating

5.6.1 Introduction

Amino acid racemisation dating or direct aspartic acid racemisation dating was developed in the early 1970s to provide absolute dates for bone which, at that time, could not be dated by the C–14 method. Compared to conventional C–14 dating, its two big advantages were, firstly, that it enabled small samples to be dated, since normally less than 10g of bone is required for each sample; and, secondly, that samples up to 100,000 years old (and possibly older) could be dated. Its big disadvantage is that the quantity measured to provide the date is highly temperature dependent, so it is necessary to know the temperature of the bone during its burial. In addition bone, which has been heated (even to temperatures less than 150°C) at any time in antiquity cannot be dated. A further problem is that the dates for each site have to be calibrated by measurements on samples of known age from that site. Thus its main role was seen as being the dating of hominid fragments from sites where other animal bones were plentiful. A C–14 date could be obtained for the most recent animal bones and used to calibrate the amino acid racemisation dates for the sites. The hominid fragments could then be dated just by the amino acid racemisation method to check that they do really belong to the same context as the other bones. Because of these problems, amino acid racemisation dating may be replaced by the recent developments in C–14 dating which enable small samples to be dated (see Chapter 2) or by ESR dating which can also be applied to small bone samples (see Chapter 3.6).

5.6.2 Chemical Formulae and Isomers

A molecule, which is the smallest part into which a chemical compound can be split without changing its properties, consists of two or more atoms joined together. Certain rules normally have to be obeyed when combining atoms to form molecules, thus restricting the chemical compounds which can exist. The bonds which join atoms together in molecules have fixed orientations in space and each atom has a fixed number of bonds. For example the four bonds of the carbon atom point towards the four corners of a tetrahedron.

The simplest way of describing a molecule is by listing all the atoms it contains in a molecular formula such as H_2O (water) or CH_4O (wood alcohol or methanol). However, in the majority of cases several ways of arranging the atoms can be found, so that several compounds have the same molecular formula. Such compounds with the same molecular formulae, but different structures, are known as isomers. A simple example is C_2H_6O

where isomers (a) and (b) are possible. (a) is the liquid ethyl alcohol or ethanol, the intoxicating component of alcoholic drinks, and (b) is a relatively unreactive gas, dimethyl ether. To save drawing the complete structural formulae (a) can be written CH_3CH_2OH and (b) as CH_3OCH_3.

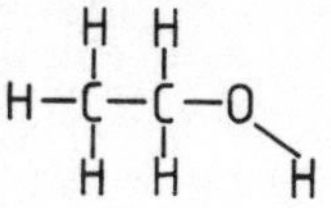

(a)

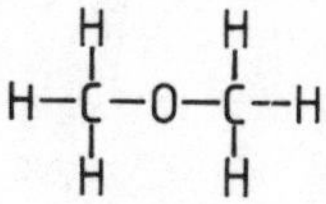

(b)

In some forms of isomerism the arrangement of the atoms in space is important and structural formulae (a) and (b) must be elaborated to represent the three-dimensional structure of the molecules. This is done by using wedges ◄ to represent bonds to atoms above the plane of the page and dashes ⅏ for bonds to atoms below the plane of the paper. Thus naturally occurring glycine may be represented as (c). Compounds such as glycine which have a carbon atom bearing four different substituents (atoms or groups of atoms) are known as chiral and show a special form of isomerism, because they can exist in two forms which are mirror images of each other. For example (d) can only be superimposed on (e) if it is reflected in a mirror and not if it is rotated about an axis through the carbon atom. Pairs of compounds related in this way are called enantiomers and have very similar properties, differing only in their interactions with other chiral systems.

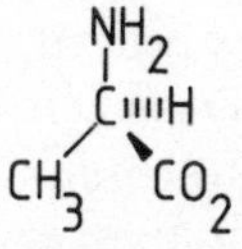

(c)

For particular classes of compound, such as sugars and amino acids, the two mirror forms are specified by prefixing D- and L- to the chemical name, hence L-aspartic acid. This system has the weakness that there is no simple relation between the structure and prefix — the assignment being for historical reasons, but the advantage that living plants and animals normally only produce L-amino acids. Molecules containing several chiral centres become

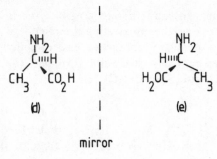

very complex with a large number of isomers being formed for each bonding arrangement. When a mixture contains equal amounts of the D- and L-isomers of a compound it is known as a racemic mixture. Further information on this subject can be found in introductory books on organic chemistry.[28]

5.6.3 Principles and Problems of Amino Acid Racemisation Dating

The existence of enantiomeric forms provides the basis of amino acid racemisation dating. When plants and animals make chemical compounds they normally produce only a single enantiomer, rather than a racemic mixture. Thus the amino acids produced by living plants and animals are made only as the L-enantiomers. However, once it is made the L-form can change into the D-form (or vice versa), so as time passes the amount of the D-form present increases. In most tissues during the lifetime of the plant or animal the amino acids are constantly being replaced, so they do not survive for long enough for a significant quantity of the D-isomer to form. But once the animal (or plant) is dead, no fresh amino acids are made so the amount of the D-isomer slowly increases until eventually there are equal quantities of the two isomers present. This process is known as racemisation, and providing that the rate at which it occurs is known, it is possible to find the date of death of the animal by measuring the amount of the D-isomer which has formed.

To date a specimen by this method approximately 10g of bone are required. At present other materials have not been dated. The sample is cut from the bone, and soil and other contaminating material are removed. The sample is then ground up and treated with various chemicals so that the amino acids are converted into forms suitable for measurement. The D/L ratio for any amino acid of interest can then be found using an automatic amino acid analyser. The process is described in more detail by Belluomini.[29] Normally only the D/L ratio of aspartic acids is of interest because it racemises most quickly, and the ratio can be measured very accurately. Sometimes measurements of the amounts of other amino acids present can also provide useful information. For example, if the bones have been heated they will be unsuitable for racemisation dating because the heating will have produced a large amount of racemisation. However, some acids such as serine and threonine are destroyed much more quickly by heating than is aspartic acid, and so if the ratio of either of these acids to aspartic acid is unexpectedly low the sample can be rejected on the grounds that it has been heated in antiquity.

Before the D/L ratio can be converted into an age for the sample, the racemisation rate has to be determined. This appears to be mainly affected by the burial temperature of the samples, with racemisation proceeding more quickly at higher temperatures. Thus if the burial temperature is known, the racemisation rate, and hence the age of the sample can be calculated. In practice, even if the modern ground temperature is known, it is unlikely that the temperature history of the site is known with sufficient accuracy for the rate to be calculated. Instead, the normal procedure is to take a bone of known age from the site (normally one which has been dated by the C–14 method) and measure the D/L ratio of its aspartic acid. The racemisation rate for this bone can then be calculated, and by assuming that it has been constant throughout the history of the site, the D/L ratios for the other samples can be converted into absolute ages. One advantage of this calibration technique is that, as long as the racemisation rate is constant at a site, it does not matter if it depends on factors other than temperature since the calibration will also correct for other site specific factors. For example, it has been suggested[30] that this is the reason why acid racemisation dates do not appear to be affected by the leaching of amino acids from the samples, i.e. the amino acids in the bones of known age will have leached in a similar way to those in the bones being dated and so the calibration procedure will correct for this effect as well as uncertainties in the burial temperature. The big disadvantage is that if the date for the sample used in the calibration is wrong, then all the dates which rely on that calibration will be wrong. In one case (see section 5.6.4) the age of human bones from North

America appears to have been overestimated by a factor of about 10.

Studies suggest that the D/L ratio for aspartic acid can be measured with an accuracy of about ±8 per cent. However the total error in the dates is likely to be larger than this as the uncertainty in the C–14 date used for the calibration must also be included. Hence in general amino acid racemisation dates should be accurate to ±15 per cent or better.

5.6.4 Applications

Amino acid racemisation has been used to date bones from North America and Italy. Bada and Masters Helfman[31] discuss the technique in some detail, and date a variety of human bones from North America. Their most important finding was that man appeared to be present in North America about 50,000 years ago, since bones from several sites gave dates between 40 and 50,000 years BP. However, all these early dates were calibrated using the same C–14 date because the sites appeared similar and there was a shortage of material suitable for C–14 dating. Recent measurements using accelerator C–14 dating, suggest that the date used for calibration was wrong and that the skeletons are in fact only 4 to 6,000 years old.[32] This does not mean that acid racemisation dating does not work, but rather that great care must be taken when choosing the sample to be used for calibration. In particular, it will always be dangerous to rely on a single C–14 date for the calibration.

Belluomini[33] has made an extensive study of samples from Italy. He compared the amino acid racemisation dates for both human and animal bones from a variety of sites with those obtained by the C–14 method on either the same bones or closely associated charcoal. In general he found good agreement between the two methods, with the average difference being 8 per cent and the greatest 18 per cent. He was also able to date directly human remains which previously had only been dated by associated material and obtained a date of 20,300 years BP for a child's skeleton.

Finally some Japanese[34] workers have used a variant of the method to find the age at death of some human skeletons. The amino acids in tooth enamel, unlike those in most other tissues, are not constantly replaced during the lifetime of the animal. Instead, while the animal is still alive, the D/L ratio in the tooth enamel steadily increases. If the time since burial and the average burial temperature are known the amount of racemisation expected to occur since burial can be calculated. The difference between this and the measured amount of racemisation can then be used to calculate the age at death of the skeleton. The authors obtained ages of between 45 and 55 years for some 700 year old skeletons from Japan.

5.7 Relative Dating of Bone

5.7.1 Introduction

Once bone is buried its chemical composition starts to change. Firstly, the protein in it decays resulting in the loss of nitrogen. Secondly, uranium and fluorine from the groundwater become incorporated in the structure of the bone. The extent to which these changes have occurred can be used to help decide whether bones found on a site are ancient and contemporary with the site, or instead are later intrusions. The rate at which these changes occur is too uncertain and too dependent on the burial conditions for them to provide absolute dates, but despite the development of techniques which can provide absolute dates, these relative techniques are still in use. This is doubtless partly because they are better established than the absolute techniques, but in addition relative dates can often be obtained more cheaply and on smaller samples than are needed for absolute dates. It is even possible to measure the uranium content of bones non-destructively. Thus one role of relative dating is to establish whether all the bones from a site are of the same age. If they are, then the less important animal bones can be sacrificed for absolute dating, while the human remains are preserved.

5.7.2 The Use of Nitrogen Content

Nitrogen is an essential element in protein and forms roughly 4 per cent by weight of fresh bone. Under normal conditions the protein content of dead bone slowly decreases so that in 10,000 year old bone there is less than 0.1 per cent nitrogen present. The nitrogen content of bone can easily be measured in the laboratory using standard techniques which require 100mg or less of bone from each specimen. This can enable modern bones to be separated from older ones.

Conclusions based solely on nitrogen measurements should be treated with caution, however, as there is some dispute as to whether the nitrogen content of bone decreases fairly uniformly, or suddenly disappears when the bone is in a comparatively advanced state of decay.

Bealey and Lunt[35] in a study on teeth of known age found that their nitrogen content depended more on the state of preservation of the teeth than on the age. Molleson,[36] examining the animal and human bones found in Quanterness chambered cairn, Orkney, found that the nitrogen content of the human bones (which were all assumed to date from the Neolithic) ranged from 0.25 to 3.89 per cent. C–14 measurements on some of the bones with a high nitrogen content confirmed their Neolithic date. Thus, at this site at least, the nitrogen content of the bones was no use in determining which animals had been placed in the cairn in Neolithic times and which had found their way in at a later date.

More encouraging results, however, were obtained by Haddy and Hanson[37] when they studied the nitrogen and fluorine content of human skeletons from Moundville in the United States. They found the expected correlation between nitrogen and fluorine content. In addition, they compared the relative dates obtained by the chemical analysis with those assigned to the bones on the basis of the associated pottery. For most samples the two methods produced similar dates, and where they did not the authors suggest that this is because some of the graves were re-used at a later date, so that the pottery dated from one burial and the bones from the other.

5.7.3 Uranium and Fluorine Dating of Bone

The inorganic component of bone is the mineral hydroxyapatite which is composed of calcium, phosphate and hydroxyl ions. When bone is buried in ordinary soil, any fluorine or uranium ions in the ground water can replace the hydroxyl or calcium ions respectively in the bone, so as time passes the uranium and fluorine content of the bone increases. Thus the fluorine content of bone ranges from 0 per cent in modern bone to a theoretical maximum of almost 4 per cent in old bone, while the uranium content ranges from 0 ppm in modern bone to 600 ppm in one million year old bone. The rate at which these elements build-up in bone depends on both the burial conditions of the bones and the concentration of fluorine and uranium in the ground water. Measurements of the concentrations of these elements in bone are thus normally only used to give relative, not absolute dates.

Originally the fluorine content of bone was measured using standard chemical techniques on a sample of 100 mg removed from the bone, but today a variety of other techniques[38] are also available, some of which require much smaller samples. The uranium content of bone is normally found from measurements of the radioactivity of the bone, and so can be measured non-destructively. Both elements tend to be concentrated at the surface of the bone, so the uranium and fluorine content of thick bones will tend to be less than that of thin ones. Thus, whenever possible, similar bones should be compared when relative dating is carried out.

One famous example of the relative dating of bone is the study of the Galley Hill skeleton and the Swanscombe skull. The Galley Hill skeleton, which is of modern *homo sapiens* type, was found in river terrace gravels which also contained hand axes and animal bones expected to date from the Lower Paleolithic. Lower in the same gravels was the Swanscombe skull. Originally the fluorine and nitrogen content of the bones was measured. The fluorine content ranged from 1.7 per cent for the Swanscombe skull and 1.5 per cent for the animal bones to 0.5 per cent for the Galley Hill skeleton. Only traces of nitrogen were found in the Swanscombe skull and the animal bones, but the nitrogen content of the Galley Hill skeleton was 1.6 per cent. This showed that the Galley Hill skeleton was much later than the other remains and presumably was a burial which had been intruded into the gravels. A C–14 date of 3310 ± 150 bp suggests that the Galley Hill skeleton dates from the Early Bronze Age. Originally only the uranium content of the Swanscombe skull was measured and was found to be 27ppm. More recently[39] the uranium content of the Galley Hill skeleton has also been measured and found to be less than 5ppm, providing further evidence for the differing ages of the two sets of bones.

Uranium relative dating was also used at Pont Newydd Cave.[40] One modern dog femur, seven bear bones from the different levels in the cave and the human mandible and vertebra were studied. All the bones, except the modern dog, contained measurable quantities of uranium, showing that they were not modern. However, the quantities of uranium in the ancient bones were so similar that no further conclusions could be drawn about their ages.

The measurements of fluorine content at Moundville are discussed in section 7.2.

Thus measurements of the fluorine and uranium content of bones still have a useful role in checking that all the bones from a single layer are likely to be of the same date, and enabling any bones that are much older or much younger than the bulk of the material to be rejected.

126   *Other Dating Techniques*

Notes

1. H.P. Schwarz, 'Absolute age determination of archaeological sites by uranium series dating of travertines', *Archaeometry*, vol. 22 (1980), pp. 3–24.
2. B. Szabo and D. Collins, 'Ages of fossil bones from British Interglacial sites', *Nature*, vol. 254 (1975), pp. 680–2.
3. Melvyn Gascoyne, Andrew P. Currant and Thomas G. Lord, 'Ipswichian fauna of the Victoria Cave and the marine paleolithic record', *Nature*, vol. 294 (1982), pp. 652–4.
4. H.S. Green, L.B. Stringer, S.N. Collcutt, A.P. Currant, J. Huxtable, H.P. Schwarz, N. Debenham, C. Embleton, P. Bull, T.I. Molleson and R.E. Bevins, 'Pontnewydd Cave in Wales, — a new Middle Pleistocene hominid site', *Nature*, vol. 294 (1984), pp. 707–13.
5. Bonnie Blackwell, Henry P. Schwartz and Andre Debenath, 'Absolute dating of hominids and Palaeolithic artifacts of the cave of La Chaise-de-Vouthon (Charente) France', *Journal of Archaeological Science*, vol. 10 (1983), pp. 493–513.
6. Henry P. Schwarz, Bonnie Blackwell, Paul Goldberg and Anthony E. Marks, 'Uranium series dating of travertine from archaeological sites, Nahal Zin, Israel', *Nature*, vol. 277 (1979), pp. 558–60.
7. H.P. Schwarz and A.G. Latham, 'Uranium series age determination of travertines from the site of Vertesszöllös, Hungary', *Journal of Archaeological Science*, vol. 11 (1984), pp. 327–36.
8. Henry P. Schwarz and Bonnie Blackwell, '^{230}Th/^{234}U age of a Mousterian site in France', *Nature*, vol. 301 (1983), pp. 236–7.
9. R.S. Harmon, J. Geazek and K. Nowak, '^{230}Th/^{234}U dating of travertine from the Bilzingsleben archaeological site', *Nature*, vol. 284 (1980), pp. 132–5.
10. H.P. Schwarz, 'Absolute age determination of archaeological sites by uranium series dating of travertines', pp. 3–24.
11. Garniss H. Curtis, 'Improvements in potassium-argon dating: 1962–1975', *World Archaeology*, vol. 7 (1975), pp. 198–209.
12. R.E. Drake, G.H. Curtis, T.E. Cerling, B.W. Cerling and J. Hampel, 'KBS Tuff dating and geochronology of tuffaceous sediments in the Koobi Fora and Shungera Formations, East Africa', *Nature*, vol. 283 (1980), pp. 368–72.
13. I. McDougall, R. Maier, P. Sutherland-Hawkes and A.J.W. Gleadow, 'K-Ar age estimate for the KBS tuff, East Turkana, Kenya', *Nature*, vol. 284 (1980), pp. 230–4.
14. Robert C. Walter and James L. Aronson, 'Revisions of K/Ar ages for the Hadar hominid site, Ethiopia', *Nature*, vol. 296 (1982), pp. 122–7.
15. R.E. Drake et al., 'KBS Tuff dating and geochronology of tuffaceous sediments in the Koobi Fora and Shungera Formations, East Africa', pp. 368–72.
16. I. McDougall et al., 'K-Ar age estimate for the KBS tuff, East Turkana, Kenya', pp. 230–4.
17. R.C. Walter and J.L. Aronson, 'Revisions of K/Ar ages for the Hadar hominid site, Ethiopia', pp. 122–7.
18. P.J. Hooker and J.A. Miller, 'K-Ar dating of the Pleistocene fossil hominid site at Chesowanja, North Kenya', *Nature*, vol. 282 (1979), pp. 710–12.
19. G. Feraud, D. York, C.M. Hall, N. Goren and H.P. Schwarz, '^{40}Ar/^{39}Ar age limit for an Acheulian site in Israel', *Nature*, vol. 304 (1983), pp. 263–5.
20. J.G. Mitchell, H. Askvik and H.G. Resi, 'Potassium argon dating of schist honestones from the Viking Age sites at Kaupang (Norway), Aggersborg (Denmark), Hedeby (West Germany) and Wolin (Poland) and their archaeological implications', *Journal of Archaeological Science*, vol. 11 (1984), pp. 171–6.
21. Robert L. Fleischer, 'Advances in fission track dating', *World Archaeology*, vol. 7 (1975), pp. 136–50.

22. A.J.W. Gleadow, 'Fission track age of the KBS Tuff and associated hominid remains in northern Kenya', *Nature*, vol. 284 (1980), pp. 225–30.

23. T.E.G. Reynolds, 'The Early Paleolithic of Japan', *Antiquity*, vol. 59 (1985), pp. 93–6.

24. Richard E. Hughes, 'Age and Exploitation of obsidian from the Medicine Lake Highland, California', *Journal of Archaeological Science*, vol. 9 (1982), pp. 173–85; Jonathon E. Ericson, 'New results in obsidian hydration dating', *World Archaeology*, vol. 7 (1975), pp. 151–9.

25. Y. Katsu and Y. Kondo, 'Dating of stone implements by using hydration layer of obsidian', *Japanese Journal of Geology and Geography*, vol. 36 (1965), pp. 45–60.

26. Joseph W. Michels, Ignatus S.T. Tsong and Charles M. Nelson, 'Obsidian dating and East African archaeology', *Science*, vol. 219 (1983), pp. 361–6.

27. J.W. Michels, I.S.T. Tsong and G.A. Smith, 'Experimentally derived hydration rates in obsidian dating', *Archaeometry*, vol. 25 (1983), pp. 107–18.

28. For example see S.S. Nathan and S.K. Murthy, *Organic Chemistry Made Simple* (W.H. Allen, London, 1968).

29. G. Belluomini, 'Direct aspartic acid racemisation dating of human bones from archaeological sites of central southern Italy', *Archaeometry*, vol. 23 (1981), pp. 125–37.

30. K. King Jr. and J.L. Bada, 'Effect of in situ leaching on amino acid racemisation rates in fossil bone', *Nature*, vol. 281 (1979), pp. 135–7.

31. Jeffrey L. Bada and Patricia Masters Helfman, 'Amino acid racemisation dating of fossil bones', *World Archaeology*, vol. 7 (1975), pp. 160–73.

32. J.L. Bada, R. Gillespie, J.A.J. Gowlett and R.E.M. Hedges, 'Accelerator mass spectrometry radiocarbon ages of amino acid extract from Californian paleoindian skeletons', *Nature*, vol. 312 (1984), pp. 442–4.

33. G. Belluomini, 'Direct aspartic acid racemization dating of human bones from archaeological sites of central southern Italy', pp. 125–37.

34. Akira Skimoyama and Kaoru Harada, 'An age determination of an ancient burial mound man by apparent racemization reaction of aspartic acid in tooth dentine', *Chemistry Letters*, (1984), pp. 1661–4.

35. J.G. Beeley and P.A. Lunt, 'The nature of the biochemical changes in softened dentine from archaeological sites', *Journal of Archaeological Science*, vol. 7 (1980), pp. 371–7.

36. Theya Molleson, 'The relative dating of bones from Quanterness chambered cairn, Orkney', *Antiquity*, vol. 55 (1981), pp. 127–9.

37. A. Haddy and A. Hanson, 'Nitrogen and fluorine dating of Moundville skeletal samples', *Archaeometry*, vol. 24 (1982), pp. 37–44.

38. R.E. Shroy, H.W. Kraner, K.W. Jones, J.S. Jacobson and C.I. Heller, 'Determination of Fluorine in food samples by the $^{19}F(p,p'\gamma)^{19}F$ reaction', *Nuclear Instruments and Methods*, vol. 149, pp. 313–16.

39. Ioanis C. Demetsopoullos, Richard Burleigh and Kenneth P. Oakley, 'Relative and absolute dating of the human and skeleton from Galley Hill, Kent', *Journal of Archaeological Science*, vol. 10 (1983), pp. 129–34.

40. H.S. Green, L.B. Stringer, S.N. Collcutt, A.P. Currant, J. Huxtable, H.P. Schwarz, N. Debenham, C. Embleton, P. Bull, T.I. Molleson and R.E. Bevins, 'Pontnewydd Cave in Wales, a new Middle Pleistocene hominid site', *Nature*, vol. 294 (1981), pp. 707–13.

6 OTHER ISOTOPIC STUDIES

6.1 Introduction

The main archaeological application of studies of the isotope ratios of elements is to enable objects and sites to be dated. The most important techniques which rely on the properties of individual isotopes such as potassium-argon, uranium series and C–14 dating have already been discussed, as has the use of potassium-argon dating in provenance studies. However, studies of the isotopic composition of samples can also provide other information for the archaeologist, and they have been applied in three main areas. The first is the use of the ratio of the stable isotopes of carbon (and more recently nitrogen) in bone to provide information about ancient diet including the importance of seafood in certain cultures and the date of the introduction of maize in America. The second is the study of oxygen isotope ratios in certain types of shells found in marine sediments to provide information about climatic conditions and in particular the surface temperature of the ocean. As well as being important in its own right, this information provides a useful relative dating technique in the Paleolithic. A variant on this technique enables the seasonal use of seafood to be studied. Finally, isotope studies have provided information about the provenance of various materials. Several different isotope ratios have been used but, as yet, the most important application has been the use of lead isotopes for metal provenance studies.

6.2 Carbon Isotope Studies and Ancient Diet

6.2.1 Variations in Carbon Isotope Ratios in Bone

In the chapter on C–14 dating it was mentioned that the ratio of the stable isotopes of carbon, ^{12}C and ^{13}C in plants and animals is not constant, but the cause of the variations was not discussed in detail. In plants, the $^{13}C/^{12}C$ ratio depends primarily on the type of plant considered, but in animal remains a major influence on the ratio is the food eaten by the animal. Hence measurements of the

$^{13}C/^{12}C$ ratio in human bones can provide important information about ancient diets, which in turn can increase our knowledge of ancient farming practices and may determine whether or not particular peoples were nomadic. Further information about ancient diet can be obtained by studying the elemental composition of bone (see Chapter 7.7.1).

The differences in the ratio arise in the following way. The $^{13}C/$ ^{12}C ratio for carbon dioxide in the atmosphere is assumed to be constant. When plants take in carbon dioxide for use in photosynthesis they preferentially absorb the light isotope ^{12}C due to an effect known as the kinetic isotope effect. This preferential absorption is known as isotopic fractionation. Further fractionation occurs during the chemical reactions by which plants convert the carbon dioxide into leaves and other tissue. There are three main photosynthetic routes used by plants, each of which produces a characteristic degree of fractionation. The C_3 (Calvin cycle) route is used by all trees, and most shrubs and grasses which are adapted to temperate or shaded environments. The most important plant to use the C_4 (Hatch-Slack) pathway is maize, but it is also used by millet, sugar cane and grasses which grow in regions with high temperatures and radiation such as the savannah regions of Africa. Finally, Crassulacean Acid Metabolism (CAM) is used by succulents.[1] The fractionation produced by these different routes is described by the number of parts per thousand (‰) by which the $^{13}C/^{12}C$ ratio of the sample differs from an agreed standard (the Chicago PDB marine carbonate standard). Hence:

$$\delta^{13}C\ (‰) = (\frac{^{13}C/^{12}C\ \text{in sample}}{^{13}C/^{12}C\ \text{in standard}} - 1) \times 1000$$

Samples which have a higher ^{13}C ratio than the standard have positive $\delta^{13}C$, while those which contain less have negative $\delta^{13}C$ values. If a process leads to a sample containing more ^{13}C than it did previously the sample is said to have been enriched with respect to ^{13}C. δ values (with appropriate standards) are also used to measure other isotopic ratios. The mean $\delta^{13}C$ values for the three pathways are $-26.5‰$ for the foliage of C_3 plants, $-12.5‰$ for C_4 plants and $-16.5‰$ for CAM plants.[2]

The differences between these values remain throughout the food chain when plants are eaten by animals or humans, though when plants or animals are eaten further fractionation of roughly

3‰ occurs. The chemical reactions involved in converting food into bone produce further fractionation, and so, compared to the $\delta^{13}C$ value for the food the $\delta^{13}C$ value for the bone collagen is more positive by about 5‰, while for bone carbonate it is more positive by 12‰. Thus animals with exclusively C_3 diets have $\delta^{13}C$ values of $-21.5‰$ for collagen and $-14.5‰$ for bone carbonate, while those with exclusively C_4 diets have values of $-7.5‰$ for collagen and $-0.5‰$ for bone carbonate. Hence, with herbivorous animals it is possible to tell whether their diet was exclusively C_3 or C_4 plants or a mixture by measuring the $\delta^{13}C$ values for their bones. With human bones the situation is more complicated, because men normally have a mixed diet containing both plants and animals. In addition, marine animals may take in carbonates dissolved in seawater, while land snails may take in limestone grit. Each of these processes produces different $\delta^{13}C$ values, so, for example, sea shells have a mean $\delta^{13}C$ value of 0‰. This means that several different human diets could produce the same $\delta^{13}C$ values. For example, a diet consisting solely of C_4 plants might be indistinguishable from one containing a mixture of C_3 plants and sea food. Thus studies of $\delta^{13}C$ values for human bones are probably of more use in detecting changes in diet over time in one group of people, or showing whether or not two groups of people had a similar diet, rather than giving the proportions of C_3 and C_4 plants or plants and animals in a diet. In addition, if it is known that a group of people had only a limited range of foodstuffs available to them it may be possible to decide the relative importance of each in the diet.

$\delta^{13}C$ values can be found fairly simply in the laboratory. Either the organic (collagen) or the inorganic (carbonate) fraction is extracted from the bone and converted into carbon dioxide. A mass spectrometer is used to measure the $^{13}C/^{12}C$ ratio of both the sample and a standard. From these measurements the value of $\delta^{13}C$ for the sample can then be found. $\delta^{13}C$ can be measured with an accuracy of $\pm 0.1‰$, so the main limitation on the information which can be gained from $\delta^{13}C$ values is set by the fact that two people eating the same diet will produce slightly different amounts of fractionation. Hence, unless large numbers of individuals are compared, differences in $\delta^{13}C$ of less than 1‰ are not significant.[3] When plenty of bone is available, the measurements are best made on collagen, rather than bone carbonate, because it is unlikely to become contaminated while the bone is buried. However, about

10g of recent bone is required for each sample, and more will be required from ancient bones because the collagen content of bone decreases as it ages. If the carbonate fraction is used, then only about 1g of bone is needed irrespective of its age. The disadvantage of using the carbonate fraction is that during burial the carbonate may undergo exchange either with the carbon dioxide in the atmosphere or with carbonate in the ground water. Thus, the $\delta^{13}C$ value measured may be more a reflection of the $\delta^{13}C$ value of the ground water than of the ancient diet. Some workers have found the inorganic fraction cannot be used in dietary studies,[4] but others have shown, by comparing the $\delta^{13}C$ values for the organic and inorganic fractions of the same samples, that both fractions reflect the ancient diet.[5] Presumably the difference is due to the samples having come from different burial conditions, since exchange would be more likely to occur in wet limestone regions than in dry sandstone areas. Burnt bones cannot be used for dietary reconstruction because the heating causes further fractionation. De Niro et al.[6] found that heating bones above 200°C for 6 or more hours made $\delta^{13}C$ values more negative by up to 5‰. Ordinary cooking did not appear to affect $\delta^{13}C$ values.

6.2.2 Applications

Carbon isotope ratios have been studied for sites in South America, South Africa and Europe. Not only do they provide information about ancient diets, but they can also be used as evidence for whether or not peoples were nomadic, and in discussions about the maximum population an area could support.

Von Schirnding et al.[7] have studied the carbon isotope ratios in ostrich eggshells, both from modern birds fed on known diets and also shells from archaeological sites. Ostriches eat a wide variety of plants, so it was hoped that measurements of carbon isotope ratios would provide information about the mix of C_3, C_4 and CAM plants in the environment. They found that, although ostriches eat limestone grit to provide calcium for shell formation, the carbonate taken in at the same time is not used and so the carbon isotope ratio of the shell reflects the plants eaten by the birds. This means ostrich shells can be used for C–14 dating. However, they also found that where there is a choice, ostriches seem to prefer shrubs to grasses so while carbon isotope ratios will reveal whether two environments are different they will not necessarily reflect the mix of plants in a single environment.

More recently, Sealy and van der Merwe[8] measured $\delta^{13}C$ values for a selection of human hunter-gatherer skeletons ranging in age from 2000 to 8000 years. It had previously been assumed that, although some came from inland and some from the coast, they all came from a single population who lived on the coast in the winter and inland in the summer so as to make best use of the available food resources. However, the $\delta^{13}C$ values fell into two distinct groups, with the values for the coastal skeletons ranging from -11.2 to $-15.1\%o$ (mean $-13.5\%o$) while the values for the inland skeletons ranged from -17.3 to $20.2\%o$ (mean $-18.9\%o$). They also measured the $\delta^{13}C$ values for a range of possible foodstuffs and found marine-based foods had $\delta^{13}C$ values ranging from -12.3 to $-19.4\%o$ (mean $-15.6\%o$), terrestial plant foods covered a range from -22.3 to $-29.2\%o$ (mean $-25.4\%o$) and terrestial animal meat a range of -20.9 to $-25.8\%o$) (mean -23.6 $\%o$). If the $+5\%o$ fractionation due to turning food into bone collagen is allowed for, the results show that the coastal dwellers ate a maximum of 50 per cent terrestial food while some ate purely marine food. The inland dwellers, in contrast, had a purely terrestial diet. This work strongly suggests that, contrary to previous theories, the coastal and inland dwellers were two separate groups of people and that the people in the region did not migrate between the coast and the mountains on a seasonal basis. $\delta^{13}C$ values from collagen reflect the diet over about 5 years, so if the people all came from the same population they should have had the same $\delta^{13}C$ values.

In Denmark Tauber[9] looked at $\delta^{13}C$ values for skeletons ranging in age from 5200 BC to AD 1750. He found that the Mesolithic skeletons formed one group and had eaten a marine based diet, while the Neolithic and later skeletons formed a second group which had a terrestial based diet. This was surprising, because all the Neolithic remains came from within 200m of the sea and so might have been expected to have included some seafood in their diet.

Finally, van der Merwe and other workers have studied the introduction of maize into diets in America. At one Woodland site[10] in North America they found $\delta^{13}C$ changed from $-21.7\%o$ in pre-maize society to $-11.8\%o$ in AD 1300 when maize formed about 69 per cent of the diet. The introduction appears to have been gradual, since in AD 1000 $\delta^{13}C$ was $-18.1\%o$, corresponding to a diet containing 24 per cent maize, and in AD 1200, $-14.0\%o$

corresponding to 45 per cent maize. Between 3000 BC and AD 200 $\delta^{13}C$ values ranged between $-20.9‰$ and $-21.9‰$, with a mean of $-21.7‰$, showing that the diet contained only C_3 plants. They also found that at Parmana in Venezuela[11] $\delta^{13}C$ changed from $-26.0‰$ in 800 BC to $-10.3‰$ in AD 400, showing that over this time the diet changed from manioc to more than 80 per cent maize. They point out that this would enable the population of the region to increase 15–fold.

6.2.3 The Use of Nitrogen Isotopes

Nitrogen also has more than one stable isotope. These are ^{14}N with a natural abundance of 99.63 per cent and ^{15}N with a natural abundance of 0.37 per cent. All proteins contain nitrogen and this nitrogen undergoes fractionation as it passes along the food chain. Studies[12] have shown that measurements of $\delta^{15}N$ can also provide dietary information. Only certain plants, in particular legumes, can use or 'fix' nitrogen from the atmosphere. Other plants and all animals have to take in fixed nitrogen, i.e. nitrogen that has already been turned into a chemical compound such as a nitrate or an amino-acid or a protein. This means that diets containing legumes can be distinguished from diets which do not because legumes produce low $\delta^{15}N$ values.[13] In addition, it has been shown that animals with a marine-based diet have a mean $\delta^{15}N$ value of $14.8\pm2.5‰$, while animals, including freshwater fish, with a terrestial-based diet have a mean $\delta^{15}N$ value of $5.9\pm2.2‰$. Consequently measurements of $\delta^{15}N$ values could also be used to distinguish between such diets.

Hastdorf and De Niro[14] studied the $\delta^{13}C$ and $\delta^{15}N$ values for some sites in the Upper Mantaro Valley region of the central Peruvian Andes. They first showed that, although many of the plant remains were burnt, those that were still recognisable could be split into three groups, leguminous C_3 plants, non-leguminous C_3 plants and C_4 plants, on the basis of $\delta^{13}C$ and $\delta^{15}N$ values. They then analysed plant remains in the soil from three successive occupation levels which were burnt beyond recognition. They found that in the middle phase legumes and C_4 plants (maize) were much more common than in either of the other phases. Finally, they analysed the plant remains burnt onto some ceramic vessels which had presumably been used for cooking, and found evidence for non-leguminous C_3 and C_4 plants but no legumes. They conclude that these vessels were not used to cook legumes. Schwarz et al.[15] have also measured $\delta^{15}N$ values for Paleoindian skeletons from Ontario, Canada, but again legumes did not appear to be an important source of protein.

6.3 Oxygen Isotopes and Climate

6.3.1 Marine Isotope Record

Oxygen has three stable isotopes ^{16}O, ^{17}O and ^{18}O with abundances of 99.76, 0.037 and 0.204 per cent respectively. Initially it was thought that the ratio of these isotopes in sea-water was constant and independent of temperature. However, when foraminfera (tiny crustaceans) remove calcium carbonate from the seawater to make their shells, fractionation occurs and the oxygen isotope ratio of their shells depends on the surface temperature of the water, since the kinetic isotope effect responsible for the fractionation is temperature-dependent. When these animals die, they often sink to the bottom of the ocean and become incorporated in the sediment there. This sediment builds up at a steady rate, so by extracting long cores from it and measuring the $^{18}O/^{16}O$ ratio for foraminfera at intervals along them, it is possible to build up a picture of past temperature variations. $\delta^{18}O$ for carbonate deposition becomes more negative by 2‰ for each 1°C increase in temperature. Unfortunately $\delta^{18}O$ of sea water is not constant, but instead becomes more negative during glaciations. This makes it difficult to calculate temperatures from $\delta^{18}O$ values in marine sediments because the two effects must be separated. Instead, $\delta^{18}O$ values are used to indicate whether the climate was warm or cool at a particular time, with highly negative values corresponding to interglacial periods, and less negative or positive values to glacials.

The climatic changes over the past 2 million years have been studied in this way using deep-sea sediment cores (see Figure 6.1). The major warm and cool periods are numbered with isotope stage 1 being the present interglacial and isotope stage 5 thought to correspond to the last interglacial. These main stages can be further subdivided according to whether the climate was warmer or cooler than average for the period in question. These subdivisions are referred to by letters, so, for example, one finds isotope stage 5e.

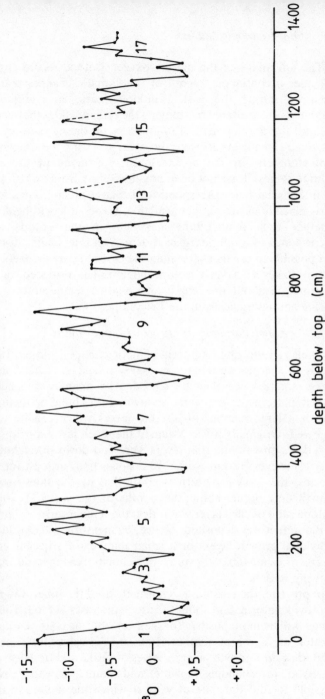

Figure 6.1 The changes in the oxygen isotope ratio for sea water as measured in a deep sea sediment core from the Caribbean covering approximately 400,000 years

The figures indicate the different isotope stages (drawn from data given in Cesare Emiliani, 'Paleotemperature analysis of Caribbean cores P6304–8 and P6304–9 and a generalised temperature curve for the past 425,000 years', *The Journal of Geology*, vol. 74, no. 2, 1966)

The advantage of the marine oxygen isotope record is that i provides a continuous record of the climatic changes that hav occurred during the past 2 million years. In addition, th sediments can be dated by studying the radionuclides they contain so until the development of uranium series dating the only date for some climatic events were those derived from these sediments Unfortunately for the archaeologist, for many of the earlie isotope stages, it has not been possible to say firmly which glacia or interglacial they correspond to, because precise dates for th early glaciations are not yet available. Hence it has to be decide whether each temperature maximum in the isotope recor corresponds to a full interglacial or just an interstadial. It is thu not possible to use dates from marine cores to date archaeologica sites. However, oxygen isotope analysis has provided valuabl information about the length and relative temperatures of th glacial and interglacials in the Paleolithic.

6.3.2 Seasonal Variation of Oxygen Isotope Ratios

As well as reflecting long-term climatic changes, oxygen isotop ratios in marine carbonates can also reflect seasonal changes These changes can then be recorded by animals with suitabl growth patterns. In particular, many molluscs build up their shell out of a large number of discrete layers which can be readil detected. Originally it was assumed that each layer corresponde to a day's growth and that layers were laid down throughout th year. However, recent work[16] has shown that, at least for som species, the growth pattern is controlled by the tides and tha growth only occurs about six months of the year. The oxyge isotope ratio of each layer will reflect the temperature of the wate at the time it was deposited. Hence, by measuring $\delta^{18}O$ values fo individual growth layers or a small number of adjacent growt layers, it is possible to study the climatic changes during th growing season.

In practice, the technique is normally used the other way roun to provide information about the use of molluscs as food. The $\delta^{18}C$ values will be more positive (or 'heavier') during cold weather an 'lighter' during warm weather. Thus, if $\delta^{18}O$ values for a shell ar plotted against growth layer, a series of peaks and troughs will b observed corresponding to winter and summer growth. It is the possible to find the time of year at which the mollusc was col lected, and also its age at that time. (Obviously, if the mollusc onl grew during the summer then it will not be possible to determine when in the winter it was collected.) By studying a large number of molluscs from a single site it can then be established whether molluscs were collected throughout the year or just for a few months and also the average age of the molluscs when they were collected.

Deith[17] describes the application of this technique to shells of Monodonta lineata from Asturian sites in Cantabria, northern Spain, which dated from between 8650 and 6800 BP. She started by studying modern shells of the same species to check that they grew throughout the year, and found that the growth rate depended on the age of the shells, with three-year-old shells growing more slowly than two-year-old. She then found that the ancient shells had been collected mainly between September and April, with none being collected in the summer. This suggests that other food sources were important at this season. Killingley[18] describes the technique he used when studying shells of a variety of species from the Punta Minitas midden site on the Pacific coast of northern Baja California, Mexico. The site was in use from 1500 to 7000 BP. He found that the majority of the shells were collected during the warm period between April and September, and he discusses the reasons for this. The technique is discussed further by Bailey et al.[19] who are critical of some aspects of Killingley's technique and in Killingley's reply.[20]

6.4 Isotopes and Provenance Studies

6.4.1 Introduction

The analysis of various different isotopes has been used in provenance studies of a range of materials. Lead isotope studies have been used to find the sources of lead, copper and silver ores, a task which had been impossible using the older trace element analysis techniques. Secondly, strontium isotope analysis has been used in studies of obsidian sources. Finally, oxygen isotope analysis has been used to show which of a group of Sidamara sarcophagi had been repaired.

6.4.2 The Use of Lead Isotopes

Probably the most important use of isotopic studies in provenance studies, has been the use of lead isotopes to locate metal ore sources. Trace element analysis techniques (see Chapter 7) had proved incapable of doing this for several reasons. Firstly trace element composition, even within a single source, showed wide variations, making it impossible to define each source satisfactorily. Then, during smelting the more volatile trace elements may evaporate and other trace elements go partly or wholly into the slag, so the trace element composition of the final metal will be very different from that of the ore from which it was made. Finally, either scrap metal or a flux which makes the smelting of the ore easier may have been added to the basic ore. Thus the trace element composition of the final metal will represent a mixture of sources rather than a single ore. Lead isotope analysis can normally overcome the first two of these problems and may also overcome the third.

Many metal ores contain lead as an impurity which is present as four isotopes, ^{204}Pb which is unstable (half-life 10^{17} years) and ^{206}Pb, ^{207}Pb and ^{208}Pb which are stable. ^{206}Pb, ^{207}Pb and ^{208}Pb are all partly derived from radioactive decay, being the final products of the decays of ^{238}U, ^{235}U and ^{232}Th respectively. Thus the ratios of the isotopes in a sample can vary by up to 5 per cent depending on its source. It has been found that lead isotope ratios are uniform throughout many ore bodies and that this ratio is unaffected by the smelting, so the lead isotope ratios in the final metal will be the same as that in the ore, provided that no other sources of lead were added to the ore during smelting. Hence, by measuring the lead isotope ratios in both the final metal and the likely ore sources, it is possible to find the source of ore for given metal artefacts. Fractionation is unlikely to be significant during smelting since the difference in mass between the isotopes is so small.

Gale and Stos-Gale[21] have studied Bronze Age copper sources in the Mediterranean and were able to locate the source of copper used for many artefacts. They point out that some copper ores can be smelted without a flux and in other cases sand, which does not contain lead, can be used, so the isotope ratios in the final metal should reflect that of the ore. With some copper ores an iron oxide flux has to be used, which may contain high quantities of lead and so would render lead isotope analysis useless. In addition, during the Greek Bronze Age chemical analysis has shown that bronze artefacts contained less than 1 per cent lead, making it unlikely that any lead was added deliberately as was done later. They also point out that the tin or arsenic alloyed with the copper to make bronze would not invalidate the isotopic analyses because the tin ore would be unlikely to contain lead. Moreover the arsenic probably came from the same ore as the copper so the lead isotope composition of the two would be the same.

Gale and Stos-Gale first showed that the Laurion and Cypriot copper ore sources could be distinguished using lead isotope analysis, and then analysed a series of Early Bronze Age Cycladic and Late Bronze Age Cretan bronze artefacts. They found the lead ratios for the artefacts fell into well defined groups, showing that the artefacts were made from metal from a single source. For the Early Cycladic objects 5 appeared to be made from Laurion ore, 2 from Cypriot ore, 4 from one unknown ore and 1 from a second unknown ore B. The authors point out that these results show that the relative importance of the Laurion and Cypriot ore sources for copper is very similar to that found in earlier work for lead and silver objects from the Cyclades.[22] Of the Cretan objects analysed 11 appeared to be made from Laurion ore, 5 from ore B and 5 from two other unknown sources. They found no objects made from Cypriot copper, a finding which may surprise some people.

Hassan and Hassan[23] have also used lead isotope studies to show that galena (lead sulphide: the main source of lead) from a pre-dynastic burial at Nagada probably came from either Zog-el-Bohar or Um Anz rather than Fuakhir which would have been a nearer source.

6.4.3 Strontium Isotope Analysis

Natural strontium occurs as four stable isotopes ^{88}Sr, ^{87}Sr, ^{86}Sr and ^{84}Sr with approximate abundances of 82.6, 7.02, 9.86 and 0.56 per cent respectively. However, with the exception of some of the ^{87}Sr which is radiogenic and is produced by the decay of ^{87}Rb with a half-life of 4.88×10^{10}yr, the isotopes of strontium are not radiogenic. Hence the $^{87}Sr/^{86}Sr$ ratio in minerals varies depending on both their initial $^{87}Rb/^{86}Sr$ ratio and their age. This is the basis of the rubidium/strontium dating method, which is widely used by geologists, but is of little interest to archaeologists because it cannot be applied to materials less than about 100 million years old. However even in newly formed volcanic rocks, the $^{87}Sr/^{86}Sr$ ratio ranges from about 0.703 to 0.720. This range of values is about 300 times greater than the accuracy with which the ratio can be measured. Hence measuring this ratio in volcanic materials, such as obsidian, found on archaeological sites can be useful in provenance studies.

Gale[24] has applied this technique to obsidian artefacts from a range of sites in the Mediterranean and also to the known obsidian sources in the area. 100mg of obsidian were required from each artefact. The strontium was chemically extracted from this sample and its isotopic composition determined using a mass spectrometer. The rubidium and strontium concentrations in the samples were also determined either by mass spectroscopy or, if sufficient sample were available, by wavelength dispersive X-ray fluorescence analysis. He found that by plotting the $^{87}Sr/^{86}Sr$ ratio against rubidium content he could distinguish all the obsidian sources known to have been important to Mediterranean cultures, though a plot of strontium content versus rubidium content could also do this. In general his analyses of artefacts agreed with the assignments made by earlier workers, but in some cases he was able to assign artefacts to a specific source rather than a group of sources. This method thus seems to offer better (or at least faster and cheaper) discrimination between sources, than does neutron activation analysis which is also widely used for this purpose (see Chapter 7) and so offers a useful way of determining the source of obsidian artefacts.

6.4.4 Isotopic Studies and Marble Provenance

Marble, like limestone, is a form of calcium carbonate and was widely used by ancient man for statues and other purposes. Because its visual appearance is important in many applications, marble would frequently have been obtained from carefully selected veins and so is likely to have been traded over long distances. Various techniques have, therefore, been used in attempts to determine marble provenance including both trace element and petrographic analysis. However both $\delta^{13}C$ and $\delta^{18}O$ are expected to depend on the conditions under which the marble was formed and so recently oxygen and carbon isotope ratios for marble have been studied in an attempt to achieve better discrimination between sources than had been achieved previously.

Coleman and Walker[25] studied marble from quarries in Greece and Turkey. They found that the $\delta^{13}C$, but not the $\delta^{18}O$ values were very scattered. They suggest this is due to the weathering of the marble, though it is difficult to see why the $\delta^{18}O$ values were unaffected. They, therefore, concentrated on measuring the $\delta^{18}O$

values. They looked at fragments of Sidamara sarcophagi and concluded, on the basis of their measurements, that some of them had been repaired using marble from a different source. They also showed that some fragments which appeared to come from the same object had very similar $\delta^{18}O$ values and so presumably did belong together.

German et al.[26] discuss some of the problems of using isotopic analysis for marble provenance studies. They studied marble from a wide range of quarries and found that even within individual quarries the isotopic composition of the marbles showed wide variations. In addition marbles from geographically separated sources may have similar isotopic compositions, thus making it impossible to assign a unique source to some marbles. They found that trace element analysis suffered from similar problems, though it could sometimes be used to distinguish between isotopically similar sources. They concluded that petrographic analysis would often distinguish between sources which could not be distinguished by either of the other methods.

Thus while isotopic analysis can solve some problems of marble provenance, it cannot solve them all. Compared to petrographic analysis, which is possibly the technique which is best at distinguishing between sources, it does, however, have the advantage that the sample required is much smaller and so the damage to the object will be less. Hence, in some circumstances at least, it may be the most suitable technique to use.

Notes

1. Y. von Schirnding, N.J. van der Merwe and J.C. Vogel, 'Influence of diet and age on carbon isotope ratios in ostrich eggshell', *Archaeometry*, vol. 24 (1982), pp. 3–20.

2. Michael J. De Niro and Margaret J. Schoeniger, 'Stable carbon and nitrogen isotope ratios of bone collagen variations within individuals, between sexes and within populations raised on monotonous diets', *Journal of Archaeological Science*, vol. 10 (1983), pp. 199–203.

3. Margaret J. Schoeniger and Michael J. De Niro, 'Carbon isotope ratios of apatite from fossil bone cannot be used to reconstruct diets of animals', *Nature*, vol. 297 (1982), pp. 577–8.

4. Charles H. Sullivan and Harold W. Krueger, 'Carbon isotope analysis of separate chemical phases in modern and fossil bone', *Nature*, vol. 292 (1981), pp. 333–5.

5. Michael J. De Niro, Margaret J. Schoeniger and Christine A. Hastdorf, 'Effect of heating on the stable carbon and nitrogen isotope ratios of bone collagen', *Journal of Archaeological Science*, vol. 12 (1985), pp. 1–7.

6. Y. von Schirnding et al., 'Influence of diet and age on carbon isotope ratios in ostrich eggshell', pp. 3–20.

7. Judith C. Sealy and Nikolaas J. van der Merwe, 'Isotope assessment of Holocene human diets in the southwestern Cape, South Africa', *Nature*, vol. 315 (1985), pp. 138–40.

8. H. Tauber, '^{13}C evidence for dietary habits of prehistoric man in Denmark', *Nature*, vol. 292 (1981), pp. 332–3.

9. N.J. van der Merwe and J.C. Vogel, '^{13}C content of human collagen as a measure of prehistoric diet in Woodland N. America', *Nature*, vol. 276 (1978), pp. 815–16.

10. Nikolaas J. van der Merwe, Anna Curtenius Roosevelt and J.C. Vogel, 'Isotopic evidence for prehistoric subsistence change at Parmana, Venezuela', *Nature*, vol. 292 (1981), pp. 536–7.

11. M.J. Schoeniger, M.J. De Niro and H. Tauber, 'Stable nitrogen isotope ratios of bone collagen reflect marine and terrestial components of prehistoric human diet', *Science*, vol. 220 (1983), pp. 1381–3.

12. M.J. Schoeniger et al., 'Stable nitrogen isotope ratios of bone collagen reflect marine and terrestial components of prehistoric human diet', pp. 1381–3.

13. Christine A. Hastdorf and Michael J. De Niro, 'Reconstruction of prehistoric plant production and cooking practices by a new isotopic method', *Nature*, vol. 315 (1985), pp. 489–91.

14. Henry P. Schwarz, Jerry Melbye, M. Anne Katzenberg and Martin Knyf, 'Stable isotopes in human skeletons of Southern Ontario: reconstructing paleodiet', *Journal of Archaeological Science*, vol. 12 (1985), pp. 187–206.

15. M.R. Deith, 'Molluscan calendars: the use of growth-line analysis to establish seasonality of shellfish collection at the Mesolithic site of Morton, Fife', *Journal of Archaeological Science*, vol. 10 (1983), pp. 423–40.

16. Margaret R. Deith, 'Seasonality of shell collecting determined by oxygen isotope analysis of marine shells from Asturian sites in Cantabria', in Caroline Grigson and Juliet Clutton-Brook (eds), *Animals and archaeology: 2 shell middens, fishes and birds* (BAR International Series 183, 1983), pp. 67–76.

17. J.S. Killingley, 'Seasonality of mollusk collecting determined from O–18 profiles of midden shells', *American Antiquity*, vol. 46 (1981), pp. 152–8.

18. G.N. Bailey, M.R. Deith and N.J. Shackleton, 'Oxygen isotope analysis and seasonality estimates: limits and potential of a new technique', *American Antiquity*, vol. 48 (1983), pp. 390–8.

19. John S. Killingley, 'Seasonality determination by oxygen isotopic profile: a reply to Bailey et al.', *American Antiquity*, vol. 48 (1983), pp. 399–403.

20. Nöel H. Gale and Zofia Stos-Gale, 'Lead and silver in the ancient Aegean', *Scientific American*, vol. 244 (1981), pp. 142–52.

21. A.A. Hassan and F.A. Hassan, 'Source of galena in predynastic Egypt at Nagada', *Archaeometry*, vol. 23 (1981), pp. 77–82.

22. N.H. Gale, 'Mediterranean obsidian source characterisation by strontium isotope analysis', *Archaeometry*, vol. 23 (1981), pp. 41–51.

23. M. Coleman and S. Walker, 'Stable isotope identification of Greek and Turkish marbles', *Archaeometry*, vol. 21 (1979), pp. 107–12.

24. K. Germann, G. Holzmann and F.J. Winkler, 'Determination of marble provenance: limits of isotopic analysis', *Archaeometry*, vol. 22 (1980), pp. 99–106.

7 CHEMICAL ANALYSIS

7.1 Introduction

This chapter discusses the techniques most widely used to determine the elemental composition of archaeological artefacts: i.e. the proportions of the different elements present in the sample. This information has been put to a variety of uses. For pottery it can be used to locate the source of clay used by the potter, and also to decide whether two apparently dissimilar pottery types could have been made from the same clay. Analysis of metals can show whether or not coinage was being debased, and also shed light on the technological standard of the metalworker. Man-made glasses have been analysed to find out what colouring agents were used at different times. Finally, analysis of human bones has been used to provide information about ancient diets.

Before samples are submitted for chemical analysis it is necessary to decide what questions are to be answered by the analysis, because this will affect the analytical technique chosen. Some techniques only analyse the surface of the artefact while others provide information about the bulk fabric so, for example, one technique would be best for analysing the glaze on a pottery sherd and another for analysing the body of the pot. Also techniques vary in their ability to detect different elements. For example X-ray techniques are poor at detecting elements with low atomic numbers: this is why X-rays are so useful in medicine as bones contain atoms of higher atomic number than do the soft tissues. Finally, some techniques are destructive in that they require material to be removed from the artefact for analysis while others, at least for small objects, are non-destructive because the entire object can be used as the sample and recovered undamaged at the end of the analysis. The most suitable technique in a particular case can frequently only be chosen after discussion with an expert as, for example, the maximum size of object which can be analysed non-destructively will depend on the equipment in use at a particular laboratory.

Elemental chemical analysis only provides limited information about the artefacts studied. It does not reveal which minerals or chemical compounds are present in the sample. Nor does it give information about the size of any crystals in pottery, or whether the pottery has been heated to such a high temperature that it has started to vitrify. This type of information can be obtained using other analytical techniques, some of which are described in Chapter 8.

The elements present in an artefact are often split into three groups: major, minor and trace elements. Major elements are those which make up 2 per cent or more of the artefact and in many cases their proportions would have been controlled by ancient man, for example when making metal alloys. Minor elements are those present in concentrations ranging from 0.1 to 2 per cent; and these may have been added deliberately, for example as colouring agents in glass, or may just be present accidentally. Finally trace elements are those whose concentration is less than 0.1 per cent and so their concentrations are often measured in parts per million (ppm). Their presence or absence would not have been controlled by ancient man, but rather have been determined by the sources of his raw materials. Hence trace element analysis is widely used in provenance studies.

The techniques used can be classified according to the precision with which they determine the composition of the sample. Most of the techniques described in this chapter are quantitative: that is the uncertainty in the values obtained is 5 per cent or less of the measured value. At the other extreme are qualitative techniques which will identify which elements are present, but give no information about their concentrations. Finally some techniques are semi-quantitative, which means that as well as identifying the elements present, they can also give a rough idea of the concentration of those elements. For example a semi-quantitative technique would show whether a bronze contained 10 or 20 per cent tin but not whether it contained 10.2 or 10.8 per cent.

Most of the techniques used for this type of chemical analysis are based on some form of spectroscopy.

7.2 Principles of Spectroscopy

7.2.1 Introduction

The techniques most widely used in archaeology for chemical analysis all measure the radiation absorbed or emitted by atoms when either the electrons or the nucleons move between different energy levels. By studying the energy involved it is possible to deduce both the type and number of atoms involved and hence determine the elements present in the sample. The techniques used fall into three groups. The first group contains those techniques where the energy involved is visible light. Originally optical emission spectroscopy (OES) was the most important technique in this group, but recent developments have resulted in it being superseded by atomic absorption spectroscopy (AAS). The second group involves more energetic radiation and contains all those techniques which involve the absorption or emission of X-rays. It includes both types of X-ray fluorescence (XRF) analysis, electron microprobe analysis and particle- (or proton-) induced X-ray emission (PIXE). The final group contains neutron activation analysis (NAA) and uses the γ-rays emitted by atomic nuclei, after they have been bombarded by neutrons from a nuclear reactor, to identify the elements present.

7.2.2 Atomic Energy Levels

When considering the radiation emitted or absorbed by different elements, it is useful to think of the atomic nucleus as being surrounded by a series of energy levels, often referred to as shells, each of which can contain only a certain number of electrons. The innermost shell can contain up to two electrons and the next up to eight. The electrons in each shell have an amount of energy corresponding to the shell in which they are situated, so to move to a different shell they have to lose or gain energy. The further away from the nucleus the shell is, the more energy the electrons in that shell have, so to move from an inner to an outer shell an election has to absorb energy, while on moving from an outer to an inner shell it will emit energy. The amount of energy required will depend on both the element involved and the energy levels the electron is moving between. This energy is absorbed or emitted in a single package known as a photon. Hence by studying the energy of the photons absorbed or emitted by a sample, it is possible to work out which elements are present in the sample and which energy levels the electrons are moving between. The radiation associated with a photon of a given energy has a fixed wavelength and frequency, so the energy involved in a given transition (movement of an electron between two energy levels) can also be described by the wavelength or frequency of the radiation involved as well as the energy difference between the two levels.

The electrons fill the shells so as to minimise their energy. Thus the innermost shell will fill completely before the next shell starts to fill. This means that, normally, all atoms of a given element will have the same number of electrons in the outermost shell containing electrons. Thus carbon always has four electrons in its outer shell, while oxygen always has six (see Figure 7.1). It is the number of electrons in the outer shell which is largely responsible for determining the chemical properties of an element. Hence elements with the same number of electrons in this shell have similar properties. For example sodium and potassium both have one electron in their incomplete shell and are soft metals which react readily with water.

Figure 7.1 A schematic representation of the lowest energy levels in carbon and oxygen

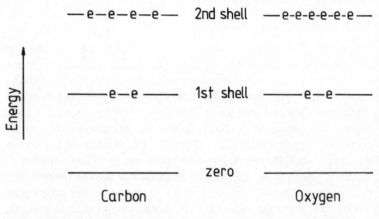

The figure shows the number and arrangement of the electrons in neutral atoms of the elements

This model of the arrangement of the electrons around the atomic nucleus can be compared to how people would occupy the flats in a tower block. Each floor of the tower block corresponds to one electron shell or energy level in the atom. Then, just as each shell can only contain a limited number of electrons, so only a limited number of people can live on each floor of the block of flats. People do not want to climb more stairs than is necessary, so the ground floor flats will fill before any of the first floor flats are occupied, in the same way that the innermost electron shell fills completely before the next one starts to fill. Finally, just as the electrons moving between the same shells always involves the same amount of energy, so people moving between floors in the block always have to climb or descend the same distance. They cannot live halfway between two floors.

Elements are often grouped according to the number of electrons in the outermost shell. The elements with one electron in this shell are known as the alkali metals. In the periodic table (see rear end paper) the elements are arranged in order of increasing atomic number so that elements with the same number of electrons in their outermost shell fall in the same column. This makes it easy to see which elements will have similar chemical properties.

Figure 7.2 The nomenclature of the lowest energy levels and transitions in an atom

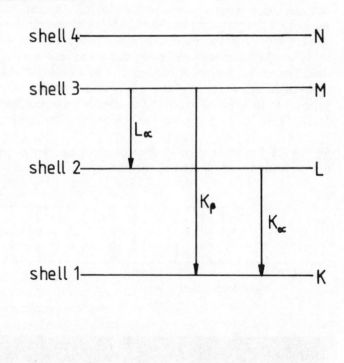

As it is often useful to know which shell an electron is in, the shells are numbered with 1 being the shell nearest the nucleus, 2 the next one and so on. Alternatively, particularly when working with X-rays, each shell is known by a letter with K being the innermost shell, L the next, M the next and so on through the alphabet. With X-rays the energy level an electron has come from is specified by a Greek letter so K_α radiation is emitted when an electron moves from the L to the K shell and K_β when it moves from the M to the K shell (see Figure 7.2).

7.2.3 Appearance of Spectra

A spectrum is produced when radiation is displayed in such a way that the wavelengths (or frequencies) present and absent can easily be seen. Thus a rainbow is a crude spectrum of the light from the Sun as each colour corresponds to a different range of wavelengths. There are two different types of spectra: absorption and emission. An absorption spectrum is produced when electrons move into higher energy levels, and so have to take in energy to do this. Thus if a spectrum is produced from a beam of white light (light of all wavelengths) after it has passed through a monatomic vapour, it will be found to contain a series of dark lines (see Figure 7.3a). These lines correspond to the energy differences between

Figure 7.3 Emission (a) and absorption (b) spectra of sodium drawn from data collected by the author

a)

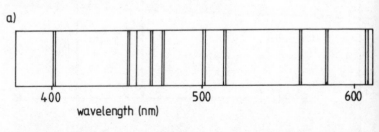

b)

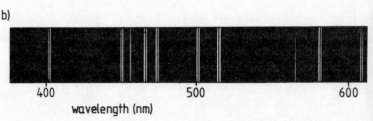

different energy levels for the elements in the sample, and so by measuring the wavelength of the absorption lines, it is possible to determine the elements present because each element produces a characteristic absorption pattern.

An emission spectrum is the reverse of this, because it is the radiation emitted when electrons move into shells of lower energy. It consists of a series of bright lines against a dark background (see Figure 7.3b). Again the elements present can be identified from the wavelength of the lines. Some elements produce such strong lines in a limited part of the visible spectrum that they can be identified by colour alone. For example sodium produces yellow light and potassium violet. Emission spectra can be produced by exciting the electrons into higher energy levels in a variety of ways. Two common ones are by heating the sample (hence cooking salt, i.e. sodium chloride, dropped in a gas flame will turn it yellow) or by bombarding the sample with particles which knock some of the electrons present into higher energy levels. This second method is most commonly used to produce X-ray spectra.

Figure 7.4 The electromagnetic spectrum showing the wavelengths of the different types of radiation

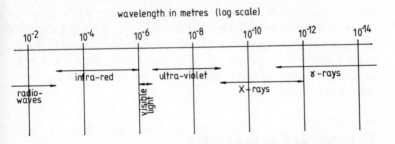

Atoms can absorb (or emit) radiation over a wide range of wavelengths or energy (see Figure 7.4). Visible light with wavelengths ranging from approximately 5×10^{-7} to 10^{-6} m is involved when electrons move between the outer electron shells. When electrons move into or out of the innermost electron shells, particularly the K shell, X-rays are emitted or absorbed. They have wavelengths ranging between approximately 10^{-9} and 10^{-12} m and are often described in terms of the energy involved, ranging from approximately 10^3 to 10^6 eV, rather than wavelength.

7.2.4 Principles of Neutron Activation Analysis

The main difference between the spectra already mentioned and that produced in neutron activation analysis is that in the latter it is the energy levels in the nucleus which are involved rather than the electronic energy levels. The protons and neutrons can be thought of as being arranged in shells of different energies in a similar way to the electrons. If a sample is then bombarded with neutrons (or other suitable particles), some of the nuclei will absorb the neutrons and may be transformed into radioactive nuclei. These artificial radionuclides then decay into stable nuclides in a similar way to natural radionuclides. The stable nuclides may initially be formed in an excited state, i.e. one or more nucleons is in a high energy level while there is a space in a lower energy level. In such a case, almost as soon as the nuclide is formed, the nucleon in the high energy level moves into a lower energy level. The excess energy is lost as a γ-ray whose energy is determined by the nuclide involved. Hence by measuring the energies of the γ-rays emitted by a sample, it is possible to determine the elements present in it. A further difference between neutron activation analysis and the other types of chemical analysis already mentioned, is that many of the radionuclides formed have half-lives ranging from a few hours to several weeks. Hence the γ-ray spectra are frequently measured some time after the bombardment of the sample. In the other methods the spectra are measured at the same time as the sample is excited because the electrons move between the levels almost instantaneously.

7.3 Techniques Commonly Used

This section does not describe all the techniques that have been used for chemical analysis, but only those most widely used at present for archaeological samples. These are neutron activation analysis, atomic absorption spectroscopy, X-ray fluorescence spectroscopy, electron microprobe analysis and particle induced X-ray emission analysis. Optical emission spectroscopy (OES), which at one time was widely used for archaeological samples, has by now been replaced by atomic absorption spectroscopy which can detect the same elements but is more accurate, particularly where high concentrations are involved.[1]

7.3.1 Atomic Absorption Spectroscopy (AAS)

For this technique between 10mg and 1g is removed from each artefact to be sampled, depending on the number and the concentration of the elements to be measured (a larger sample is required when trace elements are of interest than when only major elements are to be studied). The sample is normally drilled from an inconspicuous part of the object and the hole can later be filled, so the technique is considered to be almost non-destructive. Any glaze or corrosion should be removed before the sample is taken so that only the body and not the surface of the artefact is sampled. The sample is then dissolved in acid and diluted to a suitable concentration for the element to be measured. Elemental concentrations ranging from less than 1ppm to 100 per cent can be measured with an accuracy ranging from ± 1 per cent for major elements to ± 15 per cent for trace elements. (All errors are quoted as a percentage of the measured value.) A small quantity of the solution is turned into a fine spray and heated in a suitable flame to produce atoms of the element being studied. The flame is illuminated with a light source which produces light of a wavelength that can be absorbed by the element of interest (and only that element). The concentration of the given element can then be found by comparing the intensity of the light beam when the sample is present in the flame, with the intensity when it is not. By repeating the process using a suitable range of light sources it is possible to detect over 40 elements, mainly metals. It is particularly important for detecting metals of low atomic number such as lithium and sodium which cannot easily be detected by X-ray analysis. Normally, to reduce the time taken for each analysis, only the concentrations of a selection of elements, often about 10, are determined. These elements are selected in the light of the problem being investigated. This can have the disadvantage that if an unexpected element is present it will not be detected. AAS is discussed in more detail by Hughes et al.[2]

7.3.2 X-ray Fluorescence Spectrometry (XRF)

This technique can be carried out in a truly non-destructive way without removing any material from the artefact. However, for a variety of reasons, it may frequently be better to analyse a small

(100mg to 2g) sample removed from the artefact. Firstly, the X rays used in the analysis only penetrate about 20 to 200μm into the artefact. Hence only the surface of the artefact will be analysed. This is useful if one wants to analyse the glaze on pottery without removing it from the body of the pot. But if one wants to analyse the main bulk of an artefact, it may be necessary to remove the surface, either because it is a glaze or a slip, or else in the case of a metal object because it is corroded. With metal objects the concentration of elements frequently varies with depth, or alternatively an alloy may not be a homogeneous mixture, but may rather consist of grains of metal A dispersed in a metal B matrix even if they do not appear corroded. In addition, precious metals like gold and silver may have been applied as a thin layer over a less valuable foundation. A further problem is that prolonged exposure to X-rays can cause a slight discoloration of glass and similar materials. It would also be likely to render the object unsuitable for TL dating and ESR studies at a later date. Finally, X-rays from elements with atomic numbers less than 22 (titanium) are absorbed by air. Thus if light elements are to be detected, the measurements must be carried out with the sample in a vacuum. This may not be possible with big objects because there will only be a limited space in the vacuum chamber. Elements with atomic numbers less than 12 (magnesium) frequently cannot be detected by X-ray analysis.

In XRF spectroscopy the sample is placed in the X-ray equipment and irradiated with a beam of X-rays produced by either an X-ray tube or a radioactive source. These X-rays excite electrons in the K, and possibly L shells, into higher energy levels. The electrons then drop back into the shells from which they have come with the emission of secondary or fluorescent X-rays. The fluorescent X-rays have energies (and wavelengths) characteristic of the element from which they were emitted, so by measuring the intensity of the X-rays at different wavelengths it is possible to determine the concentrations of the different elements in the sample. The fluorescent X-rays can be detected in one of two ways. In wavelength dispersive XRF spectroscopy the fluorescent X-rays are passed through a diffraction grating which spatially spreads out the X-rays of different wavelengths in a similar fashion to the way a prism will split a beam of white light into a rainbow of different colours. The intensity of the X-rays at each wavelength can then be measured separately. Alternatively, in non-dispersive or energy dispersive XRF spectroscopy, a special detector is used which can measure the energy and intensity of the incoming X-rays simultaneously. This technique enables weaker primary X-ray sources to be used.

XRF spectroscopy can be used to determine elemental concentrations ranging from 10ppm to 100 per cent with an accuracy of ±2 to 5 per cent of the measured value under favourable conditions. One limiting factor, particularly when analysing complete objects, is that surface irregularities such as the relief on coins can make it difficult to calibrate the intensity measurements for X-rays of different wavelengths. This problem is less serious, although it still arises, when using non-dispersive techniques.

7.3.3 Other X-Ray Techniques

Two other techniques involving X-rays have been widely used for elemental analysis: electron microprobe analysis and particle- or proton-induced X-ray emission (PIXE) analysis. In both these techniques a beam of high energy particles, respectively electrons and protons or α particles are used to excite electrons from the inner shells (K and L) into higher energy levels. These electrons then emit X-rays and return to their original energy levels as in XRF analysis. Thus most of the points already made about XRF analysis also apply to them.

The main difference is that in both these techniques the particle beam can be focused, so that only a very small area of the sample is studied at once ($1\mu m^2$ for the electron microprobe and $1mm^2$ for PIXE), whereas in XRF analysis the whole surface of the sample is studied. This means that selected areas on the surface of the object can be studied so, for example, the composition of glazes of different colours on a single sherd of pottery can be compared. In addition, electron microprobe equipment is often designed so that the electron beam can be scanned over the surface of an object, enabling the distribution of an element over the surface to be studied. For example if metal objects are cut in half, it is possible to study how the concentration of different elements varies from the surface to the centre. These techniques can thus provide more information about the sample than does ordinary XRF analysis. In addition the calibration of the equipment, when calculating the concentration of the different elements present, is simpler so that often it is not necessary to compare the composition of the sample with that of a standard of known composition (see p. 157), or if this is done, the composition of the standard need not be similar to that of the sample providing they both contain the same elements.

However, both techniques do also have disadvantages when compared with XRF analysis. Firstly they are more expensive, so if XRF analysis can provide the required information this extra cost may not be justified. Secondly, sample preparation is more difficult. The area to be examined must often be polished so the damage to the sample may be greater than for XRF analysis. It may be difficult to achieve a sufficiently smooth surface, particularly with coarse ceramics, which can result in the concentrations of the elements present being underestimated. Freestone[3] reports a case where the concentrations of the various elements were underestimated by up to 30 per cent. In addition, with non-metallic samples the area to be studied must be coated with a thin carbon or metal layer, because otherwise the particles from the beam will build up on the surface and cause problems.

Electron microprobe analysis is discussed further by Freestone.[4]

7.3.4 Neutron Activation Analysis (NAA)

In this technique the samples to be analysed are irradiated with a beam of neutrons, normally produced by a nuclear reactor. The γ-rays produced by the decay of the radionuclides formed during the bombardment are studied and used to identify the elements present. NAA is particularly useful for trace element analysis because it can detect a wide range of elements in concentrations as low as 0.1ppm with an accuracy of ±5 per cent of the measured value. Some elements cannot be detected including H, B, C, N, P and Pb because they form nuclides with half-lives too short or too long for their γ-ray spectra to be studied easily. Two or more γ-ray spectra are normally recorded for each sample, because once the nuclides with short half-lives have decayed (two to three weeks after irradiation), it is easier to measure accurately the γ-rays from the longer lived nuclides.

NAA provides an analysis of the whole object, and for small objects such as beads and coins can be carried out non-destructively (at least so far as the physical appearance of the object is concerned). The objects to be irradiated are placed in metal cans, typically 3cm in diameter by 10cm in height, before being placed in the neutron beam. Thus, when NAA is to be carried out on objects larger than this, a small sample, typically about 100mg, has to be removed from them and used for the analysis. Although analysing whole objects would appear to be less destructive than removing a sample, this is not the case if further studies are to be carried out on the object. An object which has been used for NAA cannot, at a later date, be used for various techniques including TL dating, fission track dating, C–14 dating and ESR studies. In addition, its trace element composition will be changed slightly, but the changes are probably so small that they cannot be detected. Finally, NAA leaves the object in a radioactive state so it may be several years before it can be returned to the archaeologist. If the object is wanted back more quickly, this must be made clear when it is submitted for analysis, so that the time for which it is irradiated can be kept sufficiently short that the object does not become unacceptably radioactive: this may restrict the elements which can be detected.

Two variants of this technique have recently been developed. In prompt neutron activation analysis (PNAA)[5] the γ-rays emitted when the nuclei absorb the neutrons are studied. They can also reveal the elements present and their concentrations. This technique is quicker than ordinary NAA, but requires special equipment because the γ-ray spectrum produced while the sample is being bombarded has to be recorded. In proton induced γ-ray emission (PIGME) analysis the sample is bombarded with protons rather than neutrons. This will result in different radionuclides being produced, so some elements will be easier to detect. It can also be combined with PIXE analysis to provide further information.

7.4 Advantages and Disadvantages of the Different Techniques

The various techniques used for chemical analysis all have their strengths and their weaknesses and thus it is impossible to lay down hard and fast rules about which technique should be used and in what circumstances. Thus, before submitting samples for chemical analysis it is essential to have a clear idea of the questions that it is hoped the analysis will answer. A list of the elements and their concentrations in a pot sherd is unlikely to be of much use to anyone. In particular, the nature of the problem being investigated will determine whether measuring major, minor or trace elements will prove most informative and how many elements should be measured to provide the required information. Measuring more elements than necessary wastes both time and money, and may result in so much data being produced that confusion rather than clarification results. If the problem is to determine what elements were deliberately mixed together to form a metal alloy or how precisely the proportions of the different metals were controlled then a technique suitable for determining major elements should be used. Problems of this nature include whether arsenic or tin was alloyed with copper to make bronze and the extent to which gold and silver coins were being debased by the addition of less valuable metals. Also, glass can be made from a variety of materials, so that the concentrations of the oxides of sodium, potassium, calcium and lead may all be more than 10 per cent, depending on the raw materials used. In theory, for this type of problem any of the techniques described could be used, so the choice will be determined by other factors such as cost and sample size.

When investigating the debasement of gold coins or other gold objects there is an alternative technique which is cheap and quick which can be used provided that it is known that the gold has been alloyed with only one other metal, and that the metal is known. This is to determine the specific gravity or density of the coin, which can be done very simply by weighing the coin using an accurate balance first in air and then with the coin suspended in a suitable liquid. The proportions of the two metals present can then be determined once the density of gold and the other metal have been looked up in a suitable reference book.[6] Alternatively, this technique could be used to select coins for further investigation by another technique, or to check that apparently pure gold coins are not merely gold plate. This technique can also be applied to other binary alloys. Its main drawback is that if the object is corroded or contains air bubbles the proportion of the denser element (i.e. the gold) may be underestimated.

In another case the archaeologist may want to know what colouring agents were used in glass or glaze and whether a colour was always produced in the same way. Such problems involve the measurement of minor elements, as do measurements to determine the materials used as fluxes in metalworking to make smelting easier. Finally, archaeologists frequently want to know the source(s) of the raw materials used by ancient man as this can help in understanding ancient trade routes and other aspects of ancient economy and society. This is normally done by comparing the concentrations of a selection of trace elements in the final product with those in the possible sources of raw materials. It is assumed that man had no control over these elements, and so their concentrations will be unchanged by the processing of the raw material into the final object. Hence any source of raw material which has the same trace element composition as the final object is a possible source. However this assumption is not strictly true and any manufacturing process is likely to result in some change in trace element composition. For example, when making pottery the clay may have been levigated to remove the coarse material. This may also have selectively removed some elements. Then, when the clay is mixed with water, the water will contain dissolved minerals and so the concentrations of some elements in the clay may be increased. Finally when the clay is fired some of the volatile elements may escape, resulting in a reduction in their concentrations in their final pot. Fortunately, for pottery these changes are normally only small and so much work has been done on possible clay sources. With metals, however, the changes are much greater. This is partly because when metal ores are refined one element is deliberately separated from the other elements present. Any trace elements will be split between the slag and the wanted metal in unknown proportions. A further complication is that alloying and the use of scrap metal may result in the final objects containing trace elements from more than one source. Hence it is normally impossible to use trace element analysis in metal provenance studies.

Again for minor and trace element studies any of the three main groups of techniques can often be used, but if the elements are present in very low concentrations (about 1ppm) then it may be necessary to use NAA as it is more sensitive than the others.

A related problem is the accuracy with which the measurements should be made. This depends on both the element being measured and the technique chosen with, in general X-ray techniques being less accurate than the other methods. Normally, standards of similar composition to the objects of interest also have to be measured to enable the measurements to be calibrated. For example, some laboratories use pottery whose composition has been determined very accurately as the standard when studying pot sherds and other clay objects. Thus it may frequently be best to choose a laboratory which has measured similar material before, because then it will have suitable standards already available. Moreover it should be aware of any problems which may arise with that material. While in general the more accurate the measurements the better, in practice most artefacts and sources of raw materials show a range of compositions so there is no point in determining the composition much more accurately than the likely range of values. For example if the concentration of nickel in a clay source varies between 150 and 200ppm it is not necessary to measure its concentration to the nearest 1ppm, an uncertainty of ±10ppm would be sufficiently accurate. These concentration variations within clay and ore sources are one reason why analyses are normally done on large groups of similar objects, because single objects may not be representative of the group as a whole.

The accuracy with which the concentration of a given element can be measured, may be affected by the other elements present. This arises for several reasons, one of which is, that instead of emitting radiation at a single wavelength, atoms normally emit radiation over a small range of wavelengths centred on the quoted wavelength (see Figure 7.5a). If the concentration of one element is much greater than the concentration of an element which emits radiation of a very similar wavelength, then the two line widths may overlap to such an extent that the less concentrated element cannot be seen (see Figure 7.5b). Which elements are affected in this way will depend on the technique being used, as different energy levels are involved in each case. In some cases this problem can be overcome by looking at an alternative transition, for example K_β rather than K_α X-rays for an element.

The next problem to be considered is whether it is the body or the surface of the object which is to be analysed. If it is the body then it is also necessary to consider how much damage is allowable. If none, and if the object is small, then NAA will probably be the method of choice, while if a small drilling can be taken then both AAS and XRF analysis have the advantage of being cheaper (by roughly ten times) and quicker than NAA. If the surface is all that is to be analysed, either because it is expected to be the same as the body of the object, or because it is just a thin layer like a glaze or a slip, and hence of interest in its own right, then XRF analysis will normally be the best method to choose because it can be carried out non-destructively. For the other techniques it might be difficult to obtain a sample consisting only of the surface. Its main disadvantage is that it cannot detect light elements so if these

Figure 7.5 The problem of line widths

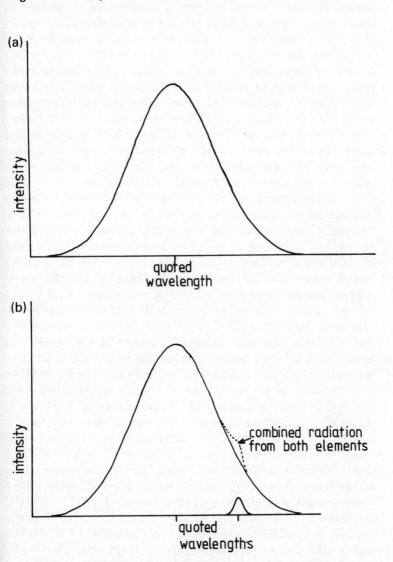

(a) Radiation from a single transition in a single element showing the range of wavelengths over which the radiation is emitted

(b) How the radiation from the element in (a) may hide the much weaker radiation centred on a slightly different wavelength from a second element

are likely to be important, then AAS will have to be used for them. However, if the artefact is corroded or weathered in any way, an analysis of the surface will give misleading results. As well as the familiar rust on iron and tarnish on silver the alkali metals may have been leached from glass and other elements may be washed into or leached out of pottery, so surface analysis would not be representative of the body of the object. In addition, many metal objects consist of a cheap core coated with a more expensive metal. For example apparently solid coins may really be cheaper metal covered with a thin layer of gold. XRF analysis would greatly exaggerate the value of such coins (specific gravity analysis would not). Some metal alloys are also affected by the fact that the alloy is not a uniform mixture but one component tends to be concentrated near the surface and the other at the centre. Copper and bronze coins do not appear to be affected by these concentration gradients but lead bronzes are. A further problem with metal alloys is that segregation of the metals can occur. This means that the two metals are not uniformly distributed throughout the object, but instead the denser metal or the one with the higher melting point may be concentrated at the bottom of the object when it cooled. Alternatively, one metal may form grains which are then coated with a film of the other metal. Thus when sampling metal objects, it may be necessary to take several samples to ensure that the concentration variations within the object are known. This problem is discussed further by Slater et al.[7] Another problem with metals is that ignoble metals frequently corrode sacrificially when in contact with noble metals i.e. the ignoble metal corrodes before the noble and also more quickly than it would have if it were pure. This can lead to the concentration of the ignoble metal being lower in the object when it is analysed than it was when the object was made. Alternatively the corrosion products may be so obvious that visual inspection of the object leads to the importance of the ignoble metal being overestimated. Sacrificial corrosion was also used deliberately in ancient times to increase the surface concentration of the noble metal so that an object appeared more valuable than it really was. Thus when sampling metal objects it is essential to ensure that the samples are representative of the whole body and not just the surface of the object. Similarly with pottery it may be necessary to increase the sample size above the minimum quoted to ensure that the results are representative of the fabric as a whole. To take an extreme example, the range of elements in a large quartz grain would be totally different to the range in the surrounding clay matrix, and so if the quartz grain alone were analysed it could lead to totally false conclusions being drawn.

Once the samples have been taken, the problem arises as to what should be done about the drill holes. If they cannot be seen when the object is on display, then it may be best to do nothing; filling them can lead to confusion if the objects are resampled at a later date. In one case[8] when several cast bronze heads from Ife were re-analysed, one was found to be made of brass although the earlier work had shown it was made of copper like the others. It was later realised that the original sample holes had been filled with brass, which was then coloured to match the rest of the artefact. Then, when the fresh samples were drilled, it was the brass that was sampled, not the copper for the anomalous object. Thus metals should not be used to fill drill holes in metals. Not only may such use confuse later studies, but it will increase the chance of the object undergoing corrosion. Instead the hole should be filled with an unreactive material, such as ground-up pot sherds or coloured wax, with a chemical composition which is obviously different to that of the object sampled. (Wax, not pot, should be used to fill holes in porcelain and other ceramics.)

So, when submitting objects for chemical analysis, the best advice is to choose the cheapest method which is likely to solve the problem in question. Frequently it may be necessary to use more than one method: AAS and XRF analysis are often used together to increase the range of elements that can be studied. Furthermore, some laboratories already have information about the composition of possible sources of raw material for particular types of artefact, for example Mediterranean obsidian, and so would be the obvious choice to carry out analysis of similar artefacts. Finally, whenever possible at an early stage the problem should be discussed with someone working in a laboratory active in the field so that advantage can be taken of the newest and most suitable technique for solving the particular problem.

7.5 Presentation of Results

The results of a chemical analysis can be presented in several different ways. Normally the analysis for each artefact starts as a list of the elements analysed and their respective concentrations, expressed either as a per cent weight of the total weight of the sample or as parts per million by weight present in the sample, although other units are occasionally used. With non-metal samples the concentrations may be listed for the oxides of the elements rather than the isolated elements. This is done by assuming that each element is only present in the sample as a specified oxide: it will produce rather different figures from those produced for isolated elements. This is because for some elements the ratio of the two types of atom in the compound is 1:1, while for others it is 2:1 or 2:3. For example, the oxides of sodium, magnesium and iron commonly quoted are Na_2O, MgO, FE_2O_3 and FeO (iron belongs to a group of elements known as the transition elements where the number of bonds per atom can change). In such cases the oxygen concentration in the sample has not been measured and so the elements could be present as other compounds, for example, chlorides.

The analysis total for the major and minor elements in a sample should be 100 per cent. Sometimes advantage is taken of this fact to enable the concentration of a major element to be estimated where its concentration cannot easily be measured. In particular, the concentration of silicon, a major element in pottery, is frequently determined in this way because it can be difficult to measure its concentration using the techniques described in this chapter. Sometimes it is also used to determine the concentration of one component of a metal alloy. Obviously the concentration of only one element in the sample can be determined in this way and then it must be a major one, because otherwise the uncertainty in the estimate will be greater than the estimate. Analyses of trace or selected elements are not expected to total 100 per cent.

Analysis of the elements present in a sample may not total 100 per cent for two other reasons than failure to analyse for all elements. Firstly, particularly with AAS, if an unexpected element is present it will not be detected and so its concentration will not be measured. Secondly, the concentrations of all the elements measured may be underestimated, again resulting in the analysis total being less than 100 per cent. This is particularly a problem with some X-ray techniques such as electron microprobe analysis where, unless the surface analysed is very smooth, some of the X-rays emitted from the sample may be deflected away from, rather than towards, the detector. This problem is frequently treated by normalising the analysis totals to 100 per cent: i.e. multiplying the concentration of each element by the same factor so that the analysis total is 100 per cent (see for example Tite et al.).[9]

Figure 7.6 Case where pottery made from different clays can be distinguished just by measuring the concentration of one element (hypothetical data)

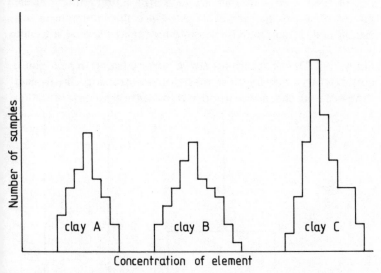

Tables of elements and their concentrations are of limited use, particularly when large numbers of samples have been analysed. They can be used to solve certain simple problems such as deciding whether artefacts are of bronze, brass or arsenical copper and also for studying whether a coinage is debased, though in the latter case, if the coins span a long period of time, it might be useful to plot gold concentration against time or type of coin to make the results clearer. Again, it may be found in provenance studies, that the range of concentrations of a single element in the different possible sources of clay is such that the clay from which the pottery was made can be established just by looking at the figures and possibly drawing a graph (see Figure 7.6). In general, however, in provenance studies, the range of concentrations of each element observed is such that the concentration range of individual elements for each source overlaps and so the concentrations of several elements must be used to separate the sources.

When the concentrations of several elements are to be used the calculations involved become very complex and so a computer is normally used to do them. Several different multivariate statistical techniques including principal components analysis (PCA) and hierarchical cluster analysis can be used and computer programs are available to perform the calculations. The differences between the different methods are not discussed here as their importance lies in their ability to split artefacts like pottery into different groups of use to the archaeologist. Once the groups have been established, it may then be possible for the archaeologist to draw

Figure 7.7 Dendrogram for some pottery found in a single context, but made by more than one potter using clay from a range of sources, some imported (hypothetical data)

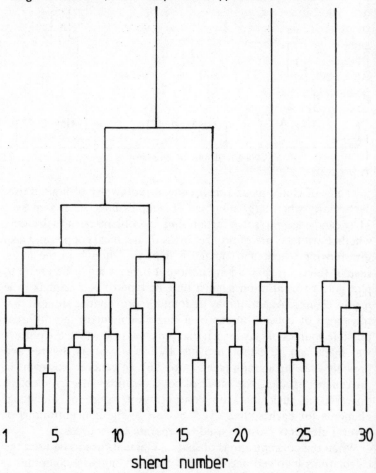

sherd number

conclusions about the trading links of a particular site or the likely sources of clay used in making a type of pottery or the development of a particular style of pottery. Frequently the results are presented graphically with dendrograms and scatter diagrams being common.

Dendrograms (see Figure 7.7) are very like family trees, in that artefacts which are similar are placed close together and are frequently joined directly to each other like siblings in a family tree, while unlike objects are placed far from each other. The longer the line joining two samples together, the less alike they are. Thus, in the example shown, sherds 1–5 came from pots made by potter A and sherds 6–10 were made by potter B, both using the same local clay. Sherds 11–15 and 16–20 were made by two other potters using different sources of local clay. Finally sherds 21–30 were imported, 21–25 from X and 26–30 from Y and so do not connect with the local wares (at least at the scale shown), i.e. they come from a different family.

Figure 7.8 Scatter diagram being used to determine the clay from which some pot sherds were made: the numbers represent the different sherds (hypothetical data)

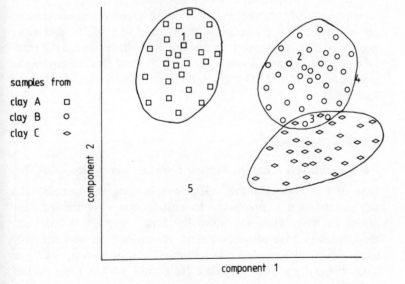

Scatter diagrams (Figure 7.8) are particularly useful when trying to locate the source of the raw materials for a particular group of objects, because they enable any overlap in concentration ranges between different possible sources to be seen easily. The axes of such a diagram may either be element concentrations, or ratios of element concentrations or, where many elements have to be studied to obtain well-defined groups, 'principal components'. 'Principal components' are a convenient mathematical way of enabling the distribution of a lot of variables, e.g. elements, to be plotted two-dimensionally on a graph. Otherwise one would need one dimension for each element of interest, which would be impossible to represent accurately on a sheet of graph paper because 10 or more dimensions (or axes at right angles to each other) would be needed. In general, the more elements included in the calculations, the better defined the groups will be, but in practice, a stage is normally reached when adding more elements produces so little improvement that the time and expense involved in including more elements is not worthwhile. In Figure 7.8 the different symbols represent samples from different clay sources, while the numbers represent analyses on a selection of pot sherds. Thus sherd 1 was most likely made from clay A and sherd 2 from clay B. Sherd 3 could have been made either from B or C. Sherd 4 is just on the edge of clay B and so could have been made from it, particularly if it is a finer ware than 2 and so made from a more processed clay because the processing might have altered the trace element distribution. Sherd 5 does not lie in or close to any of the groups and so most likely was made from a clay not included in the analysis.

7.6 New Techniques

7.6.1 Inductively-Coupled Plasma Emission Spectroscopy (ICP)

One of the problems with OES was heating the sample to a sufficiently high temperature to ensure that it contained only atoms or ions. This was normally done using an electric arc, though lasers have also been used. Recently Hart and Adams[10] used inductively-coupled plasma emission spectroscopy (ICP) to study the pottery from the Alice Holt and Overwey kilns. In this technique a solution of the sample is injected into a stream of argon to form an aerosol. This is heated using a radio frequency coil so that it becomes a plasma (a gas in which some, or all, of the electrons are separate from their nuclei) flame at a temperature of 5,000°C. The emission spectrum produced by these excited atoms and ions is then analysed to reveal the elements present and their concentrations as in OES. Plasma emission spectroscopy can be used to determine silicon, phosphorous and all significant main and trace metals except possibly rubidium. Detection limits are typically between 0.01 and 0.1ppm and concentrations can be measured to better than ±5 per cent of the measured value. Only 10mg of sample is needed and it is more accurate than OES.

Hart and Adams used ICP spectroscopy to study a selection of sherds from the waster dumps at the Alice Holt and Overwey kilns. The sherds from both sites were similar in appearance, but although the kilns were only about 5 miles apart, the authors found that the pottery from the two could be distinguished on the basis of their analyses. They also showed that the local clay had been used to make the Alice Holt pottery.

7.6.2 Auger Electron Spectroscopy (AES)

The two other techniques which have recently been applied to archaeological artefacts can provide some information about the chemical state of the elements analysed (i.e. whether they are present as oxides or chlorides etc.).

Auger electron spectroscopy (AES) has many similarities to electron microprobe analysis in that the sample is bombarded with a narrow (3μm in diameter) beam of electrons so it is possible to study the distribution of elements over the surface of the object. The electron beam ejects electrons from the inner energy levels of the atoms which are then replaced by electrons from the higher energy levels. During the transition, these electrons have to lose their excess energy. In the earlier discussion it was assumed that this energy was always lost as X-rays, but in practice, it can also be lost by transferring it directly to another electron which now has so much energy that it leaves the atom. By measuring the energies of these Auger electrons, it is possible to determine the elements present in a layer 30 Å (3×10^{-9}m) thick on the surface of the sample with an accuracy of ±5 per cent of the measured value. The detection limits are about 0.1 per cent. Polak et al.[11] applied this technique to a bronze arrow head from North Sinai and found it contained an unexpectedly high magnesium oxide concentration. The presence of the magnesium could not be due to weathering because it was the only object from the site to contain measurable quantities of magnesium.

7.6.3 X-Ray Photoelectron Spectroscopy (XPS)

X-ray photoelectron spectroscopy (XPS) can also provide some information about the oxidation state of the elements present, but only semi-quantitative information about their concentrations. In this technique a beam of X-rays is used to excite some of the electrons in the sample so that they leave the atoms. Some of these electrons move towards the detector where their energies are measured enabling the elements present in the sample and their oxidation state to be identified: for example whether iron is present as FeO or Fe_2O_3. Again, because it is necessary for these electrons to travel from the sample to the detector, with their energies unaffected by collisions en route, the technique can only be used to study the surface of objects. Gillies and Urch[12] used this technique in conjunction with other techniques to study the black surface on a variety of pottery types. They found the black coating on Little Waltham ware was due to amorphous carbon, while that on Orsett ware was due to burnishing and firing in a reducing atmosphere. For a Macedonian Early Bronze Age sherd the black colour was also caused by carbon, but for Northern Black Polished Ware from Iron Age India it was due to iron.

7.7 Applications

So many examples of the uses of chemical analysis have been published in the past few years, that it is impossible to refer to them all in this section. Instead, just a selection are included to illustrate the wide range of materials that have been analysed chemically and the information which can be obtained from such analyses.

7.7.1 Bone

The chemical analysis of bone can provide information both about ancient diet and also about pathological conditions since the amount of meat eaten affects the strontium content of bones, while the lead content of drinking water will also affect the lead content of bone. The main limitation on the use of chemical analysis in this field is that the concentrations of many elements, which could provide useful information, frequently do not remain constant after death, but instead, are either leached from the bone or are deposited in it from the ground water. The use of the fluorine and uranium content of bone for relative dating (see Chapter 5) is based on this later fact. Studies[13] have shown that strontium and zinc are the elements which are least affected by these problems. For other elements, concentration gradients are frequently found, either in the soil surrounding the bone or in the bone itself, suggesting that the elemental concentrations have not remained constant since burial. In particular copper, barium[14] and lead[15] have all been shown to be affected by post-burial changes. Thus conclusions about whether particular populations were affected by lead poisoning should be treated with caution, unless the possibility of the contamination of the bones by lead from the soil or coffin has been ruled out.

At present, the element of most use in dietary studies is strontium because its concentration is high in plants, nuts and marine invertebrates like molluscs but low in animal meat. Thus studies of its concentration can be used to indicate the main source of protein for a particular population and also to show whether or not all the groups within a population had a similar diet. Schoeniger et al.[16] measured the strontium levels in ribs from a Late Archaic hunter-gatherer population and a Mississipian period agriculturist population from the same site in the Middle Tennessee Valley. Normally, the strontium level for agriculturalists is expected to be higher than that for hunter-gatherers, since the former will have consumed more plant food than the latter. However in this case the strontium levels were 1.5 to 1.8 times higher in the hunter-gatherer bones than in the agriculturalists. The authors conclude that this unexpected result is because the hunter-gatherers ate the local freshwater molluscs, but the agriculturalists did not and so the strontium levels show the reverse effect of what would have been expected if the only difference in diet between the two groups had been that the agriculturalists ate more plants.

Lambert et al.[17] studied a range of elements in bones and soil from two sites in Illinois: Gibson and Ledders, and concluded that the analyses of strontium, zinc, calcium and sodium should reflect the concentrations at the time of burial, but that the values for the other elements studied might have, or probably had been, affected by contamination. Gibson is a Middle Woodland mound group, thought to date from approximately 200AD when the population would have been hunter-gatherers. Ledders is a Late Woodland site dated to about 1000AD when maize farming was well established. The authors found that, while the males and females from the Gibson site had identical bone compositions suggesting they ate the same diet, the Ledders male bones were lower in strontium, calcium and zinc than the female bones suggesting that here the males' diet was richer in protein than the females'. At Gibson it was also possible to classify the skeletons according to the apparent importance of the person buried into 'status', 'peripheral' and 'other' burials. The chemical analyses suggested that those in the 'other' burials had eaten a different diet to those in the 'status' and 'peripheral' classes.

Sillen and Smith[18] measured strontium levels to provide information about the age at which babies were weaned, while Lambert et al.[19] discuss some of the problems of using the elemental composition of bones to provide information about ancient diet.

Thus, providing the dangers of contamination are borne in mind, chemical analysis of bone can provide useful information about the diet of different groups of people.

7.7.2 Obsidian and Other Natural Materials

Elemental analysis has also been used to find the source of obsidian and other stone artefacts found on archaeological sites. When plenty of material is available, petrographic analysis has been widely used because it is cheap, but as a thin section has to be prepared from a slice removed from each object being analysed, it is relatively destructive. However, when a non-destructive technique is preferred or where petrographic analysis cannot distinguish between different sources, chemical analysis techniques have been found useful.

Craddock et al.[20] used AAS to measure the concentrations of seven elements (Al, Fe, Mg, K, Na, Ca and Li) in a large number of Neolithic flint axes in order to determine the source of the flint they were made from. They found only one axe at both Maiden Castle and Windmill Hill that could have been made from local flint, so the rest were presumably made from flint from mines or quarries. They then examined flint from three different mining areas and found that they could distinguish between them on the basis of the elements measured. However, individual axes could not be assigned to individual mines with any degree of confidence.

They found that the majority of the axes were from the South Downs mines in south east England and some appeared to be from an, as yet, undiscovered flint source. Very few of the axes came from the Grimes Graves or Easton Down flint mines. They suggest this is not surprising because C-14 dates suggest that both these mines were in use in the late Neolithic when polished flint axes were no longer being made, but that the South Downs mines were in use in the fourth millennium BC. They conclude that polished flint axes were made from carefully selected non-local flint.

Obsidian is another natural material which is frequently found hundreds of kilometres away from possible sources and so must have been exchanged or traded by prehistoric man. Various studies on the source of obsidian used at different sites have been carried out. In general, it appears to be necessary to use NAA to obtain the most complete assignment of artefacts to sources, though Merrick and Brown[21] found electron microprobe analysis useful in assigning preliminary sources to Kenyan obsidian artefacts, while Michels[22] found that AAS of bulk elements could distinguish different obsidian sources, but that trace element analysis by NAA was best for assigning individual artefacts to sources. Thorpe et al.[23] used NAA to study a selection of obsidian artefacts from southern France and found fifteen came from the Sardinian A source, one from the Sardinian C source, three from Lipari and two from Pantelleria. Thorpe et al.[24] then used the same technique to study the distribution of obsidian sources and artefacts in Central Europe. They found that only three of the possible obsidian sources in Central Europe were used by pre-historic man and that the Carpathian 1 or Slovakian source was the most important. Obsidian from this source can be distinguished from Mediterranean, Aegean and Near Eastern obsidian, which they showed were not used in Central or Eastern Europe. Only at the Neolithic site of Grotta Tartaruga did they find both Carpathian and Mediterranean obsidian.

Jet is another natural material used by ancient man. In particular, it was used in the Early Bronze Age to make jewellery which has been found throughout the British Isles. However, the Whitby area of Yorkshire is the only significant source of jet in England, but other materials like cannel coal which are similar to jet in appearance are more widely available. Hence, a means of distinguishing jet from these other materials is needed. Pollard et al.[25] describe the use of energy dispersive XRF analysis to distinguish between jet and non-jet artefacts. They examined the jet-like material in the Early Bronze Age collection from Devizes Museum and found that 37 out of the 72 objects were made from jet and not shale as previously assumed. Thus in the Bronze Age jet was exchanged over long distances.

Finally Thorpe et al.[26] used a combination of energy dispersive XRF analysis and NAA to show that Arran was a major source of pitchstone for archaeological sites in Scotland even when there were alternative, closer sources, while Bimson et al.[27] used XRF analysis to show that most of the Sutton Hoo garnets were Frankish rather than Russian or Gotlandic in type.

7.7.3 Glass and Related Materials

Henderson and Warren[28] used XRF analysis to study Iron Age glass beads from Meare and Glastonbury Lake Villages as the first stage in determining the compositional groups of such beads, and hence how widespread the manufacture of glass was. They found that leaded glass was used to make the yellow coloured decorations while soda-lime-silica glass low in lead was used to make clear glass. They suggest that antimony was being used as both an opacifier and as a decolourant. They also found that glasses which were visually distinct were chemically distinct.

Velde and Gendron[29] used an electron microprobe to analyse second- and third-century Gallo-Roman glass fragments from Central Western France, in an attempt to find out how tightly controlled the manufacturing techniques were. They found that both window glass and decorative glass had very similar compositions suggesting that a 'best' composition was used. Alumina (Al_2O_3) was present at approximately the 3 per cent level suggesting it was added deliberately, possibly to improve the strength and water resistance of the glass, while manganese oxide (MnO) appears to have been used as a decolouring agent to eliminate the green to brown colours that would otherwise have been induced in the glass by iron oxide impurities.

Sanderson et al.[30] used energy dispersive XRF analysis to study first millennium AD glass from a range of sites in Britain to see whether the composition changed with time. However, they found all the glass was broadly similar. In addition, they concluded that at Wroxeter glass was being recycled rather than manufactured because the composition of the cullet and the melted glass was so similar. They also found that the glasses from Hamwih

(Southampton), Dorestadt (Holland) and Helgo (Sweden) were made in different places since their composition was different.

Several studies have also been carried out on faience to discover how it was manufactured. Pollard and Moorey[31] used energy dispersive XRF to analyse Middle Assyrian faience and related materials from Tell-el-Rimah in Iraq. Copper appeared to have been used as the green colouring agent and manganese as the black. Antimony appeared to have been used as a opacifier. Foster and Kaczmarczyk[32] analysed a range of Middle Minoan faience using energy dispersive XRF and AAS. They studied both the cores and surfaces of the objects. The cores could be split into three types which could be distinguished by colour. Type 1 were white and consisted almost entirely of silicon, sulphur and calcium oxides. Type 2 were creamy due to the presence of iron oxides and also contained a wider variety of other metals. Type 3 cores came in several shades of grey and frequently contained high levels of copper and manganese. In the glaze they found copper was the main colourant in green faience. The blue faience also contained copper, as well as high levels of calcium, tin and strontium. They also found that in the early faience reduced iron was used to produce a black colour as was the practice in Mesopotamia, but that the later faience followed the Egyptian practice of using manganese as the black colouring agent.

7.7.4 Pottery

All the main techniques available have been used to determine the chemical composition of pottery. Frequently, chemical analysis is carried out in conjunction with other techniques such as X-ray diffraction analysis and scanning electron microscopy (see Chapter 8), so that the firing temperature used by the potter and minerals present in the pot can be determined as well as the elements present. As the accuracy and range of elements that can be analysed has improved, concern has been expressed as to whether weathering may affect the chemical composition of sherds and, in particular, whether some elements are leached from the pottery by the ground water.

Hatcher et al.[33] used AAS to analyse Hellenistic and Roman fine pottery from Benghazi in order to confirm the validity of some of the fabric groups which had been defined on visual grounds and also to confirm whether certain different fabrics could have a common origin. They found that two separate clay sources appeared to have been used to produce the Hellenistic black-glazed wares and that both decorated and undecorated wares were produced from each clay. Similarly the micaceous fine wares were made from a number of different clays, although the fabrics appeared visually similar. The analysis of the Hellenistic ware also suggested that one group was from the same source as similar wares from the Agora in Athens, which had previously been analysed using OES. In order to confirm this finding and to see how the two techniques compared, they re-analysed some of the sherds from Athens and also two types of pottery from Italy using AAS. They found that the different values produced by the two techniques could not be explained just by differences in calibration factors for the two techniques, because two OES measurements of 17.5 per cent Al_2O_3 are replaced by AAS values of 13.76 per cent and 15.50 per cent. In addition, the compositional groups as determined by AAS were better defined and the identity of one of the groups from Benghazi with one from Athens was confirmed. Some of the coarse wares from Benghazi and other areas in Cyrencia have been studied using NAA.[34]

Tubb et al.[35] also used AAS, but this time to analyse Roman-British pottery from kiln sites in Wales, Gloucester and the New Forest. They found the three areas produced chemically distinct pottery, but how well the source of a sherd could be determined depended on the elements studied. Measurements of the four elements iron, magnesium, calcium and potassium would enable sherds to be assigned correctly to kilns while measurements of the three elements sodium, titanium and iron would not. They also showed, by experiments in the laboratory, that barium, calcium, manganese, sodium and titanium are more affected by firing conditions and weathering than are potassium, magnesium, iron and aluminium.

Rye and Duerden[36] used PIXE to locate the sources of clay for pottery from a Papuan site. They found 36 per cent of sherds were made from local material, 45 per cent from two sources 3km distant, 17 per cent from a source 30km distant and 2 per cent could not be assigned to any known source. In the light of laboratory experiments, they discuss the elements of most use in determining the source of the pottery.

Ballié and Stern[37] used energy dispersive XRF to analyse Roman terra sigillata sherds of known origin. They found they could separate the wares from Arezzo, Italy, Lyon, La

Graufesenque and Lezoux, France on the basis of Ti/Mn and Fe/K ratios though there was a slight overlap between La Graufesenque and Lezoux. They also analysed some sherds by the potter Sentius who was reported to have worked at both Lyon and Arezzo and found two had been made at Lyon and the rest at Arezzo.

Finally Kaplan et al.[38] used NAA to study the chemical composition of Tell el Yahudiyeh ware in Cyprus, Egypt, Nubia and the Levant during the Middle Bronze Period, in an attempt to find where the ware had been manufactured. The vessels had previously been classified on typological grounds, when it had been found that some types appeared to be manufactured in the Levant and others in the Nile Valley. The authors compared the compositions they obtained for the sherds with those obtained previously for clay sources. In some cases they found sherd compositions could only be matched to clay compositions by assuming that Nile alluvium and Pleistocene clay had been mixed to make the vessel (as is the practice today), or that quantities of plant ash had been used as temper. They were able to establish the place of manufacture of most of the sherds, though a few remained unknown. They found that some types of ware were made in the Levant and other types in Egypt. In addition, there were Levantine copies of Egyptian wares, but not Egyptian copies of Levantine wares. They point out that although this period is considered to be a 'dark age' in Egypt, an active trade network appears to have existed spreading between Egypt, Nubia, the Levant and Cyprus.

7.7.5 *Metals*

While chemical analysis of metals cannot, in general, be used to determine the source of metal ores, it can still provide a wide range of useful information about metal objects.

Northover[39] discusses the types of information that can be gained from analysis of metal objects. He points out that if objects from several sites are studied it may be possible to tell whether they were all made using the same source of raw materials, while if objects covering an extended time period are studied it may be possible to identify changes in alloying practice or changes in the source of raw materials. He then discusses the development of metalworking techniques in Britain during the Bronze Age and concludes that initially the metalworking was organised on a regional basis but later on a national scale. In addition some types of bronze are found both in Britain and on the continent suggesting more extensive contacts.

Chemical analysis of metal objects can also provide information about the technological achievement of the metal workers. For example in Europe and the Middle East zinc metal was only available commercially from about the middle of the eighteenth century AD. Before that brass had to be made by heating copper with zinc ore, which produces a maximum zinc concentration of 28 per cent by weight. Thus any object containing a higher zinc concentration must be comparatively modern (unless it comes from India where high zinc brass has been made for 2,000 years). Shaw and Craddock[40] used AAS to determine the composition of some Ghanian and Coptic brass lamps. The lamps had supposedly come from old graves at Attababa in Bron country north of Kumasi and it had been suggested that they had been made in approximately the sixth century AD. However, the zinc concentrations in them were 24.95, 34.00 and 34.00 per cent which suggests they were made in the nineteenth century. Other associated objects also had high zinc contents (39, 33.55 and 33.50 per cent). AAS was also used by Stead[41] in a study of fragments thought to be from the Cerrig-y-Druidion 'Hanging Bowl'. He showed that all the fragments had the same composition and concluded that they therefore came from the bowl.

Sometimes chemical analysis can produce surprising results. Craddock[42] reports the case of a Roman mirror in the British Museum which was thought to be of bronze. However, when a sample was removed for analysis it was found that the main element was silver with some copper added. The copper had corroded preferentially, so that visually the mirror appeared to be made from a copper based alloy such as bronze rather than silver.

Mommsen and Schmittinger[43] used high energy PIXE to analyse some gold and silver coins which had previously been analysed using a variety of other techniques and found good agreement between their results and those obtained earlier. Mommsen et al.[44] also used PIXE to analyse a silver statuette of the Roman god Mercury found at Bonn in 1896. The figure of the god and a ram had been fastened to a plinth but there was some doubt as to whether they had originally belonged together, because Mercury was much better executed than the ram. The chemical analysis showed that the composition of all three components was different and so presumably had not been manufactured at the same time.

Finally, several groups of workers have compared the results of applying several different techniques to the same objects. Carter et al.[45] used seven different techniques (wet chemistry, wavelength dispersive XRF, energy dispersive XRF (radio-isotope excitation), energy dispersive XRF (tube excitation), neutron activation analysis, atomic absorption spectroscopy and activation with high energy photons) to analyse eight Roman orichalium coin fragments. They discuss the advantages and disadvantages of the different techniques and conclude the results from the different techniques agree reasonably well with each other. Hughes,[46] using AAS, re-analysed some British Middle and Late Bronze Age metalwork which had previously been analysed using OES. He found that OES underestimated lead concentrations by up to 3.5 times and concluded that OES should not be used to measure lead concentrations greater than 4 per cent. He points out that, as a result of this problem, the importance of heavily leaded bronzes in the British Bronze Age may have been underestimated by studies which used OES rather than other techniques. Fabris and Treloar[47] compared XRF and AA analysis of some Sarawakan gold artefacts. In general, they found good agreement between the two techniques but conclude that only analyses obtained using a single method should be compared.

Although in theory an analysis is either right or wrong, i.e. the composition it determines for an object either is or is not the same as the actual composition of the object concerned, in practice chemical analysis of archaeological artefacts is frequently primarily concerned with determining whether two groups of objects have the same composition. This means that providing the differences between the measured and actual values are consistent (e.g. the concentration of lead is always under-estimated by 10 per cent of the true measured value) that useful information can still be obtained. However, it also means that frequently it is not possible to compare analyses on similar objects from different laboratories or using different techniques, at least when the differences in composition between two groups of objects are small, because the concentration of an element as measured by two different techniques may differ by 10 per cent or more of the measured value.[48] Attempts are currently being made to reduce this problem by using standards whose composition is known very accurately and also by different laboratories measuring each others standards so that analyses can be corrected for systematic differences between them.[49]

Notes and Further Reading

The American Chemical Society periodically holds symposia on archaeological chemistry and publishes the proceedings in *Archaeological Chemistry*. The most recent volume, edited by Joseph B. Lambert, was *Archaeological Chemistry — III Advances in Chemistry*, Series 205 (American Chemical Society, 1984). Various examples of chemical analysis of a range of materials also appear in Jacqueline S. Olin and Alan O. Franklin (eds), *Archaeological Ceramics* (Smithsonian Institution Press, 1982); and Patricia Phillips (ed.), 'The Archaeologist and the Laboratory', *CBA Research Report*, No. 58 (Council for British Archaeology, 1985).

1. M.J. Hughes, 'British Middle and Late Bronze Age metalwork: some re-analyses', *Archaeometry*, vol. 21 (1979), pp. 195–202.

2. M.J. Hughes, M.R. Cowell and P.T.C. Craddock, 'Atomic absorption techniques in archaeology', *Archaeometry*, vol. 18 (1976), pp. 19–37.

3. I.C. Freeston, 'Applications and potential of electron probe micro-analysis in technological and provenance investigations of ancient ceramics', *Archaeometry*, vol. 24 (1982), pp. 99–116.

4. I.C. Freestone, 'Applications and potential of electron prove micro-analysis in technological and provenance investigations of ancient ceramics', pp. 99–116.

5. M.D. Glascock, T.G. Spalding, J.C. Biers and M.F. Cornman, 'Analysis of copper-based metallic artifacts by prompt gamma-ray neutron activation analysis', *Archaeometry*, vol. 26 (1984), pp. 96–103.

6. See, for example, Robert C. Weast (ed.), *Handbook of Chemistry and Physics* (CRC Press, published annually), pp. B6–B41.

7. E.A. Slater and J.A. Charles, 'Archaeological classification by metal analysis', *Antiquity*, vol. 44 (1970), 207–13.

8. F. Willet, 'The anomalous Ife alloy: a conflict of evidence resolved', *Archaeometry*, vol. 21 (1979), p. 247.

9. M.S. Tite, M. Bimson and I.C. Freestone, 'An examination of the high gloss surface finishes on Greek Attic and Roman Samian wares', *Archaeometry*, vol. 24 (1982), pp. 117–26.

10. F.A. Hart and S.J. Adams, 'The chemical analysis of Romano-British pottery from the Alice-Holt Forest, Hampshire by means of inductively-coupled plasma emission spectroscopy', *Archaeometry*, vol. 25 (1983), pp. 179–85.

11. M. Polak, J. Baram and J. Pelleg, 'Auger electron spectroscopy applied to the analysis of archaeological artifacts', *Archaeometry*, vol. 25 (1983), pp. 59–67.

12. K.J.S. Gillies and P.S. Urch, 'Spectroscopic studies or iron and carbon in black surfaced wares', *Archaeometry*, vol. 25 (1983), pp. 29–44.

13. Joseph B. Lambert, Sharon Vlasak Simpson, Carole Bryda Szpunar and Jane E. Buikstra, 'Ancient human diet from inorganic analysis of bone', *Accounts of Chemical Research*, vol. 17 (1984), pp. 298–305.

14. J.B. Lambert, S.V. Simpson, C.B. Szpunar and J.E. Buikstra, 'Copper and barium as dietary discriminants: the effects of diagenesis', *Archaeometry*, vol. 26 (1984), pp. 131–8.

15. H.A. Waldron, 'On the post-mortem accumulation of lead by skeletal tissues', *Journal of Archaeological Science*, vol. 10 (1983), pp. 35–40.

16. Margaret J. Schoeniger and Christopher S. Peebles, 'Effects of mollusc eating on human bone strontium levels', *Journal of Archaeological Science*, vol. 8 (1981), pp. 391–7.

17. J.B. Lambert, C.B. Szpunar and J.E. Buikstra, 'Chemical analysis of excavated human bone from Middle and Late Woodland sites', *Archaeometry*, vol. 21 (1979), pp. 115–29.

18. Andrew Sillen and Patricia Smith, 'Weaning patterns are reflected in strontium-calcium ratios of juvenile skeletons', *Journal of Archaeological Science*, vol. 11 (1984), pp. 237–45.

19. J.B. Lambert et al., 'Ancient human diet from inorganic analysis of bone', pp. 298–305.

20. P.T. Craddock, M.R. Cowell, M.N. Lease and M.J. Hughes, 'The trace element composition of polished flint axes as an indicator of source', *Archaeometry*, vol. 25 (1983), pp. 135–63.

21. H.V. Merrick and F.H. Brown, 'Rapid chemical characterization of obsidian artifacts by electron microprobe analysis', *Archaeometry*, vol. 26 (1984), pp. 230–6.

22. Joseph W. Michels, 'Bulk element composition versus trace element composition in the reconstruction of an obsidian source system', *Journal of Archaeological Science*, vol. 9 (1982), pp. 113–23.

23. Olwen Williams Thorpe, S.E. Warren and Jean Courtin, 'The distribution and sources of archaeological obsidian from Southern France', *Journal of Archaeological Science*, vol. 11 (1984), pp. 135–46.

24. Olwen Williams Thorpe, S.E. Warren and J.G. Nandris, 'The distribution and provenance of archaeological obsidian in Central and Eastern Europe', *Journal of Archaeological Science*, vol. 11 (1984), pp. 183–212.

25. A.M. Pollard, G.D. Bussell and D.C. Baird, 'The analytical investigation of early Bronze Age jet and jet-like material from the Devizes museum', *Archaeometry*, vol. 23 (1981), pp. 139–67.

26. Olwen Williams Thorpe and R.S. Thorpe, 'The distribution and sources of archaeological pitchstone in Britain', *Journal of Archaeological Science*, vol. 11 (1984), pp. 1–34.

27. M. Bimson, S. La Neice and M. Leese, 'The characterisation of mounted garnets', *Archaeometry*, vol. 24 (1982), pp. 51–8.

28. J. Henderson and S.E. Warren, 'X-ray fluorescence analyses of Iron Age glass: beads from Meare and Glastonbury Lake villages', *Archaeometry*, vol. 23 (1981), pp. 83–94.

29. B. Velde and C. Gendron, 'Chemical composition of some Gallo-Roman glass fragments from Central Western France', *Archaeometry*, vol. 22 (1980), pp. 183–7.

30. D.C.W. Sanderson, J.R. Hunter and S.E. Warren, 'Energy dispersive X-ray fluorescence analysis of 1st millenium AD glass from Britain', *Journal of Archaeological Science*, vol. 11 (1984), pp. 53–69.

31. A.M. Pollard and P.R.S. Moorey, 'Some analyses of Middle Assyrian faience and related materials from Tell Al-Rimah in Iraq', *Archaeometry*, vol. 24 (1982), pp. 45–50.

32. K.P. Foster and A. Kaczmarczyk, 'X-ray fluorescence analysis of some Minoan faience', *Archaeometry*, vol. 24 (1982), pp. 143–57.

33. H. Hatcher, R.E.M. Hedges, A.M. Pollard and P.M. Kenrick, 'Analysis of Hellenistic and Roman fine pottery from Benghazi', *Archaeometry*, vol. 22 (1980), pp. 133–51.

34. W. Krywonos, G.W. Newton, V.J. Robinson and J.A. Riley, 'Neutron activation analysis of Roman coarse ware from Cyrencia', *Archaeometry*, vol. 22 (1980), pp. 189–96.

35. A. Tubb, A.J. Parker and G. Nickless, 'The analysis of Romano-British pottery by atomic spectrophotometry', *Archaeometry*, vol. 22 (1980), pp. 153–71.

36. O.S. Rye and P. Duerden, 'Papuan pottery sourcing by PIXE: preliminary studies', *Archaeometry*, vol. 24 (1982), pp. 59–64.

37. P.J. Baillié and W.B. Stern, 'Non-destructive surface analysis of Roman terra sigillata: a possible tool in provenance studies', *Archaeometry*, vol. 26 (1984), pp. 62–8.

38. M.F. Kaplan, G. Harbottle and E.V. Sayre, 'Multi disciplinary analysis of Tel El Yahudiyeh ware', *Archaeometry*, vol. 24 (1982), pp. 127–42.

39. J.P. Northover, 'The exploration of the long-distance movement of bronze in Bronze and Early Iron Age Europe', *Institute of Archaeology Bulletin*, vol. 19 (1982), pp. 45–72.

40. Thurstan Shaw and Paul Craddock, 'Ghanian and Coptic brass lamps', *Antiquity*, vol. 58 (1984), pp. 126–8.

41. I.M. Stead, 'The Cerrig-y-Druidion "Hanging Bowl"', *Antiquaries Journal*, vol. 62, part II (1982), pp. 221–34.

42. P.T. Craddock, 'A Roman silver mirror "discovered" in the British Museum: a note on its composition', *Antiquaries Journal*, vol. 63, part I (1983), pp. 131–2.

43. H. Mommsen and T. Schmittinger, 'Test analysis of ancient Au and Ag coins using high energy PIXE', *Archaeometry*, vol. 23 (1981), pp. 71–6.

44. H. Mommsen, M. Befort, Q. Fazly, T. Schmittinger, and A.-B. Follmann-Schulz, 'Analysis of a silver statuette of Mercury from Bonn', *Archaeometry*, vol. 22 (1980), pp. 87–92.

45. G.F. Carter, E.R. Caley, J.H. Carlson, G.W. Carriveau, M.J. Hughes, K. Rengan and C. Segebade, 'Comparison of analyses of eight Roman orichalcium coin fragments by seven methods', *Archaeometry*, vol. 25 (1983), pp. 201–13.

46. Hughes, 'British Middle and Late Bronze Age Metalwork', *Archaeometry*, vol. 21 (1979).

47. G.J. Fabris and F.E. Treloar, 'X-ray fluorescence and atomic absorption analysis of Sarawak gold artifacts', *Archaeometry*, vol. 22 (1980), pp. 93–8.

48. Suzanne P. De. Atley, M. James Blackman and Jacqueline S. Olin 'Comparison of data obtained by neutron activation and electron microprobe analyses of ceramics', in J.S. Olin and A.O. Franklin, *Archaeological Ceramics* pp. 79–87.

49. Garman Harbottle, 'Provenence studies using neutron activation analysis the role of standardization', in J.S. Olin and A.O. Franklin, *Archaeologica Ceramics*, pp. 67–77.

8 OTHER ANALYTICAL TECHNIQUES

8.1 Introduction

The last chapter discussed the analytical techniques used to quantify the elements present in different types of artefact and the wide range of uses of such information. However, other analytical techniques also have an important role to play in the study of archaeological remains, because they can provide information about the technological achievements of different cultures, and also about the use to which different artefacts were put. Various types of thermal analysis have been used to establish the firing temperatures used to produce ceramic objects and also to show whether or not ceramics have undergone post-burial alteration. Scanning electron microscopy is capable of revealing surface detail on artefacts, which is invisible using an optical microscope, and so has been used in attempts to discover how different materials were produced, as well as in studies of the firing conditions used to produce various types of ancient pottery. It has also been used to reveal how prehistoric man used different flint implements. X-ray diffraction analysis will identify the minerals present in a wide range of materials and so has been used to determine firing conditions, in provenance studies and to determine how the composition of niello has changed over the past 2,000 years. Mössbauer spectroscopy can give highly detailed information about the iron present in objects, and so again, is used to study ancient firing temperatures. These techniques have all been used, primarily, to study inorganic remains such as pottery and flint. Recently, however, studies on organic remains such as the food residues on pots and the lacquer used to coat wooden objects have also been reported; some of the techniques used in this field are therefore also described.

For reasons of space many important techniques have had to be excluded from this chapter. The principal omissions are petrographic analysis, metallurgical studies and radiography. For information about these topics the reader must look elsewhere (see further reading).[1]

8.2 Thermal Analysis

8.2.1 Principles

The various types of thermal analysis are primarily used to determine the firing temperature of pottery. They depend on the complex physical and chemical changes that occur when pottery is fired. They can also indicate the extent to which pottery has weathered or altered during burial. Different changes occur at different temperatures: for example free water is removed by heating the pottery to temperatures below 100°C, while the water trapped in the crystal lattice is normally lost at temperatures between 100 and 200°C. In addition, many of the carbonates present in the pottery will decompose and release carbon dioxide; for example calcite decomposes at about 800°C. At high temperatures many minerals exist in different phases (i.e. the atoms are arranged in a different way in the crystals) from those which are present in unfired clay. Thus a knowledge of the temperatures at which different phase changes occur, can also help when determining firing temperatures. Finally, when pottery is heated to temperatures approaching 1,000°C it becomes vitrified (i.e. some of the minerals it contains start to melt and on cooling become glassy, rather than crystalline). The temperature at which vitrification starts to occur depends on the minerals present in the pottery and can be as low as 750°C. Most of these changes are permanent and are accompanied by the absorption or emission of energy or by a weight change. Hence, when pottery is heated its weight will remain constant until the firing temperature is reached and any changes in energy will be explicable in terms of the changing temperature of the pottery. Thermal analysis involves the determination of the temperatures at which these changes start to occur. The degree of vitrification is normally measured using a scanning electron microscope (section 7.3), while changes in the minerals present can be determined using X-ray diffractograms (section 7.4) or Mössbauer spectroscopy (section 7.5).

Three types of thermal analysis are commonly used: differential thermal analysis (DTA), differential thermogravimetric analysis (DTG or DTGA) and thermogravimetric analysis (TG or T_G). DTA looks at the energy changes which occur when pottery is heated. In an exothermic reaction, such as the burning of organic material, heat is given out, while in an endothermic reaction, for example the decomposition of calcite, energy is taken in. The energy changes are measured by comparing the temperature of the pot sample with that of an inert sample which absorbs heat at the same rate as pottery (i.e.

has the same specific heat capacity) when it is heated using identical conditions. Pottery or clay that have already been heated to high temperatures make suitable inert samples. The temperature difference between the two samples is then plotted against the temperature of the pottery sample, because during an exothermic reaction the temperature of the pottery will be greater, while during an endothermic reaction it will be less than that of the inert sample. In theory, the temperature of the two should remain the same until the firing temperature of the pottery sample is exceeded. Then chemical and physical changes will start to occur and produce endo-and exothermic peaks. In practice, weathering may result in the absorption of water and other changes in the pottery during its burial, so that when it is heated endo- and exothermic reactions can occur below the original firing temperature. Thus DTA curves should be interpreted with caution. Only about 100mg of pot is required for each sample being studied.

In DTG and TG the weight changes which occur when the sample is heated are studied. In TG only the pottery sample is heated and its weight, while it is being heated, is measured as a function of temperature, using a special balance. The main cause of weight changes is the loss of water, which can occur at various temperatures depending on whether the water is just trapped in the crystal lattice or the atoms which form the water are actually chemically bonded to the crystal. In the former case, the main weight loss occurs between 100 and 200°C, and in the latter between 500 and 700°C. Thus, in principle, the minimum temperature at which weight loss occurs experimentally is the maximum temperature to which the sample had been heated in antiquity, though again allowance must be made for the effects of weathering. In DTG the same procedure is followed, except that the weight of the pottery sample is compared with the weight of an inert sample heated under identical conditions. Only about 10mg of pottery is required for each sample though larger quantities may be required to ensure that the sample is representative of the complete pot.

In general, thermal analysis is best suited to determining the firing temperatures of pottery fired at low temperatures, because in pottery fired at high temperatures no changes that can be detected by these methods are observed. Thermal analysis can only provide an estimate of the temperature used in antiquity, because the actual temperature required to produce the changes observed will depend on various factors, including whether or not the pot was fired in a reducing atmosphere and how fast it was heated.

8.2.2 Applications

Thermal analysis has been used to determine the firing temperatures of a variety of objects, though recently its main use has been to check for post-burial changes such as re-hydration in pottery.

Mejdahl[2] used DTA to determine the firing temperatures of 14 objects from Glozel. He compared their DTA curves with DTA curves for unfired Glozel clay and Glozel clay which had been fired at 700°C for two hours in the laboratory. He concluded that ten of the objects had been fired above 400 °C and hence would be suitable for TL dating, because their geological TL would have been drained by the firing, but that the remainder were poorly fired and hence would be unsuitable for TL dating.

Kardos et al.[3] used X-ray diffraction analysis to determine the firing temperature of the pottery from the Sopron-Krautacker Iron Age pottery workshop. They concluded that a firing temperature of 600–700°C had been used, though in some cases overfiring had occurred, because some sherds had been heated to 1,000°C. They used DTG, DTA and TG to show that few post-burial changes had occurred in the clay. Edwards et al.[4] used the scanning electron microscope to show that fourth millennium (or possibly earlier) pottery from the Chalcolithic site of Teleilat Ghassul (Jordan) had been fired at about 1,000°C, which would mean that the potters were highly skilled for such an early period. DTA and TGA curves contained only small changes showing that the pottery had not re-hydrated during burial.

Finally Enriquez et al.[5] used DTA to study the extent to which Amazonian pottery, ranging in age from 600 to 3,000 years BP, had re-hydrated during burial. Earlier studies had suggested that the firing temperature was less than 700–800°C. (The lower the firing temperature, the more likely the pottery is to undergo re-hydration and other forms of weathering.) They found a marked endothermic peak between 100 and 200°C in the older samples and a smaller one in the younger samples. The size of the peak appeared to depend on the age of the samples, suggesting that re-hydration occurs throughout the burial of the pottery. Such re-hydration is likely to turn iron oxides into hydroxides and so change the magnetic properties of the pottery. Along similar lines, Flamini et al.[6] used DTA and TG to compare ancient Etruscan pottery and modern imitations. They found the ancient pottery could be distinguished from the modern, because the former re- hydrated much more readily than the latter.

8.3 The Scanning Electron Microscope

8.3.1 Introduction and Principles

The scanning electron microscope (SEM) has many similarities to the optical microscope; the main difference being that a beam of electrons, instead of visible light, is used to illuminate the object. This is because in a microscope only those details in the object being studied further apart than the wavelength of the illumination used, can be resolved. Hence, the finer the detail being studied, the shorter the wavelength of the illuminating source must be to reveal it. The wavelengths associated with electrons are much shorter than the wavelengths for visible light and so if a beam of electrons, rather than a beam of visible light, is used to illuminate the sample a much larger magnification can be achieved. Thus the SEM is a powerful tool for the study of the surface detail and microstructure of a wide variety of materials. Magnifications of up to 50,000 can be produced, enabling features as small as $1.5 \times 10^{-2} \mu m$ to be seen, though normally, for archaeological work smaller magnifications are used. In particular, it can be used to study the effects of different firing conditions on the microstructure of pottery and the various microscopic wear marks produced on flint implements by different types of use.

The SEM is just one type of electron microscope and owes its name to the fact that the electron beam is scanned over the surface of the object being studied, enabling a much larger surface area to be studied than is possible with a standard electron microscope. For archaeological purposes, this more than compensates for the fact that a comparatively broad beam of electrons ($2.5 \times 10^{-2} \mu m$ diameter) is used, so that the magnification of the surface is less than can be achieved with a standard electron microscope. When the beam of electrons used to illuminate the object being studied reaches the surface of that object several things can happen. Firstly, some of the primary electrons are deflected from the surface by the charge on the atoms, as a ball thrown at a wall bounces back. Such electrons are known as back-scattered electrons. The probability of an electron being back-scattered depends on the atomic weight of the atoms it hits, with heavy atoms being more likely to deflect electrons than light atoms. These back-scattered electrons can be detected, and by observing how the numbers of back-scattered electrons vary over the surface being studied, it is possible to build up a picture of how the elements are distributed in that surface. Others of the primary electrons penetrate into the surface and, as a result of their collisions with the atoms present, the atoms lose electrons. Some of these secondary electrons, which have lower energies than the primary electrons, then escape from the surface of the object. The numbers of these escaped secondary electrons can then be counted using suitable detectors. The number of secondary electrons detected from any given point depends on the angle between the primary electron beam and the part of the surface hit by the beam, so by comparing the number of electrons detected from different parts of the surface, it is possible to build up a detailed picture of the microstructure of the surface. The results of SEM studies are frequently published as photographs, which makes it easy to compare the effects of, for example, heating a given type of pottery to different temperatures.

The SEM is closely related to the electron microprobe, whose use for elemental analysis has already been discussed (Chapter 7). The main difference is that in the SEM the back-scattered and secondary electrons are detected, while in the electron microprobe it is the X-rays which are emitted after electrons have been knocked out of the inner energy levels which are studied. The two instruments can thus be combined, but because the conditions under which the surface detail is seen most clearly are different from those under which the different elements present are measured most accurately the two techniques are normally best carried out separately.

Samples for the SEM can take several forms. In the first, the exposed surface or the surface of a slice removed from the object of interest is examined. In some cases it may be possible to examine the object as it is, but frequently a slice will have to be removed from it so that a sample of a size that will fit in the SEM is obtained. In addition, the surface of a natural break may be so irregular that most of it would be out of focus when examined. (The depth of focus of the SEM is less than $10\,\mu$m.) In other cases it may be necessary to examine polished sections which, will again, require the removal of a sample from the object being studied. Finally, with some materials it may be possible to make a 'cast' (normally an acetate peel) of the surface of interest. This can be done with stone artefacts and has the advantage that the object is not damaged by having a slice removed to provide the sample. In addition, when using a peel, the whole object can be studied, whereas if the object itself were examined, part of it would be destroyed in the preparation of the sample. The making of acetate peels suitable for use with the SEM is described by Knutsson et al.[7] Whichever type of sample is used, it may be necessary to coat the surface to be examined with carbon or another conducting material, so that electrons from the primary beam do not build up on the surface and cause problems.

8.3.2 Applications

SEM studies have been carried out on a wide variety of materials for a range of purposes, only a few of which are mentioned here. One of the main uses of the SEM has been in determining the temperature to which a variety of materials has been heated. Flint which has been heated is easier to work than unheated flint, but more likely to break in use. Thus, in some but not all circumstances, it is advantageous to heat flint before working it. Olausson et al. used the SEM to compare flint from Neolithic and Mesolithic implements from Sweden with samples from the implements heated to known temperatures in the laboratory and found that the implements had been made from unheated flint. Price et al.[9] also used the SEM, along with other techniques, to show that flint from Havelte in the Netherlands was unheated. The SEM has also been used to provide information about how and on what materials flint implements had been used. Meeks et al.[10] studied modern replica flint sickles whose method of use was known and compared the polish on them with that on Israeli and Egyptian reaping knives, Danish sickles, polished Neolithic axes and naturally polished flint. They found they could distinguish the polish produced by use from deliberate or natural polish. In addition, the striations in the microwear marks gave information about the manner in which the knives were used. They were, thus, able to distinguish between use on wild grasses and on cereals. The optical microscope has also been used for this type of work, though its lower magnification will limit the detail which can be seen. Keeley et al.[11] used it to study the microwear polishes on 1.5 Myr old stone tools from Koobi Fora, Kenya. Only a few tools had identifiable wear marks, but four of them had been used for cutting meat, two for cutting grasses or reeds and three for working wood.

The SEM has also been used in a range of work on ceramics. Tite et al.[12] examined faience made in the laboratory by a variety of methods, and compared it with that produced in ancient Egypt. They concluded that the Qom technique, in which the object is fired while buried in a glazing mixture, could have been used to produce all the objects, but that some of them could also have been produced using the efflorescence technique, in which the glaze mixture is mixed with the body material and allowed to dry naturally. This results in the glaze components migrating to the surface, so that a surface glaze is produced when the object is fired. Manitas et al.[13] used the SEM to identify the firing conditions used when producing a wide range of Neolithic and Bronze Age pottery from central and south-east Europe, Greece and the Near East. They compared the original pottery with samples from it re-fired in the laboratory at various temperatures and under both reducing and oxidising conditions. They found that the use of a reducing atmosphere led to vitrification starting at lower temperatures and the occurrence of bloating. They concluded that firing temperatures ranged from less than 800°C in much of south-west and central Europe to 850–1,050°C for some Bronze Age pottery from Jericho. Both oxidising and reducing atmospheres were used, with an oxidising atmosphere being preferred in Anatolia, Jericho and Thessaly and a reducing atmosphere in much of south-west and central Europe. In general there appeared to be few changes in the techniques for manufacturing pottery in these regions between the Neolithic and Bronze Ages. The use of the SEM to study refractory ceramics from metal-production and metalworking sites in discussed by Tite et al.[14]

8.4 X-Ray Diffraction

8.4.1 Introduction and Principles

The main use of X-ray diffraction analysis (XRD) is in identifying the crystalline minerals present in a sample. Not only will it reveal whether an element is present as an oxide or other compound, but also the phase of the mineral present. In many minerals it is possible for the same proportions of atoms to be arranged in different ways, so that the mineral can exist in more than one crystal form. For example, if a mineral consists of equal numbers of two types of atom they can be arranged, either so that each atom in the crystal has eight nearest neighbours cubically arranged (see Figure 8.1a), or else so that each atom has six nearest neighbours octahedrally arranged (see Figure 8.1b). These different structures are known as different phases of the mineral.

Figure 8.1 Two different types of crystal lattice

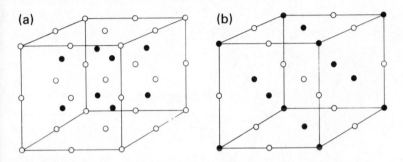

(a) The eight nearest neighbours of each atom are arranged cubically;
(b) The six nearest neighbours of each atom are arranged octahedrally

Identifying the mineral phases present in a sample has a variety of uses. Firstly, it may help to show what material a particular sample is. Secondly, it has been used in provenance studies on both pottery and stone artefacts, because the proportions of the different minerals present will depend on the source of the raw materials. Finally, it has been used to estimate the firing temperatures used when making pottery, because both the minerals present in the clay and their phase will depend on the temperature to which the sample has been heated.

XRD analysis is normally carried out using the powder diffraction method. In this method a representative sample is removed from the object of interest, powdered and between 5 and 10mg is turned into a rod-shaped specimen, either by mixing the powder with a suitable adhesive or else by sealing the powder in a glass capillary tube. The sample is then placed at the centre of a cylindrical X-ray camera and illuminated with a beam of monochromatic X-rays (i.e. X-rays of a single wavelength). The layers in any crystals present can be thought of as acting like

Figure 8.2 How two beams of X-rays behave when they meet

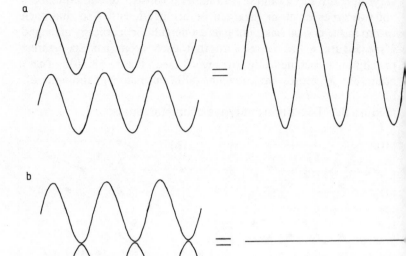

(a) The two beams are in phase, i.e. peaks coincide with peaks and troughs
    with troughs. The beams, therefore, reinforce each other and the
    resultant beam has twice the amplitude (or intensity) of the initial beam;
(b) The two beams are completely out of phase, i.e. peaks coincide with
    troughs. The beams, therefore, cancel out and produce a beam of zero
    amplitude (or intensity)

mirrors and reflecting the X-rays, as visible light is reflected by an
ordinary mirror. The beams of X-rays reflected from each layer
interact with each other and either reinforce each other to produce a more intense X-ray beam or cancel each other out so that
no X-rays are detected. (If the incident X-ray beam is thought of
as being made of a series of waves of X-rays then if the peaks in the
reflected beams coincide as in Figure 8.2a they will reinforce each
other, but if a peak in the beam from one layer coincides with a
trough in the beam from the next layer as in Figure 8.2b then the
two beams will cancel each other out.) Whether or not the reflected X-ray beams reinforce each other depends on both the
angle between the incident X-ray beam and the layers (or planes)
in the crystal from which it is reflected, and the distance between
adjacent crystal planes. Put mathematically, X-rays will only be

observed when $n\lambda = 2d\sin\theta$, where n is a whole number, λ the wavelength of the X-rays, d the distance between the lattice planes and θ the angle between the incident (or reflected) X-ray beam and the crystal plane (see Figure 8.3). The sample in the X-ray camera is rotated so that all the crystals present will, at some time, reflect the X-rays at such an angle that the reflected X-rays reinforce each other. The film in the X-ray camera will, therefore, record a series of bright lines. In reality, these are pairs of arcs centred on where the unreflected X-ray beam emerges from the camera (see Figure 8.4). By measuring the distance between the pairs of arcs it is possible to calculate the lattice spacing of any crystals present (i.e. the distance between successive layers of atoms in the crystal) and hence, with the aid of suitable tables or reference photographs, to identify the minerals present. If more than one mineral is present, the relative intensities of the different pairs of arcs will enable a rough estimate of the concentrations of the different minerals to be made. The minimum concentration that can be detected ranges between 1 and 10 per cent depending on how well crystallised the mineral is.

Figure 8.3 The conditions under which two X-ray beams will reinforce each other when reflected by a crystal

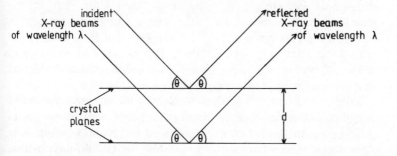

8.4.2 *Applications*

XRD analysis has most frequently been applied to pottery, but it can also be used to study a variety of other materials including stone and decorative inlays on metals.

Maggetti et al.[15] used XRD studies, in conjunction with other techniques, to compare the 'geriefte' fine pottery from the Heuneburg with similar looking Iron Age pottery from

Figure 8.4 The production of an X-ray diffractogram

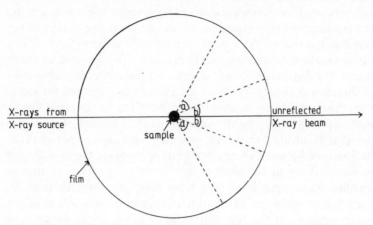

X-rays from
X-ray source

sample

unreflected
X-ray beam

film

------reflected X-ray beams (really cones of X-rays centred on sample)

Châtillon-s-Glâne. Some of the other pottery types at Châtillon-s-Glâne had obviously been imported, but it was unclear whether the 'geriefte' ware had also been imported or instead made locally. The X-ray diffractograms for the pottery from the two sites showed some similarities, but there were also important differences including more plagioclase then kalifelspar in the sherds from Châtillon-s-Glâne. This, along with other differences between the two types of pottery, suggests that they were made from local clays and not imported. The presence of calcite and dolomite, but not calcium-silicates, in the diffractograms suggest that the maximum firing temperature was 600–650°C.

Kohl et.[16] used XRD analysis to identify the minerals present in a highly distinctive type of decorated, green, soft stone vessel produced in the mid-third millennium BC and found in south west Asia from Mesopotamia to the Indus Valley. While possible sources of the stone could be identified on the ground, it was impossible to distinguish those sources quarried in ancient times from those worked only in more recent times. In an attempt to identify the source, and in particular, to establish whether Tepe Yahya in the Soghun Valley of Iran was the sole or primary source of the vessels, a variety of analytical techniques including XRD was used. The XRD analaysis of some of the vessels from Tepe Yahya showed that they were made from chlorite, rather than steatite as had previously been assumed. Vessels from a range of sites were then analysed and it was found, that while the majority were made from relatively pure chlorites, 17 per cent were made from steatite or other minerals. Using multivariate statistical techniques, the authors were able to subdivide the vessels made from chlorites into smaller groups, which showed that the vessels were made from stone from a variety of sources. In particular, it was found that sites with local sources of suitable stone normally used just one type of stone, presumably local, but on the islands in the Gulf, where the stone to make the vessels would have to be imported, stone from a range of sources was used.

Finally La Neice[17] used XRD analysis to determine the composition of the neillos (a black compound inlaid as decoration on metal objects) on a range of objects in the British Museum dating from Roman times to the present century. True niello is a metal sulphide, with different metals and mixtures of metals having been used at different times, but the term has also been applied to other decorative black inlays. While XRF analysis would have distinguished between the different metals present, it would not have distinguished niello from other black metal compounds like oxides and so XRD analysis was chosen for this study. She found that in Roman times the metal in the niello was normally the same as the metal to which it was applied, although silver sulphide is difficult to work with. Thus, silver sulphide was found on silver, copper sulphide on copper, copper/tin/zinc sulphide on brass and one case of gold sulphide on gold. She suggests that this was because the smith used scrap metal to make the niello. There were also some examples of copper/silver sulphides but this may have been due to the use of base metal. In medieval times the type of niello seems to have been chosen for its ease of use with copper/silver sulphide becoming common in early medieval times and copper/silver/lead sulphide starting to occur in the late medieval period. This form continued to be used until recently, presumably because its low melting point makes it easier to work than silver sulphide.

8.5 Mössbauer Spectroscopy

8.5.1 Introduction and Principles

Mössbauer spectroscopy (MS) uses nuclear transitions to provide information about the chemical environment close to the nuclides excited. So far, in the archaeological field, only iron has been studied, but the technique can be applied to the majority of other elements, in particular tin. Mössbauer studies on iron can provide information about the firing conditions used when making pottery and the extent to which the chemical composition of the pottery has been affected by its burial, because it will show which particular iron compounds are present in the sample. It can also show what fraction of the iron is present in a ferromagnetic form and hence is capable of contributing to the magnetic moment of a sample. This information can be of use in archaeomagnetic studies (see Chapter 4).

Mössbauer spectroscopy is based on a similar principle to AAS, but studies the nuclear energy levels rather than the electronic levels. The principles behind it are best understood by considering the example of ^{57}Fe, the nucleus most commonly studied. An excited state, ^{57}Fe* (* is frequently used to denote an excited state of a nuclide), is produced by the decay of ^{57}Co and this ^{57}Fe* decays to the ground state, ^{57}Fe, by the emission of a γ-ray. Normally, when a nucleus decays from an excited state it recoils, analogously to a gun when it is fired. This means that part of the energy liberated in the decay is used in producing the recoil, so the energy of the γ-ray emitted is less than the difference in energy between the two energy levels involved in the decay. Similarly when a nucleus absorbs a γ-ray and enters an excited state it also normally recoils, so the energy of the γ-ray must be greater than the energy difference between the two states (see Figure 8.5). Thus a γ-ray emitted by a nucleus on decaying from a state x cannot excite a similar nucleus into state x, because it has too little energy. This situation is rather like changing money at a bank, in that if the quoted exchange rate is $1.39 to £1, you will only get $1.38 for each £1 you give the bank. If you then change the $1.38 back into pounds you will only get 98p. The 'missing' money has been taken by the bank to pay for its services just as the 'missing' energy has been used in the recoil of the nucleus.

However, under certain circumstances, both the decaying and the absorbing nuclei (i.e. ^{57}Fe produced by the decay of ^{57}Co in the cobalt source and ^{57}Fe in the sample) are so firmly attached to the crystal lattice that they cannot recoil and instead the whole crystal recoils. Surprising as this may seem, this involves an energy distribution far more in favour of the γ-ray and so γ-rays emitted by ^{57}Fe in the cobalt source can be absorbed by ^{57}Fe in the sample.

Figure 8.5 Production of Mössbauer spectra

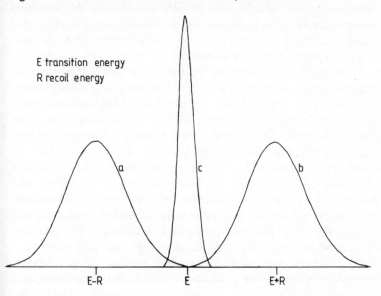

E transition energy
R recoil energy

Curves *a* and *b* are the range of energies involved in the normal absorption and emission, respectively, of γ-rays in a transition of energy E. *c* is the energy range involved for the same transition in recoil-free emission and absorption

This process is known as the recoil-free emission of γ-rays, or the Mössbauer effect. If however, the ^{57}Fe in the sample is present in a different chemical form to that in which it is present in the cobalt source, then there may be a small energy difference between the transition in the two cases, and so the sample will not absorb the emitted γ-rays. Then, if the cobalt source is moved slowly towards (or away from) the sample, a speed will be found at which absorption occurs. This is because, when a radiation source is moving towards an observer the wavelength of the radiation is shortened and hence its frequency and energy is increased, while if the radiation source is moving away from the observer its wavelength is increased so its frequency and energy is decreased. This effect is known as the Doppler effect and can be observed when a whistling train passes. As the train passes, the sound of the whistle will drop in pitch (i.e. the frequency of the note decreases), because the train has changed from moving towards to moving away from the observer. Thus, in Mössbauer spectroscopy if the speed of the source is plotted against the number of γ-rays absorbed by the sample, it is possible to measure the transition energies for the ^{57}Fe in the sample and by studying the shape and number of the absorption peaks to determine in which chemical form and mineral phase it is present.

Mössbauer spectroscopy is frequently carried out at low temperatures: for example 4.2 and 77K. (Kelvin (K) is a temperature scale favoured in physics in which the degrees are the same size as on the centigrade scale, but are counted from absolute zero, the lowest theoretically attainable temperature, corresponding to −273°C.) The use of low temperatures makes the data collected easier to interpret and can also provide additional information about the sample. Mössbauer spectroscopy is particularly useful for identifying the iron minerals in poorly crystallised materials, because even in crystals too small to be identified using an optical microscope, ^{57}Fe can undergo recoil-free absorption. Unless the material being analysed has an unusually low iron content, a 100mg sample is required from each artefact being analysed. Mössbauer spectroscopy is discussed further by Manitas et al.[18]

8.5.2 Applications

The main application of Mössbauer spectroscopy has been in determining the firing conditions used to produce ancient ceramics. Gancredo et al.[19] studied the pottery from a fourth-century BC level in a site at Seville. They found that the Fe^{2+}/Fe^{3+} ratio (i.e. the ratio of doubly charged iron ions to triply charged iron ions) in the 'grey' pottery was high, showing it had been fired under reducing conditions, while the 'painted' ware had a lower $Fe^{2+}/Fe^{3}+$ ratio, and hence, had been fired under less reducing conditions. They then re-fired some of the pottery at 850°C and found that produced changes in the Mössbauer spectra, so they concluded that originally the pottery had been fired at a lower temperature than this. Bakas et al.[20] also used Mössbauer spectroscopy to determine the firing conditions used to produce one of the tablets from Glozel. They compared the spectra obtained from the original tablet with those obtained from fractions which had been refired at 200, 400, 600, 800 and 1,000°C and concluded that the original firing temperature for the tablet was definitely less than 600°C and probably more than 400°C. By studying the shape of the spectra for the original tablet, they also concluded that the original firing had used oxidising conditions and that 40 per cent of the iron present in the sample was probably the product of weathering.

Manufacturing conditions can also affect the colour of glass. Longworth et al.[21] studied medieval stained glass from Elgin and St Andrews' cathedrals. They found both Fe^{2+} and F^{3+} in the green glass, but only Fe^{3+} in the purple and emerald glasses, showing that the latter had been produced using more oxidising conditions than the former.

8.6 Analysis of Organic Remains

8.6.1 Infra-Red Absorption Spectroscopy

Most molecules are not rigid structures, but instead the atoms which compose them vibrate relative to each other. The frequencies at which the vibrations occur are not random, but instead, depend on the atoms (or groups of atoms) at either end of the bond which is vibrating. This can be compared with the way a violin string will only vibrate at certain frequencies (produce certain notes), which depend on its length. If energy of a suitable frequency is available the bond will absorb energy and begin to vibrate. In addition to these simple vibrations, more complex modes involving several atoms may occur. Thus different molecules have different sets of vibrational energy levels. These energy levels lie in the infra-red (IR) region of the spectrum between visible light at the high energy end and micro- and radiowaves at the low energy end. By studying the IR absorption spectrum of a sample, it is possible to identify some of the groups of atoms present and hence to identify the molecules in the sample. Lines in an IR spectrum are frequently described in terms of wave number which is the inverse of the wavelength, rather than frequency. For example carbonyl groups absorb between $1,600 \text{cm}^{-1}$ and $1,700 \text{cm}^{-1}$, so their presence in a sample is easily detected in an IR spectrum.

One big advantage of IR spectrometry is that the sample can normally be recovered once the analysis is complete. About 10mg of material is required from each specimen of interest. If the sample is a gas, liquid or solution it can be placed directly in the spectrometer in a suitable container, but if it is an insoluble solid it will be ground up, mixed with potassium bromide and formed into a disc which is placed in the spectrometer. Once the analysis is complete the potassium bromide can be dissolved and the sample recovered, though in a fragmented condition. IR spectroscopy can be used to study both organic and inorganic samples because the hydroxyl (OH) group, which may be present in both types of material, is easily identified.

Evershed et al.[22] used IR spectroscopy, in conjunction with other techniques (see sections 8.6.2 and 8.6.3), to show that the pitch from the Mary Rose was similar in composition to early medieval pitch from York and pitch from an Etruscan shipwreck dating from about 6,000 BC found off the Island of Giglio, Italy and also to modern 'Stockholm tar'.

Manitas et al.[23] used IR spectroscopy to show whether hydroxyl groups were present in Late Bronze Age terracotta statues from Ayia Irini, Kea in the western Cyclades. The absence of hydroxyl groups would imply a higher firing temperature was used than if they were present, because they are not normally present in clay fired above 600°C. On the basis of the presence or absence of hydroxyl groups and SEM studies, they were able to divide the statues into groups according to the firing temperatures used to produce them. These groups coincided with the grouping of the statues on archaeological grounds. The firing temperatures found ranged from less than 600°C to between 750 and 800°C.

8.6.2 Mass Spectroscopy and Pyrolysis Mass Spectroscopy

The mass spectrometer has already been mentioned as the means of determining the isotopic composition of samples (see Chapter 6). However, its main use is as an aid to identifying organic molecules. Although it is a destructive technique, it can work with extremely small samples (less than 0.1mg). However, in general, larger samples are better, because such small samples are invisible to the naked eye and so the risk of contamination by fingerprints etc. is very great.

The mass spectrometer works by measuring the masses of the molecules and molecular fragments in the sample. When a sample is placed in the spectrometer it is first vaporised and then bombarded by an electron beam, which ionises the molecules by knocking off an electron. Some of these ions break up and give fragment ions. Thus, the mass spectrum will contain not only M^+ (singly charged molecular ions), but also a host of fragment ions characteristic of the structure of the molecule, because even molecules with the same molecular weight will produce different fragments. Thus, by measuring the masses of the molecule and the fragments, and then determining the structure of the fragments, it is possible to identify the original molecule. One aid in identifying the fragments is that their accurate molecular weights are not the same as the sum of the mass numbers of the constituent atoms. Thus, while for many purposes, it is reasonable to assume that 1 molecule of H_2O (water) has a molecular weight of 18 amu (atomic mass units) and 1 molecule of CH_4 (methane) has a mass of 16 amu, in practice, an accurate mass for water would be 18.010564 amu and for methane 16.0313 amu. Hence, methyl acetate ($C_3H_6O_2$) can be distinguished from diethyl ether ($C_4H_{10}O$), because the former has a mass of 74.036778 amu and the latter a mass of 74.073164 amu.

Evershed et al.[24] used mass spectroscopy (MS) to measure the molecular weights of the components of the pitch from the Mary Rose. Gas chromatography (see section 8.6.3) had revealed 8 components which MS showed had molecular weights and formulae as follows: 256 ($C_{19}H_{28}$), 254 ($C_{19}H_{26}$), 256 ($C_{19}H_{28}$), 252 ($C_{19}H_{24}$), 238 ($C_{18}H_{22}$), 220 ($C_{17}H_{16}$), 234 ($C_{18}H_{18}$) and 248 ($C_{19}H_{20}$), where all the masses are in amu. Further work also showed the presence of a compound with molecular weight 314 amu and formula $C_{21}H_{30}O_2$.

Burmeister[25] used pyrolysis mass spectroscopy (PMS), a technique which is used for samples which cannot easily be vaporised to produce a molecular beam, to study Far Eastern lacquers. In PMS the sample is heated until it decomposes and then the masses of the decomposition products are studied to provide information about the original sample. Far Eastern lacquer comes from the Far Eastern lacquer tree and has been used to coat wooden objects for over 2,500 years. Because the lacquer is still available for use, it can be difficult to tell whether an object is ancient or a modern forgery, and if ancient, the extent to which it has been restored or repaired. Burmeister found that the lacquer samples he studied could be split into groups with the aid of multi-variate statistics, on the basis of the fragments produced. In general, he found that samples from a single object or adjacent layers on an object were very similar, while samples from objects of different dates fell into different groups. Thus PMS seems to offer a way of detecting repaired or restored lacquer and possibly also modern forgeries. In the latter case more work needs to be done to establish why the lacquers differ: possible causes of the differences include workshop practices varying with time and differences between individual trees.

8.6.3 Chromatography

There are various types of chromatography: some are normally used to identify unknown compounds, while others are used to purify single compounds or to separate mixtures of compounds. A simple example of chromatography is what occurs when a blob of ordinary black writing ink is placed on a piece of blotting paper. If the paper is then suspended in water so that the ink blot is just above the water level, water will travel up the paper and past the ink. When the water has travelled some way beyond the initial blot, it will be found that between the blot and the water front are a series of coloured blobs. These are due to the dyes which make up the ink separating out, because some of them have a greater affinity for the moving phase (the water), while others have a greater affinity for the stationary phase (the paper). Those with the greatest affinity for the moving phase get carried furthest. Both the moving and stationary phases can take various forms, with the most commonly encountered variations being gas chromatography (gc), also known as liquid gas chromatography (glc), in which the moving phase is a gas and the stationary phase a viscous liquid coating a solid; and high pressure liquid chromatography (hplc) in which the moving phase is a liquid and the stationary phase a solid.

Gas chromatography/mass spectroscopy (GC/MS) in which MS is used to identify the compounds produced by GC was used by Evershed et al.[26] to identify some of the pitches and tars found on the Mary Rose. The authors found the samples contained di-terpenoid hydrocarbons, methyl dehydroabietate and de-hydroabietic acid in similar proportions to those in modern 'Stockholm tar' which is made from pine wood. They concluded, therefore, that the pitch and tar found on the Mary Rose were made by the destructive distillation of pine wood as is Stockholm tar. The pitches already in use for caulking, luting and on the anchor rope were less like Stockholm tar than that being stored in barrels. The authors suggest that these differences were just due to weathering or the means of preparing them for use, rather than any differences in origin. Shackley[27] also used GC to identify a resinous deposit in a sixth-century storage jar from En Boqeq in Israel. She concluded it was pine resin and suggests that it would have been used to make unguents. A further example is the use of GLC by Patrick et al.[28] to analyse residues found on pottery from an open-air coastal site on the Vredenburg Peninsula at

Kasteelberg in the south western Cape, South Africa. They identified the fatty acids present in the residue and concluded they came from a marine animal, possibly seal. Seal bones were amongst the animal remains found on the site so they suggest the pot had been used to cook seal meat.

8.6.4 Nuclear Magnetic Resonance Spectroscopy

Many nuclides and all electrons possess magnetic dipole moments, so that when they are placed in a magnetic field they behave rather like tiny bar magnets and take up a fixed orientation parallel to the field. For each nuclide only a certain number of orientations are possible so, for example, the proton (nucleus of a hydrogen atom) can only be aligned parallel or anti-parallel to the magnetic field. The energy of the proton depends on which way it is aligned and so if energy of a suitable frequency (i.e. wavelength) is available the proton can flip between the two possible alignments. The energy difference between the two alignments depends on the intensity of the magnetic field at the proton which depends on two factors: firstly, the external magnetic field, which is the same for all the nuclei in a compound; and secondly, the magnetic field produced by the electrons and the other magnetic nuclei in the molecule. This second component of the field is different for protons in different environments or parts of the molecule. Thus, the different protons in a molecule are in different local magnetic fields and so require different amounts of energy to allow them to flip from one alignment to the other.

This principle is used in nuclear magnetic resonance (nmr) spectroscopy, probably the single most powerful technique for identifying organic molecules. The most basic form of an nmr spectrometer contains an energy source of fixed frequency and a magnetic field of variable intensity. If the magnetic field intensity is slowly varied, different protons will be in the right magnetic field for them to change orientation at different times; and so they will also absorb energy from the energy source at different times. If the energy absorbed is then plotted against magnetic field intensity, a series of absorption peaks will be produced. By studying this spectrum it is possible to identify the organic molecules present in the sample. In practice, mainly because of the extreme weakness of the absorptions being observed, far more elaborate, computer-based spectrometers are now used.

Although, in principle, nmr spectra can be obtained for any

nuclide which processes a magnetic moment, some nuclei give very weak or poor signals or have only a low abundance in nature and so are not normally studied. However ^1H and ^{13}C give clear spectra and so are frequently used. (Carbon and hydrogen are the two most common elements in organic molecules.)

Lambert et al.[29] used nmr spectroscopy to study amber from the Dominican Republic, Mexico and the Baltic. They found the Dominican amber could be distinguished from that from the other areas and also that some, but not all, of the amber mines within the Dominican Republic could be distinguished from each other. Cassar et al.[30] used ^{13}C-NMR spectroscopy to determine the material used to make several English seals. They studied seals of Kings Stephen, John and William IV and also modern and ancient bees wax. They found that all the seals were made of bees wax and that the only difference between the ancient and modern wax was a slight oxidation. The William IV seal also contained a rosin component which they suggest could be deteriorated colophony.

Notes and Further Reading

1. For example, on petrography see *The petrology of archaeological artefacts*, edited by D.R.C. Kempe and A.P. Harvey, (1983); on metallurgical studies see R. Tylecote, *Metallurgy in Archaeology* (Edward Arnold, London, 1962); on radiography see David Graham and Thomas Eddie, *X-ray techniques in art galleries and museums* (Adam Hilger, 1985).

2. V. Mejdahl, 'Further work on ceramic objects from Glozel', *Archaeometry*, vol. 22, no. 2 (1980), pp. 197–203.

3. J. Kardos, K. Zimmer, L. Kriston, O. Morozova, T. Träger and E. Jerem, 'Scientific investigation of the Sopron-Krautacker Iron Age pottery workshop', *Archaeometry*, vol. 27, no. 1 (1985), pp. 83–93.

4. W.I. Edwards and E.R. Segnit, 'Pottery technology at the Chalcolithic site of Teleilat Ghassul (Jordan)', *Archaeometry*, vol. 26, no. 1 (1984), pp. 69–77.

5. C.R. Enriquez, J. Danon and M. Da C.M.C. Betrão, 'Differential thermal analysis of some Amazonian archaeological pottery', *Archaeometry*, vol. 21, no. 2 (1979), pp. 183–6.

6. A. Flamini and P. De Lorenzo Flamini, 'Discrimination between Etruscan pottery and recent imitations by means of thermal analyses', *Archaeometry*, vol. 27, no. 2 (1985), pp. 218–24.

7. K. Knutsson and R. Hope, 'The application of acetate peels in lithic usewear analysis', *Archaeometry*, vol. 26, no. 1 (1984), pp. 49–61.

8. Deborah Seitzer Olaussan and Lars Larsson, 'Testing for the presence of thermal pretreatment of flint in the Mesolithic and Neolithic of Sweden', *Journal of Archaeological Science*, vol. 9 (1982), pp. 275–85.

9. T. Douglas Price, Sylvia Chappell and David J. Ives, 'Thermal alteration in mesolithic assemblages', *Proceedings of the Prehistoric Society*, vol. 48 (1982), pp. 467–85.

10. N.D. Meeks, G. de G. Sieveking, M.S. Tite and J. Cook, 'Gloss and use

Other Analytical Techniques 203

wear traces on flint sickles and similar phenomena', *Journal of Archaeological Science*, vol. 9 (1982), pp. 317–40.

11. Lawrence H. Keeley and Nicholas Toth, 'Microwear polishes on early stone tools from Koobi Fora, Kenya', *Nature*, vol. 293 (1981), pp. 464–5.

12. M.S. Tite, I.C. Freestone and M. Bimson, 'Egyptian faience: an investigation of the methods of production', *Archaeometry*, vol. 25, no. 1 (1983), pp. 17–27.

13. Y. Maniatis and M.S. Tite, 'Technological examination of Neolithic-Bronze Age pottery from Central and Southeast Europe and from the Near East', *Journal of Archaeological Science*, vol. 8 (1981), pp. 59–76.

14. M.S. Tite, I.C. Freeston, N.D. Meeks and P.T. Craddock, 'The examination of refractory ceramics from metal-production and metalworking sites', in Patricia Phillips (ed.), *The Archaeologist and the Laboratory*, CBA Research Report no. 58 (Council for British Archaeology, 1985), pp. 50–5.

15. M. Maggetti and H. Schwab, 'Iron Age fine pottery from Châtillon-s-Glâne and the Heuneburg', *Archaeometry*, vol. 24, no. 1 (1982), pp. 21–36.

16. P.L. Kohl, G. Harbottle and E.V. Sayre, 'Physical and chemical analyses of soft stone vessels from Southwest Asia', *Archaeometry*, vol. 21, no. 2 (1979), pp. 131–59.

17. Susan La Neice, 'Neillo: an historical and technical survey', *Antiquaries Journal*, vol. 63, no. 2 (1983), pp. 279–97.

18. Y. Maniatis, A. Simopoulos, and A. Kostikas, 'The investigation of ancient ceramic technologies by Mössbauer spectroscopy', in Jacqueline S. Olin and Alan D. Franklin (eds.), *Archaeological Ceramics* (Smithsonian Institution Press, 1982), pp. 97–108.

19. J.R. Gancedo, M. Gracia, A. Hernandez-Laguna, G. Ruiz-Garcia and J. Palomares, 'Moessbauer spectroscopic, chemical and mineralogical characterization of Iberian pottery', *Archaeometry*, vol. 27, no. 1 (1985), pp. 75–82.

20. Th. Bakas, N-H. Gangas, I. Siglas and M.J. Aitken, 'Mössbauer study of Glozel tablet 198b1', *Archaeometry*, vol. 22, no. 1 (1980), pp. 69–80.

21. G. Longworth, N.H. Tennent, M.J. Tricker and D.P. Vaishnava, 'Iron-57 Mössbauer spectral studies of medieval stained glass', *Journal of Archaeological Science*, vol. 9 (1982), pp. 261–3.

22. R.P. Evershed, K. Jerman and G. Eglinton, 'Pine wood origin for pitch from the Mary Rose', *Nature*, vol. 314 (1985), pp. 528–30.

23. Y. Maniatis, A. Katsanos and M.E. Caskey, 'Technological examination of low-fired terracotta statues from Ayia Irini, Kea', *Archaeometry*, vol. 24, no. 2 (1982), pp. 191–8.

24. R.P. Evershed et al., 'Pine wood origin for pitch from the Mary Rose', pp. 528–30.

25. A. Burmeister, 'Far Eastern Lacquers: classification by pyrolsis mass spectroscopy', *Archaeometry*, vol. 25, no. 1 (1983), pp. 45–58.

26. R.P. Evershed et al., 'Pine wood origin for pitch from the Mary Rose', pp. 528–30.

27. Myra Shackley, 'Gas chromatographic identification of a resinous deposit from a 6th century storage jar and its possible identification', *Journal of Archaeological Science*, vol. 9 (1982), pp. 305–6.

28. M. Patrick, A.J. de Koning and A.B. Smith, 'Gas liquid chromatographic analysis of fatty acids in food residues from ceramics found in the Southwestern Cape, South Africa', *Archaeometry*, vol. 27, no. 2 (1985), pp. 231–6.

29. J.B. Lambert, J.S. Frye and G.P. Poinar Jr., 'Amber from the Dominican Republic: analysis by nuclear magnet resonance spectroscopy', *Archaeometry*, vol. 27, no. 1 (1985), pp. 43–51.

30. M. Cassar, G. V. Robins, R.A. Fletton and A. Alstin, 'Organic components in historical non-metallic seals identified using ^{13}C-NMR spectroscopy', *Nature*, vol. 303 (1983), pp. 238–9.

9 TECHNIQUES FOR LOCATING AREAS OF ARCHAEOLOGICAL INTEREST AND ARCHAEOLOGICAL FEATURES

9.1 Introduction

Various techniques have been used to locate those archaeological sites which are not so easily visible on the ground as are many hillforts and barrows. These include fieldwalking to recover pottery and other finds brought up by ploughing or moles or rabbits from sites now buried under farm land; and also aerial photography, which reveals cropmarks and slight irregularities in the ground caused by archaeological sites which cannot readily be seen at ground level. However, both these techniques have their disadvantages. Fieldwalking will only reveal sites where artefacts are plentiful and sufficiently close to the surface to be brought up by ploughing, while aerial photographs need to be taken when shadow-, soil- or cropmarks are pronounced. In addition, in some years cropmarks are more prominent than others. Moreover farming practices change, so air photographs taken in any year may reveal hitherto unknown sites. Finally, once a site has been discovered on an air photograph, complex calculations may still be needed before it can be located precisely on the ground, though computer programs are available to help with the calculations.[1] The use of aerial photography is discussed further by Wilson.[2]

Geophysical surveying techniques, which are discussed in this chapter, provide alternative means of locating archaeological remains. These techniques measure the electrical and magnetic properties of the ground and thus enable geophysical anomalies, i.e. areas where the electrical or magnetic properties of the ground are different to normal, to be located. These anomalies can be caused by a variety of factors, with some being due to human activity and others to natural variations in the soil and bedrock. For example, the soil within a pit or ditch normally has different electrical and magnetic properties to the surrounding soil or bedrock (the natural). In addition, stone structures such as roads and walls have different electrical properties to the natural while fired structures such as kilns and hearths will have different magnetic properties. Hence if a geophysical survey is carried out all these products of human activity may produce anomalies. Unfortunately for the archaeologist, natural features such as hollows in the bed rock, igneous boulders and iron rich areas of soil can also produce anomalies in a geophysical survey and so this type of survey must be interpreted with care if anomalies produced naturally are not to be confused with those produced by human activity.

Providing this is done geophysical surveying offers a useful way of locating those areas it would be most worthwhile to excavate and offers several advantages over the techniques already mentioned. Firstly, it can locate sites which are not visible from the air, though aerial photographs may also show sites that are not easily detected by geophysical surveying. Secondly, because the surveying is carried out at ground level, it is a simple matter to locate any features found by the survey. Finally, the survey can be carried out by the archaeologist himself, or at least when he wants it, rather than being dependent on when cropmarks are easily visible and when there is an aeroplane equipped for photography in the area, or when a field has been ploughed. The area which can be covered in one day by geophysical surveying is, however, much smaller than that covered in only a single air photograph, and so it is normally only carried out in areas of specific interest. It is particularly useful in locating sites of archaeological interest in open countryside which is about to be developed or to have roads built over it, so that they can be properly excavated before construction work starts. Its other big role is in planning the excavation of known archaeological sites. If carried out before an excavation, it can reveal those areas which would be most worthwhile digging, while if carried out afterwards it can provide information about those areas which could not be excavated due to a shortage of time. While a geophysical survey will not provide as much information as a full-scale excavation — in particular no artefacts will be recovered — it should reveal traces of human activity, and it can be carried out much more quickly than an excavation. In favourable circumstances, the plots produced may be sufficiently clear to enable the ground plans of buildings and the layout of field systems to be identified.

Three main techniques are in use. In resistivity surveying the ease with which an electric current can travel through the ground is measured. It is best suited to finding structures made of stone and defining the limits of linear features, because although the equipment needed is comparatively cheap, the survey itself is time consuming. Magnetic surveying uses the differences in magnetic properties between man-made structures and the natural to reveal features of archaeological interest. The equipment required is normally more expensive than that used for resistivity surveying, but a survey can be completed more quickly. Finally, in electromagnetic surveying the instrument used emits a signal which induces different signals in archaeological features and the natural. Thus by studying the induced signals it is possible to locate buried remains. This technique is both relatively quick and relatively cheap, but it suffers from the disadvantage that it can only be used on sites where the archaeological features are near the surface. Thus, which technique will prove most suitable will depend on a variety of circumstances and there is no guarantee that any technique will produce useful results. For example, if a lot of structures overlap it may be impossible to disentangle them except by excavation. In addition, if there is irregular bedrock close to the ground surface the signals produced by the irregularities may be confused with the signals from archaeological features. Finally the magnetic properties of the bedrock may vary from place to place.

Other techniques have also been proposed for the location of buried remains, but most of them have still to prove their worth. These include soil-sounding radar[3] and thermal prospection on bare soils.[4] The only other technique which is discussed in detail in this chapter is phosphate analysis.

9.2 Planning and Layout of a Survey

Once it has been decided to carry out a geophysical survey of an area, the next stage is to plan where the measurements are to be made. This process is the same for all the geophysical surveying techniques and also for phosphate analysis and so is described before the individual techniques are discussed. The survey needs to be carefully planned to enable the best possible results to be obtained. Most importantly, unless the measurements are made and recorded in a systematic way, the results will be difficult to interpret. For this reason, a grid is normally laid out on the site to mark these points at which readings are to be taken. The first stage in laying out this grid is to decide how frequently the measurements are to be made. If the space between measurements is too large important information may be lost, while if the space is too small time may be wasted taking unnecessary measurements.

Figure 9.1 Lay out of part of the grid for a geophysical survey

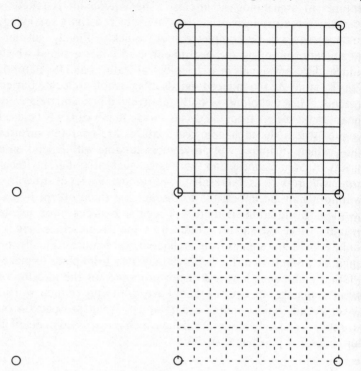

○ posts marking main survey grid
— first position of string grid
- - second position of string grid

For geophysical surveying measurements are ideally made every 0.5 or 1m, but for phosphate analysis the interval may be up to 5m.

The best way of marking the points on site will depend on how frequently the measurements are to be made. If the interval is small (around 1m), then a grid should be made of stout string with sides 10m by 10m. More strings can be run from side to side and up and down at 1m intervals so that a grid is produced. If the points half-way between each intersection are also marked, the grid can be used for taking measurements at either 1m or 0.5m intervals. Before the string grid can be used, it will be necessary to lay out on the site a grid of squares 10m by 10m. This can be done using wooden pegs. The string grid can then be placed on the ground with its corners touching four of the pegs and measurements made at the marked points. Once the area covered by the string grid has been surveyed, the grid is moved along one square so that the next area can be surveyed (see Figure 9.1). If the survey is being carried out at 5m intervals the string grid can be dispensed with and wooden pegs only used. In addition, some instruments for geophysical surveying produce continuous readings. In this case all that is needed are two parallel lines of wooden pegs on either side of the area to be surveyed with 1m (or whatever the measurement interval is) between the pegs. Strings can then be stretched between the pegs and the survey carried out by walking up and down the strings carrying the survey instrument. It is important that the position of the grid is accurately marked on the site plan so that any features found during the survey can be located on the ground at a later date. If a magnetic or electromagnetic survey is being carried out, iron nails must not be used to attach the string grid to the pegs or elsewhere in the lay out of the survey.

9.3 Geophysical Surveying: Principles and Techniques

9.3.1 Resistivity Surveying

It is a well-known fact that some materials carry an electric current more readily than others, i.e. they have a lower resistance to the electric current. For example, an electric flex is normally made of several metal wires, each coated with plastic, because metal has a low resistance (or high conductivity), while plastic has a high resistance (or poor conductivity). Thus the electric current can flow easily along the metal but not through the plastic. Soils and rocks are generally thought of as being poor conductors of electricity. However, particularly when wet, soils have a lower resistance than rocks and so by measuring the ease with which an electric current passes through different areas of an archaeological site, it is possible to locate those areas in which there are stone built structures. If the survey is carried out in a systematic way, it may be possible to build up quite a detailed plan of the roads, walls and any other stone built structures on the site. In addition, ditches and pits cut into rock or soil will be filled with different material to the undisturbed ground. This material may have a different resistance to the surrounding soil or alternatively the disturbed ground will be better drained than the undisturbed ground, so again such features may be detected by a resistivity survey. The resistance of the ground is normally measured in Ohms (Ω) or a suitable multiple thereof.

The differences in the resistance of the ground can be detected using a resistivity meter consisting of four metal electrodes attached to cables of suitable length, an ac power source and a meter to measure the resistance. To carry out a survey a grid is laid out as described in section 9.2 and measurements are made at appropriate intervals. To do this all four electrodes are inserted in the ground and a current is applied to two of them. This current speeds through the ground and produces a voltage between the other two electrodes, proportional to both the resistance of the ground between them and to the current used. The size of the resistance is, therefore, displayed on the meter and is either recorded automatically by some instruments or else is marked manually on a site plan. One or more of the electrodes are then repositioned so that the next measurement can be made. This procedure is repeated until the whole site has been surveyed.

The main advantage of resistivity surveying, when compared with magnetic surveying is that the equipment required is comparatively cheap. Commercially available resistivity meters cost roughly £300 to £800 (1985 prices), though if the measurements are recorded automatically the cost of a data logger or computer must be included. It is also less subject to interference from power lines and metal objects. Its big disadvantage, when compared with the other geophysical techniques is that it is a slow process. For example Linnington[5] found that it took roughly four times as long

o carry out a resistivity survey of a given area as it did to perform
a magnetic survey. This is because in a resistivity survey a large
proportion of the time is taken up pushing the electrodes into the
ground before each reading and pulling them out afterwards.
When the electrodes are inserted, care has to be taken to ensure
that they are properly in contact with the ground and that there are
no air gaps, because air has a very high resistance. Thus poor
contact between the ground and the electrodes will result in a high
resistance being measured even when the resistance of the ground
is normal.

Figure 9.2 The Wenner electrode configuration for resistivity
surveying

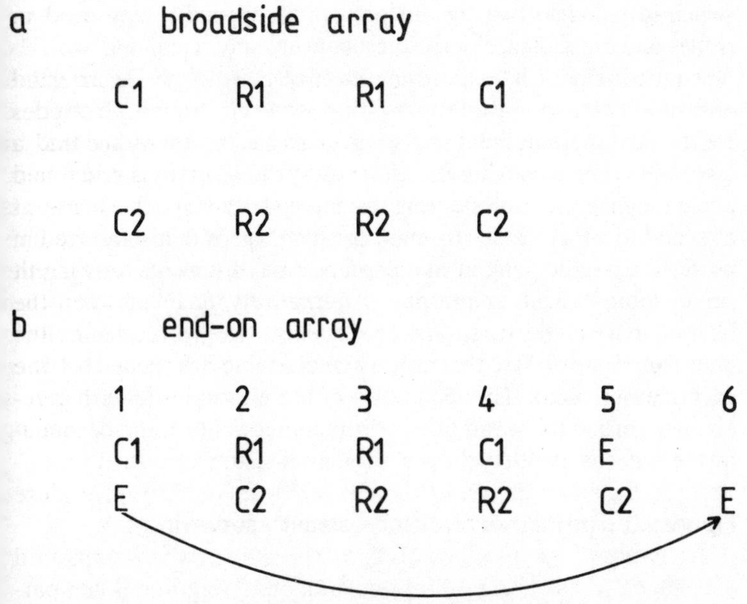

a   **broadside array**

C1   R1   R1   C1

C2   R2   R2   C2

b   **end-on array**

1	2	3	4	5	6
C1	R1	R1	C1	E	
E	C2	R2	R2	C2	E

C indicates electrodes to which the current is applied and R the electrodes
between which the resistance is measured. Electrodes labelled 1 are used for
the first measurements and 2 for the second
(a) The broadside array. All four electrodes have to be moved from C1 and
    R1 to C2 and R2 before the second measurement is made
(b) The end-on array. No electrode has to be moved between the first and
    second measurements, but the spare electrode, E, is moved from
    position 1 to position 6 while the second reading is made

The time taken moving electrodes was particularly great in early resistivity surveys because all four electrodes had to be moved between each reading. This was because the electrodes were arranged in the 'Wenner configuration' in which the electrodes are equally spaced The current is then applied between the two outer electrodes and the resistance measured between the two inner ones. The separation of the electrodes was normally chosen to be the same as the expected depth of any features, because a smaller separation would result in deeper features being missed, while a wider separation would result in small features being missed. These electrodes can be moved in two ways. In the broadside array (see Figure 2a) all four electrodes are moved forward after each reading. This has the advantage that each archaeological feature only produces one peak (or trough) in the resistance readings but the disadvantage of being very time consuming. In the end-on array, five electrodes can be used and a rotary switch included so that the current can be applied to any two electrodes and the resistance measured between any remaining two. The first measurement is made using electrodes 1–4 (see Figure 9.2b), electrode 1 is then moved to position 6 while electrodes 2–5 are used for the next measurement and so on. This has the advantage that far less time is spent moving the electrodes, though care is required to avoid tangling the cables during the survey because each electrode is attached to a long cable. Its main disadvantage is that some features produce a double peak in the resistance measurements, making the survey more difficult to interpret. Alternatively the Palmer array can be used in which the electrodes are fastened together mechanically in pairs (see Figure 9.3) so that only two movements are needed between each measurement. The separation of the electrodes in each pair is about 0.5m and the separation of the pairs about 1 to 2.5m, depending on the expected depth of the archaeological features.

Figure 9.3   The Palmer array for resistivity surveying

The electrodes are joined in pairs as indicated. Nomenclature as in Figure 9.2

Today the preferred arrangement is to have two pairs of electrodes, as in the Palmer array, but one pair is left permanently in the ground so that only one pair is moved between readings. The separation between the pairs is large, being typically more than 15m (see Figure 9.4). This has the advantage that the relative orientation of the two pairs of probes is unimportant and that single peaks are always obtained from single features. While the measured changes in resistance are much smaller than with the other arrangements, this does not matter because the sophisticated electronic equipment available today can measure resistances very accurately. A further advantage of this type of equipment is that computer programs[6] have been written to produce dot density plans from the readings while on site. This makes it easier to see as the survey is progressing whether useful results are being produced and also reduces the time taken for a survey.

Figure 9.4 The electrode arrangement favoured today

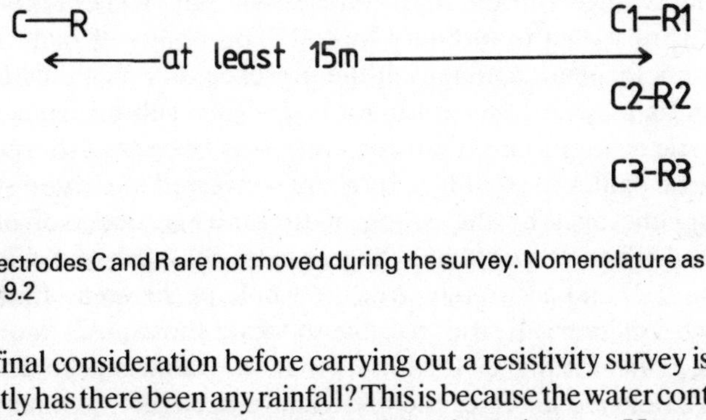

```
C—R                                          C1—R1
  ←————at least  15m ————————————→
                                             C2-R2

                                             C3-R3
```

The electrodes C and R are not moved during the survey. Nomenclature as in Figure 9.2

A final consideration before carrying out a resistivity survey is: how recently has there been any rainfall? This is because the water content of the ground is the main factor determining its resistance. Hence, after recent rainfall, stone structures will show up clearly because they will contain no water in contrast to the soil which will have a high water content. By contrast, if the ground is water-logged features cut through soil or gravel may show up less well than if the excess water has had time to drain away. In addition, water may be trapped in hollows in the bedrock, which again could produce misleading results. Equally in very dry conditions the water content of the ground may be so low that the contrast between different features may be too small to be easily seen.

9.3.2 *Magnetic Surveying*

Magnetic surveying provides an alternative means of revealing archaeological sites and has several advantages over resistivity surveying, though these may be outweighed by the greater cost of the equipment required. It utilises the fact that if the magnetic field at the surface of the Earth is measured very accurately (to the nearest nT, or nanoTesla) it will be found to vary over even quite short distances (less than 1 m). These variations are frequently due to the presence of archaeological features and arise from two causes. The stronger effect is produced by features which have been heated and hence are permanently magnetised due to the phenomenon of thermoremanent magnetisation (see Chapter 4). The magnetic field due to this remanent magnetisation combines with the Earth's magnetic field to produce the magnetic field in the immediate vicinity of the feature. A weaker effect is produced by the soils in ditches and other areas disturbed by man. This arises because all soil contains magnetic iron oxides which can acquire a magnetic moment when a magnetic field, in this case the Earth's, is present. It has been found that the more disturbed the soil, the larger this moment is. Thus the weakest effect is found in subsoil, and the strongest in the fill of ditches and pits, while a moderate effect is observed in ordinary topsoil. This ability of materials to acquire a magnetic moment in the presence of a magnetic field is known as magnetic susceptibility (χ_m). Thus subsoil has a lower magnetic susceptibility than top soil. This is because the weakly magnetic oxides present in subsoil are converted into more strongly magnetic ones by the action of fire and the decay of organic material. Thus by measuring the magnetic field systematically (see section 9.2) and accurately over the whole of the area of interest, at say 0.5 m intervals, it is possible to locate those areas where the magnetic field is higher (or lower) than the value expected for the Earth's field alone. Once the results have been plotted it may then be possible to identify features such as pits (including post holes under favourable circumstances) and ditches and to locate them on the ground.

In practice, there may be various complications. Firstly, in the first part of this section, it was assumed that the Earth's field is constant. As was discussed in Chapter 4, this is not the case. While the long-term changes used for dating will not affect a magnetic survey, there are various short-term changes that may. The most important of these are the diurnal changes which arise because the magnetic field which is measured at the surface of the Earth and is normally referred to as the Earth's magnetic field is not due purely to the Earth, but also includes contributions from the Sun and other bodies. Hence, because magnetic fields are vector quantities and so their directions as well as their magnitudes are important when they are added together, the measured intensity of the Earth's magnetic field shows regular daily variations. This is because of the rotation of the Earth about its own axis. The other important source of variations is magnetic storms in which the intensity of the Earth's magnetic field undergoes sudden and unexpected changes. These variations can be corrected for (or at least detected) by re-measuring and noting the field strength at a fixed point throughout the day (for example after every 10 or 20 measurements). The survey values can then be adjusted to have the values they would have had if the Earth's magnetic field had remained constant. Alternatively, equipment is available in which the correction is carried out automatically.

Another potential source of problems is that the magnetic anomaly will not be identical in shape with the archaeological feature nor will its centre lie exactly over the centre of the feature. In particular, in Europe, because of the shape of the magnetic field associated with the feature, the maximum of the anomaly will normally lie to the south of the feature by roughly one-third of the depth of the feature. In addition, a reverse anomaly (i.e. a minimum in the field strength) will lie to the north of the feature. For archaeological features this reverse anomaly will normally be less than 10 per cent of the normal anomaly and so may not be noticed. However, provided the whole of an anomaly is excavated there should not be any problems over locating the archaeological feature.

Finally archaeological features are not the only source of magnetic anomalies. Iron, because of its high magnetic permeability, distorts the nearby magnetic field. Thus even quite small objects such as modern nails can produce large anomalies. Fortunately such anomalies can usually be easily recognised, because the reverse anomaly is much bigger than would be expected for an archaeological feature. In addition, the area affected by the anomaly will probably be small, so only one or two readings will be affected. More serious problems are caused by recent scrap because it may be distributed over a large surface area. For example, rusty wire netting or barbed wire may spread some way from a fence line, making it time consuming, if not impossible to separate the anomalies due to archaeological features from those due to scrap iron. In particular, Clark et al.[7] concluded that they detected mainly chicken wire when they surveyed Mount Down, Hampshire. Buried iron pipes, iron fences and buildings containing large quantities of iron or steel can also cause serious problems because they will produce strong anomalies affecting large areas of the site. Serious problems can also be caused by iron rich pockets of soil in clay or hollows in limestone because they can produce anomalies which could be confused with archaeological features. Another possible source of unwanted iron is the survey itself. Cars and other forms of transport normally contain large amounts of iron and so should not be parked close to the area to be surveyed. In addition, many tools are made of iron or steel and so should not be left lying around. For similar reasons the survey grid should not be marked using iron or steel nails, but rather wooden posts. Any moveable metal objects to which a small magnet will stick (and the magnet) should be removed from the site while the survey is being carried out. Igneous rocks can also cause problems because they carry TRMs just like hearths and other heated clay. Magnetic surveying may therefore be impossible in those areas where there are significant quantities of such rocks. This is because the magnetic field from the rocks will mask the smaller anomalies due to archaeological features. In particular, the anomalies from igneous rock dykes could be confused with ditches while a scatter of igneous boulders could also cause problems. Finally ac power lines or radio transmitters near to the area being surveyed may prevent the instruments working properly, while dc power lines create magnetic fields which must be distinguished from those due to archaeological features.

Two main instruments have been used for magnetic surveying: the proton magnetometer and the fluxgate magnetometer. Both can be used either as absolute instruments (i.e. they measure the field value at each point surveyed) or as gradiometers (i.e. they measure the difference between the field strength at the survey point and a fixed point). The latter technique has the advantage that the long- and short-term variations of the Earth's magnetic field do not affect the readings, so it is no longer necessary to keep measuring the field at one point to provide a record of such variations. In addition, magnetic anomalies will be easily detected because they will produce positive or negative readings, while undisturbed areas will produce zero readings. A gradiometer requires two magnetometers, one to measure the field at the fixed point and the other to measure the field at the survey point. The associated electronics then compare the second value with the first in order to find the required reading. In practice, rather than leaving one magnetometer fixed and moving the other one, it is normally more convenient to attach them both to opposite ends of a long pole (2m or more in length) which is then carried vertically. The field as measured by the magnetometer close to the ground will be affected by any magnetic anomalies present, but the magnetometer at the top of the pole will just measure the Earth's field and so serves as the fixed magnetometer. So far as the archaeologist is concerned the main difference between the proton magnetometer and gradiometer on the one hand and the differential fluxgate magnetometer on the other is that the former provides single readings from fixed points, while the latter provides a continuous measurement of the magnetic field. Thus with the former it is necessary to stop at pre-marked points to take the measurements, while with the latter the field value can be recorded continuously on magnetic tapes or a chart recorder attached to the instrument. This enables a survey to be carried out more quickly using a fluxgate magnetometer, and in addition, a more detailed survey is carried out, at least in one dimension. Moreover, if a continuously reading instrument is used to carry out a survey in two directions at right angles to each other a three-dimensional graph of the results can be prepared. Such a graph has a greater visual impact than the more normal two-dimensional plots (see Chapter 10.3). For details of how the proton and fluxgate magnetometers work the reader must look elsewhere.[8] Commercially available magnetometers cost £2,000 or more.

A unit commonly encountered in magnetic surveys is the γ (gamma), which is equivalent to 1 nanoTesla (10^{-9}T) or 10^{-5} Oersted. This is because typical magnetic anomalies are 10 to 100γ in size and so the γ is a convenient size for recording magnetic anomalies directly onto a plan.

9.3.3 Electromagnetic Surveying

Electromagnetic surveying has been less widely used than either resistivity or magnetic surveying. This is because, while it combines the cheapness of resistivity surveying with the speed of magnetic surveying, it can normally only detect archaeological features within 0.5m or less of the ground surface. The metal detector, nowadays most commonly associated with treasure hunters, is currently the best known electromagnetic survey instrument, but other equipment has also been developed specifically for use on archaeological sites. All electromagnetic survey instruments contain a transmitter coil and a receiver coil so designed (either spatially or temporally) that the receiver coil does not respond to the signal from the transmitter coil. Instead the signal from the transmitter coil induces signals in the ground which are then picked up by the receiving coil. If the receiving coil is connected to a suitable electronic processor, the induced signal can then be interpreted to provide information about buried remains. Two properties of the ground affect the induced signal: its magnetic susceptibility and its resistivity, with their relative importance depending on the frequency of the transmitted signal. At low frequencies (about 4kHz) the magnetic susceptibility is the more important, but at high frequencies (around 100kHz) the resistivity is the more important. In addition, the strength of the signal also depends on the depth of the topsoil, at least for depths of less than 1m. Thus, under suitable conditions electromagnetic surveying should provide an alternative to either magnetic or resistivity surveying.

Unfortunately, the depth of features that can be detected using electromagnetic surveying is severely limited. At high frequencies the limit is about 0.3m, while at low frequencies it is rather better, being about 0.6m. These depths can be increased by increasing the separation between the transmitter and receiver. This, however, would normally result in unwieldy equipment, because in many instruments the transmitting and receiving coils must be kept at right angles to each other, to ensure that the receiving coil does not pick up the signal from the transmitting coil. In some instances the transmitting coil transmits a pulsed signal, so providing the signal at the receiving coil is only measured when the transmitter is off, the relative orientation of the two coils does not matter. The use of this technique enables larger coil separations to be used and hence features at greater depths to be detected.

It was originally hoped that electromagnetic surveying would provide a faster alternative to resistivity surveying. However, because the depth at which features can be detected is so limited when high frequencies are used, this is not practical. Instead, it is normally carried out at lower frequencies to provide a cheap alternative to magnetic surveying, though again it will not detect such deep features as can be detected by magnetic surveying. The other use of electromagnetic surveying is in detecting metal objects. While treasure hunters have given this use a bad name, it can serve a useful archaeological purpose by increasing the proportion of metal objects that are recovered from a site. In particular, in a rescue excavation where mechanical stripping of the topsoil is being carried out, if an electromagnetic survey is done first any metal objects present can be located and recovered before the stripping starts. This will mean that the location of the finds will be known more accurately than if they were recovered later from the spoil heap and it may be of great help in dating the site if coins or distinctive metal work are recovered.

Various instruments have been developed for electromagnetic surveying. These include the soil conductivity meter (SCM, also known as the soil anomaly detector or banjo)[9] which despite its name detects changes in magnetic suspectibility not resistivity, and the Colani pulsed magnetic induction detector.[10] Finally, as well as being used to detect metal objects, commercially available metal detectors can also be modified to respond more to archaeological features.

9.3.4 Presentation and Interpretation of Results

Once a survey is complete the archeologist will be faced either with a site plan covered with a mass of figures (see Figure 9.5a), or with one or more pieces of paper covered with a series of wiggly lines (see Figure 9.5b). The former is more common with instruments such as the proton magnetometer which only produce readings at fixed points, while the latter is more common with continuously reading instruments like the fluxgate magnetometer, though in practice either form of result may be produced by either type of survey. Initially, at least, the latter is easier to interpret because any anomalies will appear as peaks or troughs in the lines, with the height of the peak being proportional to the strength of the anomaly, and its width to the size of the feature. For example in a resistivity survey of the avenue heading to Stonehenge the chalk banks show up as two parallel rows of peaks.[11] In such cases, where any possible archaeological features are immediately obvious their positions can be marked on a site plan and they can be excavated at a later date to check the interpretation. On a complex site the interpretations may be less simple because it may be unclear which parts of the lines represent undisturbed ground or whether very strong anomalies mask weaker ones. The interpretation will also be difficult if the measured value of the resistivity or magnetic field at a fixed point is changing from day to

Figure 9.5 Two ways of recording the measurements from a geophysical survey (a)

390	394	387	396	392	396	395	398	394	389	388
390	393	391	397	412	410	409	408	399	394	395
392	394	400	407	417	428	439	428	409	396	391
395	401	411	427	445	469	486	464	415	393	391
395	405	416	428	441	468	489	461	415	391	388
393	406	415	420	427	436	426	405	386	384	382
388	398	407	406	408	389	378	372	478	377	383
386	390	390	389	379	369	366	371	376	379	385
388	383	382	377	372	370	374	375	378	385	388
389	388	385	382	380	382	383	386	388	391	391
390	390	387	384	384	384	385	386	389	389	391
390	390	389	385	383	382	384	385	401	359	406
391										

Readings made at individual points. These figures are based on a survey of a pottery kiln made using a proton magnetometer

day because then the plots will need to be corrected for this effect before they can be interpreted. In such cases it may be easier to plot the value of the quantity measured at say 1m intervals onto a site plan and treat this as though it was the original form of the data.

If the data from a survey is presented as an array of numbers the first step is to correct for any drift in the measurements that occurred while they were being made (i.e. adjust all the values so that the value at a fixed point becomes constant). The values to the left of the grid in Figure 9.5a represent the values of the magnetic

Figure 9.5b Two ways of recording the measurements from a geophysical survey (b)

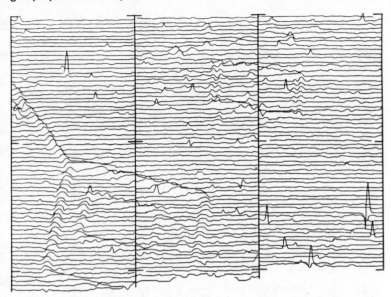

Readings made continuously. The figure shows a magnetic survey done with a fluxgate gradiometer with a sensitivity of 7.5 nT/0.5m. It revealed the foundation trenches of a probable church (note the apsidal east end) in a ditched churchyard enclosure (lower left) and a rectangular building with double foundation trenches (upper right). The buildings were of timber construction. The spikes were due to iron. The traverses were made at 1m intervals within each 30m square and the sensitivity was set so that 7.5 nT was equivalent to the standard spacing between the traces. (Courtesy Dr A.J. Clark and the Ancient Monuments Laboratory)

field at a fixed point and measured before each new row of the grid was surveyed. Only the final three figures for each reading have been recorded because the first two figures should be constant throughout the survey. The first step in the correction procedure is to find the average value of the field at the fixed point. In this case 393γ. In order to keep the calculations of the corrections for the other values as simple as possible it will be better to round the average to the nearest 10γ so it becomes 390γ. This value is then compared with the values for the fixed point at the start of each row. If two consecutive values are the same as the average, i.e. they are both 390γ, then the row between them needs no correction. If they are both 5γ higher than the average, then all the

Figure 9.6   The figures in Figure 9.5a after correction for diurnal variations etc.

394 387 396 392 396   395 398 394 389 388
                       0

393 391 397 411 409 408 407 397 392 393
      0   -1   -2

392 398 406 414 425 435 424 405 391 386
   -2   -3   -4   -5

396 406 422 440 464 481 459 410 388 386
                       5

400 411 423 437 464 485 457 412 388 385
      -5   -4   -3

403 413 418 426 435 426 405 387 385 384
 -3   -2   -1   0   1   2

400 409 408 411 392 381 375 382 381 387
      2   3   4

394 394 393 382 372 369 374 378 381 387
      4   3   2

385 384 379 374 372 375 376 379 386 389
         2   1

389 386 383 381 383 383 386 388 391 391
         1   0

390 387 384 384 384 385 386 389 389 391
                       0

390 389 385 383 382 383 384 400 358 405
         0   -1

The small figures are the corrections applied

values in the row between should be decreased by 5γ. If the first value is 2γ lower than the average and the second 4γ lower, then the first three values in the row should be increased by 2γ, the middle four by 3γ and the last three by 4γ. Figure 9.6 shows the corrected value from Figure 9.5a with the corrections applied in brackets.

Once all the data has been corrected and plotted on a site plan the next stage is to identify possible archaeological features. This involves making those regions where there are anomalies obvious to the eye and can be done in several ways. One method is to plot the contours of equal magnetic field strength or resistivity (see

Figure 9.7a). However drawing in contours correctly is a lengthy process and once it has been done it may still be difficult to identify features unless some sort of shading is also used. In particular, it is useful to mark either the high values or the low values (see Figure 9.7b). A quicker technique is just to mark all those values which deviate significantly from the value for undisturbed ground (or the average value). If the site is fairly simple it may be possible to interpret the survey when only one symbol is used, but on complex sites it may be necessary to use a series of symbols corresponding to increasing deviations from the average (see Figure 9.8). As an alternative the areas corresponding to different measurements can be shaded using different colours for different deviations. If the value expected for undisturbed ground is unknown, then the same procedure can be adopted, but starting by marking all the values above a certain value and continuing downwards using different symbols or colours every 10 or 20 units as appropriate. If too many different symbols are used the plan may become very confusing. It may be useful if positive and negative anomalies can be readily distinguished from each other, for example by using open symbols for one and closed for the other.

A final technique which has been frequently used is the dot density diagram. In this technique the ground area on the plan corresponding to each reading is randomly filled with dots whose number is related to the reading obtained. The number of dots per unit reading will depend on both the scale of the plan and the range of values covered by the readings. The use of too many dots per unit not only wastes time, but may also obliterate any features present because the result will be an almost totally black piece of paper. If too few dots per unit are used the features may be too faint to be readily seen, but at least the number of dots per unit can easily be increased. The dotting should also be done in such a way that the number of dots per square range from none to a lot. In particular, if all the readings lie between 350 and 450 it will be best to take 350 from all the readings and use the values so produced when calculating the number of dots per area. Figure 9.9 shows the data from Figure 9.6 plotted in this way.

Under favourable circumstances, once the survey is plotted in one of these ways, features such as ditches, walls and foundation trenches of buildings will be immediately obvious as straight or curved lines, while kilns, hearths, refuse or storage pits and areas of rubble or stone flooring will appear as blotches. However, in other cases it will not be possible to identify individual features, but instead all that can be done is to say that the area were anomalies are present was probably a focus

Figure 9.7 Contour plots of the measurements in Figure 9.6

(a)

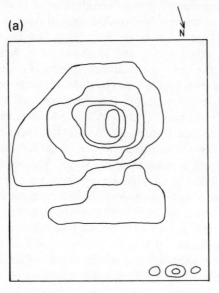

(b)

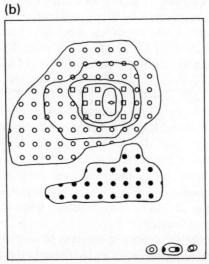

o	400–440γ
□	440–480γ
◇	480–520 γ
●	340–380γ

(a) The anomalies can be clearly seen, but it is unclear whether any of them are reverse anomalies

(b) The reverse anomalies have been marked to make the survey easier to interpret. The small anomaly was caused by a horse shoe and the large by the pottery kiln

Figure 9.8 A different way of plotting the data in Figure 9.6, in which every reading has been replaced by a symbol

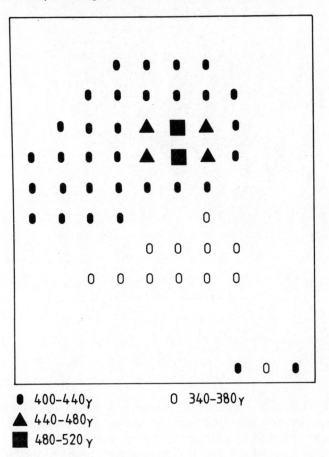

● 400–440γ   O 340–380γ
▲ 440–480γ
■ 480–520γ

Again the anomalies can be clearly seen

of human activity. In addition, it must always be remembered that a geophysical survey cannot tell the whole story of a site and so whenever possible the interpretation of the survey should be checked by excavation. In particular, a geophysical survey cannot provide dating evidence for the site, nor will it detect very small features such as stake holes or features which lie underneath other features. Equally, it is always possible that a geophysical survey will miss large features because their properties are the same as the surrounding

Figure 9.9 A dot density plot of the data in Figure 9.6

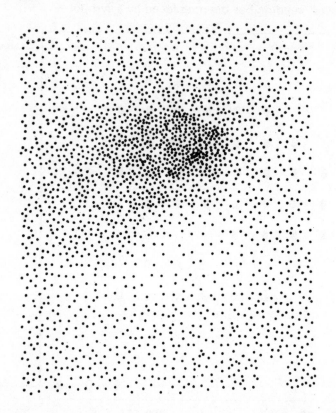

material. Finally, on a geophysical survey it is possible to mistake natural features such as hollows in uneven bedrock or iron rich pockets in soil for features produced by human activity.

While the results of a survey can frequently be interpreted using the plotted methods described above, in some cases a clearer picture may emerge if any features which are of no interest to the archaeologist are removed from the plot. For example if the survey is carried out in a ploughed field a series of parallel lines which correspond to the furrows may appear on the plot. Alternatively, if a large mass of igneous rock is affecting the magnetic field over part of the area surveyed, it may be possible to remove its effect from the final plot. The calculations involved in such procedures take a long time and so computer programs have been written to perform them.[12] Preparing dot density diagrams or contour plots manually is also a time consuming process so again, if the initial readings are fed into a suitable computer, either automatically during the survey or by hand at a later date, programs are available to produce the final plots. Geophysical surveying is discussed further by Clark.[13]

9.3.5 Applications

Despite the early success of geophysical surveying at sites like Dorchester (Oxon), Dragonby and Cadbury/Camelot, not many examples of its use have been published recently. The reasons for this are unclear. It may be that on the type of excavation being carried out at present archaeologists feel that geophysical surveying would serve no useful purpose. Alternatively, it may be that the geophysical surveys which have been carried out recently have not yet been published, or it may be that on those sites where geophysical surveying has been carried out no useful results were produced. For example a geophysical survey at Fortevoit, Perthshire, a historically documented royal centre of the early Middle Ages, using both a proton magnetometer and an SCM (banjo) failed to detect even the ditch visible on air photographs.[14] However, on other sites geophysical surveying has been more successful.

One site where magnetic surveying was of particular use was at Dragonby in Lincolnshire (now South Humberside).[15] Roman and Iron Age pottery had been recovered from two fields to the south of the modern village of Dragonby which were threatened by ironstone mining. Previous excavations had revealed Romano-British buildings, roads and pottery kilns and an Iron Age ditch, but the full extent of the settlement was unknown. In particular air photographs provided no useful evidence about its extent. Therefore, before a large scale excavation was undertaken to provide more information about the settlement and in particular about Iron Age activity at the site, it was decided to carry out a geophysical survey of as large an area as possible in order to define the limits of the settlement and also to indicate which areas it would be most profitable to excavate. Most of the area was surveyed in the mid-1960s using an absolute proton magneto-meter, though a small part was examined by a proton gradiometer. The magnetic field intensity was measured at 5 feet intervals and a complex pattern of both normal and reverse anomalies was revealed (see Figure 9.10). Excavation of two areas showed that the

Figure 9.10 The magnetic survey of Dragonby

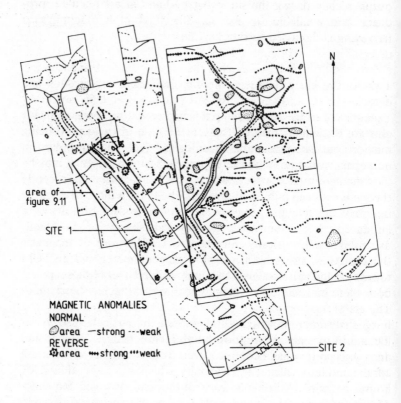

MAGNETIC ANOMALIES
NORMAL
⊘area —strong ---weak
REVERSE
✪area ⊮⊮⊮strong ⊮⊮⊮weak

area of figure 9.11

SITE 1

SITE 2

N

(courtesy Jeffrey May)

linear normal anomalies were due to ditches, while the linear reverse anomalies were due to stone roads. Similarly, the area normal anomalies correspond to either pits and wells, or to fired-clay structures such as pottery kilns and ovens, while the area reverse anomalies correspond to areas of stone rubble from destroyed buildings.

Figure 9.11 shows the results of excavating part of site 1 and provides an illustration of the extent to which a geophysical survey may reveal the features of archaeological interest on a site. In particular, not all of the buildings and ditches found by excavation appear on the geophysical survey. The absence of some of the Iron

Age ditches can be explained by their lying under later features, but the missing buildings are more difficult to explain. Some of the ovens, wells and pits have also been missed but this is probably due to their small size, so they might have been detected if more frequent readings had been made. The roads appear to have been detected fairly well. For this site the geophysical survey was thus able to define the major limits of the occupation and establish the approximate plan of the settlement, even if it did not reveal its full details.

Another site where an extensive geophysical survey was carried out was Cadbury/Camelot.[16] Here air photographs had shown many rock-cut features in the interior of the hillfort, but because no vertical photographs were available, it was difficult to locate individual features on the ground. Because the area enclosed by the defences was approximately 18 acres, it would have been impossible to excavate the whole of the interior. However, such a large area can be covered fairly quickly (approximately 20 weeks) using geophysical surveying and this was done in order to locate those areas that would be most worthwhile to excavate. The topsoil on the site was comparatively shallow (less than 30 cm) so both electromagnetic and magnetic surveying were carried out. The electromagnetic readings were made at 0.5 m intervals in the hope that features as small as individual post holes could be located. However, although the survey revealed a wealth of pits and ditches (see Figure 9.12) and also circular anomalies corresponding to some, but not all of the Pre-Roman Iron Age houses it failed to detect many small gullies and post holes. In addition the excavation showed the danger that the archaeologist will interpret the survey in terms of what he expects to find. For example three sets of anomalies which were thought to be rectangular halls turned out instead to be a field ditch, a chance alignment of refuse pits and, most unexpectedly, a cruciform foundation trench, probably for a Late Saxon church. Thus again, while the geophysical survey proved valuable in revealing the area of human activity and provided some indication of the type of features to be expected, it did not provide as full a picture as could be obtained from excavation.

Magnetic surveying was also used to locate features for excavation in the interiors of several hillforts in south east England. At Bigberry near Canterbury[17] the excavation of the anomalies revealed eaves drip gullies, a hearth, a clay lined water-hole or

Figure 9.11 Plan of part of site 1 at Dragonby showing the features revealed by excavation that might have been detected by the magnetic survey

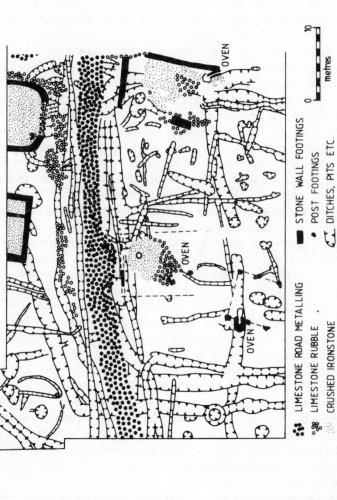

•••• LIMESTONE ROAD METALLING
•°°° LIMESTONE RUBBLE
CRUSHED IRONSTONE

▬ STONE WALL FOOTINGS
• POST FOOTINGS
〰 DITCHES, PITS ETC.

0   10
metres

My thanks to Jeffrey May for providing access to the plans on which this figure is based

Figure 9.12 Geographical Survey of Cadbury/Camelot

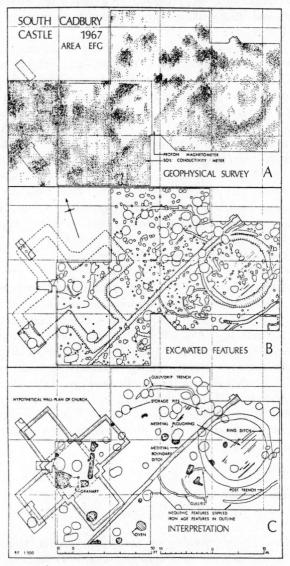

(A) Dot density plot of part of the geophysical survey at Cadbury/Camelot showing a wealth of archaeological features
(B) Plan of features revealed by excavation of the same area
(C) Interpretation of features found by excavation (courtesy Professor L. Alcock)

small reservoir and an anvil embedded in clay with a gulley on one side, suggesting the presence of a temporary smithy. At Holmbury and Hascombe in Surrey[18] the excavated anomalies all appeared to be due to hearths.

Jones et al.[19] used resistivity surveying to define areas of occupation on Roman sites in Catalunya, north east Spain. At the late Roman villa of Vilauba they were able to locate walls, paths, opus signum floors and rubble spreads, and so were able to deduce the ground plan of the villa and its associated outbuildings and enclosures. At the Roman site of Cors the resistivity survey was only able to define the limits of the site.

Resistivity surveying was also used by Pitts[20] to study the Avenue leading to Stonehenge. His article compares the results from resistivity and magnetic surveys of the same area and found that the chalk bank showed best on the resistivity survey, but the ditches best on the magnetic survey. Other anomalies were also found which might represent pits, but would need to be excavated before final conclusions could be drawn.

Finally, along rather different lines, Gregory et al.[21] employed local metal detector users to locate metal objects on sites they were excavating. In particular, by locating any metal objects in the topsoil they were able to recover them before the topsoil was stripped mechanically. At a site at Thetford, Norfolk, where they were excavating a triple ditch enclosure shown on an air photograph, the coins recovered during the metal detector survey provided the only evidence for late Roman use of the site, while at Middle Harling, Norfolk the use of metal detectors increased the number of metal objects found, because only 18 per cent of the objects recovered were in features, while 25.1 per cent were in the machined topsoil.

9.4 Phosphate Analysis

9.4.1 Principles

Phosphate analysis provides an alternative means of locating areas of human activity and may also enable deductions to be made about the types of activities carried on in different areas. Phosphorus is an essential element for all plants and animals and is normally present in the soil in a variety of phosphate salts. Under natural conditions, the phosphorous distribution within a given area remains constant, because there is a phosphorus cycle like the carbon cycle. Hence the phosphorus continuously circulates from the soil to plants to animals and back to the soil again. However, human activities can disrupt this process and produce local increases or decreases in the phosphorus content of the soil. Domestic refuse, food wastes, plant and animal remains and excreta are all sources of phosphorus, and hence, if they are deposited in a restricted area, will lead to an increase in the phosphate concentration in that area. Thus any area within which animals have been enclosed, such as a byre or a field, is likely to have an enhanced phosphate level, as are middens and houses; equally the spreading of manure on early field systems will also lead to increased phosphate levels. By contrast, over-grazing of pasture can remove phosphorus from the area and so lead to a reduction in phosphate levels.

Because many of the phosphates in soil have only a low solubility, any local excess or deficiency of phosphorus tends to be long lasting and so by measuring the phosphate levels in a systematic way over an area it is possible to locate those areas where the phosphate levels are abnormal and hence find possible areas of human activity. Alternatively, if closely spaced samples are taken from an area of known human activity it may be possible to draw conclusions about what activities were carried out at different points in the area.

In the former case, a sampling interval of 5m may be sufficiently close, while in the latter an interval of 1m or less will be needed if detailed information is to be obtained. In both cases a grid should be laid out as described in section 9.2 so that the samples can be obtained in a systematic way.

As well as the samples from the area of archaeological interest, control samples of the same soil type, but from an area supposedly unaffected by human activity will also be required. This is because human activity is only one of a variety of factors which affect soil phosphate levels and so areas of human activity can only be detected by phosphate analysis if the phosphate levels in two areas of a site which are identical except that one was affected by human activity and the other was not are significantly different. In addition measurement of the control samples gives the range of phosphate levels expected in that area from undisturbed soil and so helps show whether any variations found in the archaeological features are significant.

One complication with phosphate analysis is that phosphate levels can be measured in more than one way. The quantity most commonly measured by soil scientists is 'available' or 'extractable' phosphate which is a measure of the phosphorus available to plants, and so is the most relevant quantity when deciding whether a phosphate fertilizer should be applied to a field. It is the quantity measured by commercially available phosphate analysis kits. Some archaeologists have obtained useful results by measuring available phosphate levels in the field.[22] Schwarz describes how this can be done.[23] However, for archaeological purposes 'total' phosphate is probably the more relevant quantity, because it measures all the phosphate in the soil sample, which can be 100 times the extractable value. Unlike available phosphate, total phosphate analysis can only be performed in an appropriately equipped laboratory by someone specialising in the technique. The specialist may want to come to the site and collect his own samples. If, however, the archaeologist is collecting the samples, approximately 100g of soil should be taken from each sampling point, bagged and carefully labelled with its position — clearly if the position of the samples cannot be located, it will be impossible to plot the phosphate distribution at the site and hence all the effort involved in obtaining the samples will have been wasted. It should also be remembered that the samples for phosphate analysis are bulky and heavy. For example if an area 100m by 100m is sampled at 5m intervals over 50kg of soil will be collected. If transport of such a large amount of material is likely to prove a problem, it might be possible to do the preliminary processing of the samples on the site, because the actual measurement of the phosphate content can be done on much smaller samples. Large samples are taken initially to ensure that the measured phosphate level is representative of the point sampled.

When obtaining samples for phosphate analysis, the archaeologist must ensure that they come from the levels of interest and are not just modern topsoil or undisturbed subsoil. Phosphate analysis will only reveal areas of human activity if the areas affected are sampled. In addition, the archaeologist should be certain that any high phosphate levels are due to ancient rather than modern activities. For example, even on open moors, sheep tend to congregate under rock overhangs and in the shelter of walls and so high phosphate levels could be produced in areas unaffected by human activity. Obtaining samples for phosphate analysis is a time consuming process, being likely to take even longer than carrying out a resistivity survey of a similar area. The laboratory analysis of the samples will add further to the time before a distribution map can be obtained. Hence, before collecting samples the archaeologist should be certain that the survey is likely to produce useful results. Finally, because the rate at which phosphates accumulate in soil depends on so many factors, phosphate analyses from different sites should not be compared. The problems of phosphate analysis are discussed further by Proudfort.[24]

Although phosphorus is the element most frequently studied to provide information about human activity, other elements including organic carbon, nitrogen, calcium, potassium, magnesium, iron, copper and zinc have also been studied.[25]

9.4.2 Applications

So far phosphate analysis does not appear to have been widely used, probably because it takes so long to do and it is uncertain whether useful results will be produced. However, in areas where geophysical surveying is impossible or unsatisfactory it may provide an alternative means of locating areas of human activity. It can also provide information about human activities not obtainable using geophysical surveying. Two recent applications were as part of the Shaugh Moor project and at Cefn Graeanog, North Wales.

In the Shaugh Moor project[26] phosphate samples were taken at 5m intervals from both the field system and an enclosure containing round houses. In the field system the only high phosphate levels were close to a round house, while elsewhere they were the same as the levels in the area outside the system. The authors, therefore, conclude that the field system was not used for penning animals, nor was it manured over long periods. In the enclosure containing the round houses, again the only high phosphate levels were in and close to the houses. This suggests that stock was not kept in the enclosure so the authors suggest the wall was in fact for keeping animals out.

Phosphate analysis was also used to study some of the buildings found at a native farm of Roman period at Cefn Graeanog, Gwynedd, North Wales.[27] Samples were taken at 1m intervals and their total phosphate content measured. Conway then used

trend surface analysis to help interpret the distributions obtained
In a domestic building thought to have been occupied throughou
the use of the site, he found a circular distribution with the
highest phosphate levels being close to the walls. He also found
high levels of phosphates near the entrance. He suggests this
distribution was caused by the erosion of a dung-tempered clay
floor and that the phosphate analysis also provides evidence for
benches or bed platforms close to the wall. In addition, he found
high phosphate levels near burnt clay and charcoal. In another
building, which had been divided into two halves, and was
thought to have been used as a barn the phosphate distribution
was more complex. One half of this barn was devoid of internal
features and so may have been used for storing grain, while the
other half contained a post hole and a transverse drain. On the
basis of the phosphate distribution, Conway suggests that this
latter half had been divided into two animal stalls by a partition
attached to the post. The final building investigated had only
been occupied during the later stages of the occupation. Here he
found high phosphate levels in the midden area and also in two
hearths.

Thus at both these sites phosphate analysis helped to shed light
on the activities carried out in different areas.

Notes

1. J.G.B. Haigh, 'Practical methods for the rectification of oblique aerial
photographs', *Abstracts of the 22nd Symposium on Archaeometry* (University of
Bradford, 1982).

2. D.R. Wilson, *Air photography interpretation for archaeologists* (Batsford
1982)

3. M.R. Gorman, 'An archaeological soil-sounding radar: preliminary results'
Abstracts of the 22nd Symposium on Archaeometry (University of Bradford, 1982).

4. M.C. Périsset and A. Tabbagh, 'Interpretation of thermal prospection on
bare soils', *Archaeometry*, vol. 23 (1981), pp. 169–88.

5. R.E. Linnington, *Quaderni di geofisica applicata*, vol. 22 (1961).

6. M.A. Kelly, P. Dale and J.G.B. Haigh, 'A microcomputer system for data
logging in geophysical surveying', *Archaeometry*, vol. 26 (1984), pp. 183–91.

7. A.J. Clark, J.N. Hampton and M.F. Hughes, 'Mount Down, Hampshire
the reappraisal of evidence', *Antiquaries Journal*, vol. 63, part 1 (1983), pp. 122–
4.

8. M.J. Aitken, 'Magnetic prospecting IV — the proton magnetometer'
Archaeometry, vol. 2 (1959), pp. 40–2; M.J. Aitken, 'Magnetic prospecting: the
proton gradiometer', *Archaeometry*, vol. 3 (1960), pp. 38–40; J.C. Alldred, 'A
fluxgate gradiometer for archaeological surveying', *Archaeometry*, vol. 7 (1964)
pp. 14–9.

9. M. Howell, 'A soil conductivity meter', *Archaeometry*, vol. 9 (1966), pp. 20–3.

10. C. Colani, 'A new type of locating device. I — the instrument', *Archaeometry*, vol. 9 (1966), pp. 3–8.

11. M.W. Pitts, 'On the road to Stonehenge', *Proceedings of the Prehistoric Society*, vol. 48 (1982), pp. 75–132, in particular pp. 90–3.

12. I. Scollar and F. Krückeberg, 'Computer treatment of magnetic measurements from Archaeological sites', *Archaeometry*, vol. 9 (1966), pp. 61–71; Irwin Scollar, 'Some techniques for the evaluation of archaeological magnetometer surveys', *World Archaeology*, vol. 1 (1969), pp. 77–89.

13. Anthony Clark, 'Archaeological prospecting: a progress report', *Journal of Archaeological Science*, vol. 2 (1975), pp. 297–314.

14. Leslie Alcock, *Survey and excavation at Fortevoit, Perthshire 1981* (Department of Archaeology, University of Glasgow, 1982), pp. 5–6.

15. Jeffrey May, 'Dragonby: an interim report on excavations on an Iron age and Romano-British site near Scunthorpe, Lincolnshire, 1964–9', *Antiquaries Journal*, vol. 50, part II (1970), pp. 222–45.

16. Leslie Alcock, '*By South Cadbury is that Camelot*' . . . *excavations at Cadbury Castle 1966–70* (Thames and Hudson, 1972), pp. 51–62 and 70–2; Leslie Alcock, 'Excavations at South Cadbury Castle, 1967', *Antiquaries Journal*, vol. 48 (1968), pp. 6–17, esp. 8–10.

17. F.H. Thompson, 'Excavations at Bigberry, near Canterbury, 1978–80', *Antiquaries Journal*, vol. 63, part II (1983), pp. 237–78.

18. F.H. Thompson, 'Three Surrey hillforts: excavations at Anstiebury, Holmbury and Hascombe, 1972–1977', *Antiquaries Journal*, vol. 59, part II (1979), pp. 245–318.

19. R.F.J. Jones, S.J. Keay, J.M. Nolla and J. Tarrús, 'The Late Roman villa of Vilauba and its context', *Antiquaries Journal*, vol. 62, part II (1982), pp. 245–82, in particular p. 255 and pp. 259–61.

20. M.W. Pitts, 'On the road to Stonehenge', pp. 75–132.

21. T. Gregory and A.J.G. Rogerson, 'Metal-detecting in archaeological excavation', *Antiquity*, vol. 58 (1984), pp. 179–84.

22. Ralph Allen and Hary Hamroush, 'The application of geochemical techniques to the investigation of two Predynastic sites in Egypt', *Archaeological Chemistry*, vol. 3 (1914), pp. 51–66.

23. G.T. Schwarz, 'A simplified chemical test for archaeological field work', *Archaeometry*, vol. 10 (1967), pp. 57–63.

24. B. Proudfort, 'The analysis and interpretation of soil phosphorous in archaeological contexts', in D.A. Davidson and M.A. Shackley, *Geoarchaeology* (Duckworth, 1976), pp. 93–114.

25. William I. Woods, 'Soil chemical investigation in Illinois archaeology: two example studies', *Archaeological Chemistry*, vol. 3 (1984), pp. 67–78.

26. N. Balaam, K. Smith and G.J. Wainwright, 'The Shaugh Moor project — fourth report', *Proceedings of the Prehistoric Society*, vol. 48 (1982), pp. 203–78, in particular pp. 215–9.

27. J.S. Conway, 'An investigation of soil phosphorous distribution within occupation deposits from a Romano-British hut group', *Journal of Archaeological Science*, vol. 10 (1983), pp. 117–28.

10 COMPUTERS IN ARCHAEOLOGY

10.1 Introduction

The aim of this chapter is not to provide a beginners' introduction to computing, but rather to point out to the archaeologist some of the things he could do if he had access to a microcomputer and also to highlight some of the other developments which are affecting archaeology rather more indirectly.

A computer is a device for handling large quantities of information and is thus rather like a very sophisticated card index system. It is much better at performing some jobs than a human being because it can carry out simple or repetitive tasks very quickly. Thus it can sort lists of data into alphabetical order or provide a list of all the Roman sites in a county (providing it is given suitable instructions and has been given enough information to enable it to decide which archaeological sites are Roman and which county they are in) much more quickly than can be done by hand. It is also very good at doing arithmetical calculations such as are involved in analysing the pottery or other artefacts found on an archaeological site. However, computers are not intelligent and they are very literal minded, so they obey precisely the instructions they have been given. Thus a computer asked to list all the sites where Roman pottery has been found will not include sites where Samian ware was found, unless it has also been told that Samian ware is a type of Roman pottery. Nor can it normally cope with typographic errors. For example, if the list of finds at one site included Simian (sic), ware, but no other pottery, the computer would not include it in the list. Thus when feeding information into a computer, it is essential to ensure that there are no typographic errors. In addition if a computer is expecting capital letters it may be confused if lower case letters are used; nor will it accept the letters O and l as numbers. If the number of bronzes found in a feature was entered as l, the computer might complain that it had been given incorrect information but it might just assume that because no number had been entered, no bronzes had been found in the feature. This could have serious consequences when attempting to interpret the distribution of finds on the site. Similarly 12 pieces of pottery would be 2 to the computer.

Another difference between computers and people is that computers solve equations using numerical methods, while whenever possible people use analytical methods. All this means is that if a person has to solve the equation $x^2 - 4x + 4 = 0$ he will say there is a formula for solving this type of equation $x = (- b \pm \sqrt{b^2 - 4ac})/2a$ so x must equal 2. A computer, however, guesses at the answer and if it is wrong tries a different value. It could start by calculating whether the equation was true if $x = 1$. $1^2 - 4 + 4 = 1$ so it would have to continue trying different values until it reached one which fitted. While this might seem a slow way of doing things, computers can do such calculations so fast that, in general, a computer will solve such an equation far more quickly than a human being.

Computers can be divided into two types: mainframes and microcomputers. Microcomputers contain a single chip to do all the calculations and data handling, while mainframe computers contain several. This makes modern mainframe computers more powerful (i.e. they can do a wider range of jobs or do the same jobs more quickly) than microcomputers, but also more expensive. Thus mainframes are normally only owned by institutions such as universities, while microcomputers are frequently owned by individuals or may be distributed to sub-departmental levels in large institutions. The home computer is one type of microcomputer. Microcomputers, although less powerful than modern mainframes, are many times more powerful than the early mainframes (and are increasing in power all the time), and so jobs which at one time would have been thought of as requiring a large computer, can today be done by a microcomputer. Even if the microcomputer is slower than the mainframe, this is frequently outweighed by the microcomputer being used by fewer people than the mainframe so that there is less competition for time on it. *Mini*computers which are also available can be thought of as extra large microcomputers.

The power of computers is frequently described in bytes, which is a measure of the amount of information a computer can hold in its memory at one time. Modern microcomputers frequently have 32 or 64 kilobytes (1 kilobyte = 1024 bytes) of memory, though larger ones are appearing all the time. Because of the way computers work, the size of a computer memory is normally a power of 2: i.e. 2, 4, 8, 16, 32, 64, 128, 256, 512 or 1024 kbytes. Each byte contains 8 bits (binary digits which can have the value 0 or 1, i.e. off or on).

Thus the bits in each byte can be arranged in 256 different ways Normally one byte is used to store each character (i.e. letter, number space, etc.), so a short sentence would take up about 50 bytes o memory.

Most microcomputers can do a wide range of tasks, but some are specifically designed to do one particular job and so could no normally be used for other work. Word processors, which are particu larly good at handling text and editing articles for journals, and microprocessors which are designed to control individual pieces o equipment such as spectrometers are the most common examples.

Finally, electronic calculators can be considered to be microcomputers designed specifically for doing calculations and so their ability to handle words is normally non-existent. In recent years there have been many developments in calculators so that now the choice ranges from ones costing under £10 and capable only of doing simple arithmetic, to ones costing around £100 which are more like small computers since they can perform advanced statistical and othe calculations. Some can be attached to printers so that permanent copies of the calculations can be obtained, while others have smal screens on which simple graphs or short sentences can be displayed Finally, for programmable calculators it is possible to obtain modules or magnetic cards which will instruct or program the calculator to carry out a range of more lengthy calculations.

Although the range of tasks that can be carried out by a calculator is more limited than those that can be done by computer, there are many situations in which a calculator may be more convenient to use Calculators are more portable and robust than computers and so may be better for use in the field. In addition, they will be faster for doing some types of calculation because they will have to be given less information by the operator than would be required by a computer. I may also be easier to write programs for them because they wil require only one instruction to do some jobs for which a compute would have to be given two or three. Thus, if the archaeologist ha only a limited amount of money available it might be best to spend it on a good calculator rather than a cheap computer.

In order to have a usable computer system the archaeologist wil need to buy more than just a microcomputer. Firstly he will require other hardware (i.e. machines or physical equipment) to interface (i.e physically attach) to the computer, so that he can communicate with it and obtain permanent copies of information from it. A simple com puter system has four parts (see Figure 10.1): the microcompute itself, a printer, a cassette tape recorder and a VDU (visual display unit). The microcomputer itself consists of the central processing unit, which is the 'brains' of the system and does all the calculations and other data handling: a memory in which the computer can store the data it is handling at that time; and a keyboard, like an ordinary typewriter keyboard but with some extra keys, to enable the operator to type information into the computer, give it instructions and reply to any questions the computer asks. The printer enables the computer to produce permanent or 'hard' copies of whatever it has been doing and also to ask the operator questions. Two types of printers are in common use: dot matrix printers which are cheap and fast, but produce only poor quality print unsuitable for reproduction, and daisy wheel printers which are expensive and slower but can reproduce a variety of type faces ready for publication. Because a computer does not store permanently all the information and programs it needs to operate, this information has to be stored in some other form so that it can be fed into the computer when required. The cheapest way of doing this is with ordinary cassette tapes so that an ordinary cassette recorder can be used to transfer the information to the computer. Finally, the VDU provides an alternative to the printer for displaying the results obtained by the computer and questions for the computer to answer. An ordinary television set can be used, although if the computer is to be used to produce detailed diagrams a VDU or monitor specifically designed for use with computers will be needed. Much useful work can be done with this type of simple system.

However, to increase the range of jobs which the computer can undertake, further hardware will be required. Probably the most important piece of additional hardware is a disc drive (or preferably two) to replace the tape recorder. A disc drive is a device for transferring information stored on floppy discs to the computer and vice versa. Floppy discs look rather like small gramophone records in sleeves, but are designed to store programs and data in a form easily used by a computer. Hence information can be transferred much more quickly from disc to computer than from a cassette, which makes jobs involving the handling of large quantities of information easier and faster to perform. Lists of information stored on floppy disc (or otherwise) which the computer can use to answer specific questions, such as the largest hillfort in England or sites where bronze daggers have been found, are known as files. Secondly, if the computer is to be used to

Figure 10.1 Components of a computer system

(a)

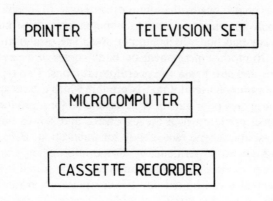

(b)

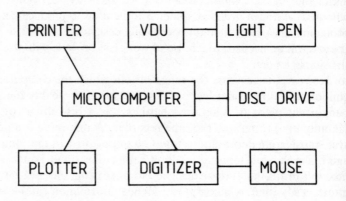

(a) A simple but cheap system.
(b) A more sophisticated system capable of doing a wide range of jobs

produce graphs and plans a plotter will be needed. These come in varying degrees of sophistication: some can only draw lines in single colours, but more expensive ones can produce full colour pictures. To obtain full benefit from the computer's ability to handle plans and diagrams, a digitizer will also be needed to enable the details of plans and diagrams to be transferred to the computer. A digitizer looks rather like an ordinary drafting table but contains an electronic grid. When a special pointer (often called a mouse) is held against a point on the diagram and a button pressed the co-ordinates (i.e. position) of the point are transferred into the computer. Hence by tracing the lines on a plan with the mouse and pressing the button at appropriate points a complete plan can be transferred to the computer.

The other item that a computer system requires before it will work is software: that is programs or instructions to tell the computer how to carry out the job the archaeologist wants done. Programs can be obtained from various sources. The first is to buy pre-recorded cassettes or discs from a computer software company. This is the simplest way of obtaining programs, since providing the program is written for the type of computer owned by the archaeologist, it should work without any problems. The danger of buying programs in this way is that if the programs were not originally written to solve archaeological problems the assumptions upon which they are based may not apply in archaeological situations. The second source of programs is people who have written programs specifically to solve archaeological problems. Occasionally the program listing (i.e. the precise form the program must take for it to work) may have been published so that it can be typed into the computer and then transferred to disc to make a permanent copy. More often the program listing or a copy of the program on disc will need to be obtained from the person who wrote the program. In all the above cases care must be taken to ensure that the program is compatible with the computer system it is intended to run on. Not only must it be in a language and dialect that the computer can understand, but also it must give instructions in the correct form to the printer or other hardware interfaced to the computer. Otherwise the program will not run. Finally the archaeologist can write his own programs. This is not difficult for simple but repetitive tasks such as calculating the amount of grain that could be stored in pits of different size. However, if complex calculations are to be carried out or large quantities of data have to be sorted, the archaeologist would be better leaving the program writing to an expert, because it is a skilled job to produce a program to do such a task efficiently.

Many commercially available programs are designed to be used by people with no previous computing experience. Such programs are known as 'user-friendly' and frequently make use of interactive computing techniques. These enable the computer to guide the user into providing the correct information for the program to run. This is done by the computer asking a question on the VDU, to which the user types in the answer. The question will often include details of the form the answer should take: for example, 'width of ditch to nearest 10cm'. Alternatively, the computer will offer a choice of possible answers and the user will have to select the correct one. Thus to use a well-designed interactive computer system the archaeologist does not have to have any prior knowledge of computing or computing languages. All he has to know is how to switch the computer on and load the program, which is no more difficult than using a radio. After that the computer will help him to do the job. A further use of interactive computing is in manipulating diagrams, since if the computer system includes a light pen and a suitable VDU, parts of plans can be moved around on the screen just by using the light pen to indicate where they are to go to.

Microcomputers are developing so fast at present and prices changing so rapidly that it is impossible to state how much an archaeologist would need to spend in order to obtain a useful computer system. Thus, before buying a system, the archaeologist should talk to other people who already own systems to find out what they think of them and also investigate what is currently available in the shops before making a final decision. If possible he should try out the computer system by himself to check that he can understand the instruction book, since some sets of insructions are clearer than others. An expensive computer with clear instructions would be a better buy than a cheaper one with unintelligible instructions.

The rest of this chapter is devoted to the archaeological applications of computers and is divided according to where they are most likely to be carried out, namely on site, in the office and in the laboratory. Applications such as word processing and book keeping, while of use to archaeologists, are not specifically archaeological in their applications and they are therefore not discussed. While some of the applications mentioned involve programs designed to run on mainframes, the speed with which computing is developing means that it soon may be (or already is) possible to adapt such programs for use on smaller computers. Alternatively, the archaeologist may be able to arrange access to a mainframe if he wants to make use of such a program.

10.2 Computers on Site

This section is intended to cover possible uses of a computer from the initial survey of a site through to the completion of the excavation. While many of the applications ideally require the computer to be taken to site, in other cases it is possible to record the data on site and transfer it to the computer at a later stage. If purely numerical data are to be recorded, for example measurements during a survey, data loggers are available which can automatically record readings in a form that can later be fed directly into a computer. However, if details of an excavation are to be transferred to the computer they will probably need to be recorded on cards in a standardised form and typed into the computer at a later stage.

One of the areas of archaeology in which computers are already widely used is surveying, particularly geophysical. Scollar[1] and Clark[2] both discuss the way in which 'filtering techniques' can make geophysical surveys easier to interpret. These techniques can remove the unwanted causes of variations in the measured values of the magnetic field or resistivity such as change in topsoil depth, the diurnal variation of the magnetic field, instrumental drift (i.e. changes in the readings due purely to changes in the instrument) or changes in the underlying background to leave only these anomalies due to archaeological features. This makes it easier to plot the readings so that the archaeological features stand out clearly from the background. Simple filtering can be done by hand but the calculations involved are tedious, even if done by a pocket calculator. More complex filtering can be done quickly by computer. Many of the programs also produce contour or dot density plots of the results, thus freeing the archaeologist from another time consuming and tedious chore. Some of the programs will only run on mainframes, but Kelly et al.[3] have written a program to enable an on-site microcomputer to record the data from a resistivity survey. The data is stored on microcassette, with one cassette being capable of storing 400 measurements (i.e. the readings at 1m intervals from a 20m square). The printer connected to the computer can produce either a dot density plot or the numerical values of the readings while on the site. It is also possible to transfer the data to a mainframe if a contour plot is required, because they have not yet written a microcomputer program to do this. The use of the microcomputer reduces the time taken to complete a survey because less time is spent recording the measurements. In addition, dot density diagrams can be produced while the survey is still in progress so it is possible to check that the survey is producing useful results and to see if any area needs to be surveyed in greater detail or in which direction the survey should be extended. Bradford have also written a computer program to enable a portable computer to produce contour plots in two colours.

Another survey technique where microcomputers have a role to play is aerial photography. Here a major problem is locating on the ground features visible on oblique air photographs. Haigh[4] has written a program to enable a microcomputer interfaced to a digitizer and plotter to handle this problem. When attempting to rectify air photographs manually the archaeologist is frequently faced with the problem that he lacks the data to use standard photogrammetric techniques and so uses the four-point projective transformation which is subject to a wide variety of errors. Haigh's program is based on the four-point technique, but can use more control points if they are available. The results are reported to be comparable with those from photogrammetric methods.

Contour surveys are another place where both computers and programmable calculators have been found useful. The calculations involved in converting the readings obtained into heights is time consuming so Hogg[5] has published a program to enable a programmable calculator to do this for both anchored tape and tacheometric surveys. As well as giving the program listings he also discusses the recording of the measurements on site. At present the use of computers is restricted to drawing contour maps once the height of suitable points have been calculated: for example, Lock[6] has examples of contour plots produced by a commercially available graphics package (see Figure 10.2). However, it would seem to be a fairly simple task for someone to write a program to produce a contour plot from the readings taken on site and so save the time spent at present turning the readings into heights and feeding the heights and their positions into a computer.

Figure 10.2 An example of the type of plot that can be obtained using a modern computer and plotter

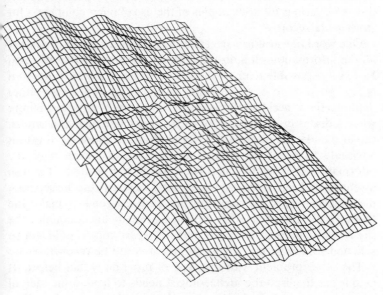

It shows the results of a contour survey at Stafford Castle. Alternative plots of the same data can be seen in note 6 (courtesy Dr G. Lock)

During an excavation a microcomputer can provide a convenient and quick way of storing site records. Booth et al.[7] describe the system used when excavating a site at Maxey in Cambridgeshire, which had features ranging in age from Neolithic to Medieval. Details of features, layers and finds were recorded on separate cards in a standardised form and then typed into the computer and stored on disc by the excavator when the weather was unsuitable for digging. This transfer of information was carried out interactively. Once this has been done the computer can then produce a list of all the features which contained Roman pottery, or similar information, as required by the archaeologist. One advantage of this system is that, because it is so simple to get information from the computer, it is no longer necessary to mark each find with site code, finds, features, layer and section numbers and put this information plus depth record, eight-figure grid reference and brief description on the find bag. Instead only the find number and site code are put on both find and bag and the rest of the information is obtained from the computer when required. This results in a great saving of time. This particular system cannot handle plans and so they are stored separately. Graham et al.[8] discusses various other examples of the use of microcomputers for storing site records.

One word of warning is necessary here. It is far easier to destroy all the information on a disc than it is to destroy written records. Just as it is possible to erase the recording on a cassette tape, so it is also possible to erase the information stored on a disc either deliberately or accidentally in just a few seconds. A power failure while a disc is in a computer or physical damage such as a scratch can also make the information stored on a disc unusable. It is thus advisable to keep the original written records, even after the information they contain had been transferred to disc. It is also essential to keep more than one copy of each disc in separate places, because a spare copy only takes a few seconds to make and then, if a disaster such as fire destroying the site hut containing the site records and original disc occurs, the spare copy should still be safe and so a large part of the site records will be recoverable.

The other problem with this type of program is that before its details are finalised the archaeologist needs to have some idea of what he expects to find, otherwise the use of the program to list features or artefacts with specific properties will be limited. For example, if when the excavation was started, it was not thought necessary to include Samian as a possible choice for classifying the finds, then it will not be possible to obtain a list of features that contain Samian pottery. Instead the computer would have to be asked to list a broader class such as features that contain Roman pottery and the archaeologist would then have to separate those containing only Samian by hand. It is, however, possible to write a program in which new categories can be added later when it is discovered that they are necessary.

Several programs have also been written to help with the interpretation of sites. Fletcher et al.[9] have developed programs to locate specific patterns of post holes on sites where post holes are too numerous for this to be done by eye. The first version of the program was designed to search for circular distributions and was intended for use at Danebury. However, at this site, the post holes were so dense that the program could not distinguish man-made alignments from chance ones and so produced no useful results. They had more success with a program to look for rectangular buildings with four or six post holes[10] and at Danebury were able to detect more rectangles than would be expected if the program was just locating chance distributions. This suggests that at Danebury the program was indeed detecting buildings. Computers were also used at Danebury to help study the pits. One program was used to help analyse the pottery from the pits, in order to arrange the pits in chronological order[11] and another was used to classify the pits by shape and provide information about how they silted up.[12]

Another site where a computer was used was Bishophill, a complex site in the heart of York. Because it was a rescue dig, it was not possible to draw the final site plans and sections at the time of the excavation. This made it time consuming to arrange the different contexts in order by hand and so the Strata program[13] was developed to do the task more quickly than it could be done by hand. This program is also discussed by Harris.[14]

10.3 The Computer in the Office

Apart from the development of the microcomputer, the recent developments in computer graphics (the use of computers to display information in tables, diagrams etc.) are likely to have the greatest influence on archaeology. However, in order to be able to make full use of all the possibilities the archaeologist will need to buy extra equipment such as a plotter and may also need access to a mainframe computer.

One big advantage of computer graphics is that, providing the computer is given sufficient information, it can produce three-dimensional perspective plots. For example, if given sufficient information about the shape of a pot, it could rotate the image so that one saw first the side view and then a view inside it. Alternatively, if given suitable drawings of a house, it could again rotate the image of the house to show what it looked like from different viewpoints. The archaeologist could then obtain a permanent copy of the view he liked best. The other use of this ability to produce perspective plots is to display contour plots and similar information in three dimensions rather than two. The image can be rotated so that the most informative viewpoint is obtained and a hard copy then produced. In addition when the plot is seen for the first time the impact of a three-dimensional image is greater than

Figure 10.3 Mirror stereo pair of the resistivity survey of Stramshall main site showing ditches and other anomalies

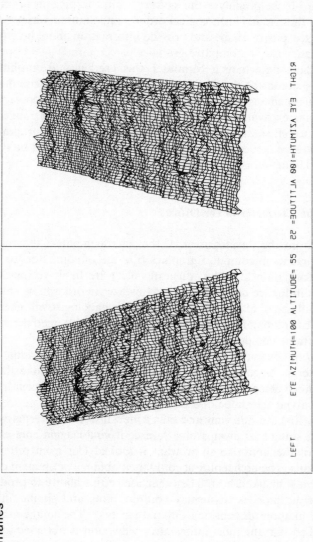

LEFT EYE AZIMUTH=100 ALTITUDE= 55

ALTITUDE= 55 ALTITUDE =100 AZIMUTH=100 EYE RIGHT

At this site a Roman fort is thought to have replaced a Romano-British farmstead. To view place a mirror facing right along the centre line and place nose on the edge of the mirror so the left eye sees the left picture normally and the right a reflection of the right picture in the mirror (courtesy Dr G. Lock) that of a two. Lock[15] discusses the use of the PICASO graphics package to produce perspective plots. The package can produce either a tiled surface or an ordinary histogram from the data supplied and the article includes examples of two sets of data plotted both ways and viewed from a variety of angles. It is also possible to use computers to produce pairs of diagrams which when viewed together in the correct way produce a stereoscopic image (see Figure 10.3).[16]

A further use of computer graphics is to manipulate site plans and sections once they are drawn. Duncan et al.[17] have produced programs to enable pencil sketches produced on site to be turned into plans and sections ready for publication. Once the original plan has been digitised and transferred to the computer, it is then possible to change its scale, add various types of shading to indicate different soil types and adjust the density of the shading as desired. Flude et al.[18] have devised a program to enable separate plans to be combined together. The plans for separate contexts are digitized and stored on disc or in a database. It is then possible for the computer to combine the plans from several contexts to produce a plan of a wider area. Alternatively, the computer can be asked to produce a plan showing all pits, all Roman features or other groups of features. One advantage of using a computer to manipulate plans in this way is that it is easy to alter details on plans or compare different interpretations of an area of the site. Both these programs have been written for mainframe computers. Computer graphics are discussed further by Barto Arnold III.[19]

At present it is not possible to use a computer to prepare site plans in the field because of the way a plan or map is stored in a computer. In particular, the plan is not stored as a series of lines, but rather the co-ordinates of a series of points on the lines are stored in the computer. When producing a copy of the plan the computer locates the points on the plotter or VDU and joins them together using a series of straight lines, rather as a child may join a series of numbered dots to produce a picture. Thus if curved lines are to be accurately reproduced by a computer it is necessary to store the co-ordinates of a large number of points on the line so that when the line is plotted by the computer, the individual straight lines merge to produce a curve when viewed by the human eye, just as the coloured dots on a television screen merge to produce a picture. To measure the co-ordinates of enough points on a feature on-site for the computer to produce an accurate plan of it would take a very long time, and in addition, a computer capable of storing and handling a large amount of data would be required if a large area was to be planned. In some cases it may be necessary to restrict the number of points per unit length of line and so when circles are plotted by the computer they will appear as polygons. If the site plan has been prepared by hand in the ordinary way and then digitized it will always be possible to check the precise shape of a feature by looking at the original plan, but if the plan was originally prepared in a digitized form this would not be possible and so valuable information might be lost.

If suitable statistical and plotting programs have been brought the computer can also be used to subdivide a group of artefacts. This use has already been discussed in connection with the classification of pottery and other materials on the basis of their elemental composition, but the same statistical and plotting techniques can be used on information gathered by the archaeologist. For example, Celoria et al.[20] recorded the outlines of a set of Neolithic polished axes on a computer and then used the PLUTARCH system (Program Library Useful To ARCHaeologists: a set of programs considered by the compilers to be of specific use in archaeology) to classify the axes according to their shape. The results were displayed as a dendrogram, which was derived without use being made of the absolute dimensions of the axes. When the groups were studied it was found that some contained only small axes and others only large, suggesting that the classification was valid. They then used the same program to study similar axes from Mexico and Guatemala and found the Mexican axes were more like the British than were the Guatemalan. Computer analysis has also been used to help classify a set of decorated Bronze Age razors from Scandinavia[21] and as part of a study of the Bronze Age pottery from the Middle East known as Tel El Yahudiyeh ware.[22]

Another important role for computers is to help build models of how particular processes worked, a function known as computer simulation. A computer could be used to help solve such problems as how many people a certain farm would support or what would be the most cost effective way of building Stonehenge or how many stone axes were likely to have been produced per year from a given flint mine and how many people would have been employed to do this. For example Carter et al.[23] have written a program to simulate the operation of a Roman mint. Die lifetimes are assumed to have an exponential distribution so that some dies will be used to strike more coins than others. Variables such as number of twelve-hour days of operation, number of anvils (work stations for striking coins), lifetime of obverse and lifetime of reverse dies, number of dies in the obverse die-box and in the reverse die-box and whether the dies are returned to the die-boxes each night can all be specified by the operator. On the first morning each worker chooses a pair of dies and goes to his work station. After each hour the computer calculates which dies have failed and these are replaced by fresh ones. At the end of the day the dies may either be returned to the die-boxes or left by the work stations. In addition, the number of dies in the die-boxes is maintained by the making of new dies, each with a specified lifetime. The computer can then calculate the average lifetime of a die combination and the number of anvils required to produce any issue of coins. In particular the authors found that when the dies were returned to the die-box each evening, the average lifetime of die combinations was nearly constant, being 8.7 ± 0.3 hours for a wide variety of parameters. Orton[24] discusses the use of computers to simulate the dispersal of artefacts from a centre and to establish whether ley lines really exist or are, instead, just chance alignments.

10.4 Computers in the Laboratory

The developments in the use of computers in the laboratory, while they do not directly affect the archaeologist, do make possible the use of new techniques or refinements of old ones. One of the most important recent advances is the use of microprocessors to control other equipment so that the turning on and off of a heater, the selection of the temperature to which a sample should be heated, the changing of samples once the measurements on one sample are complete and similar operations can all be controlled by the microprocessor. This frees the former operator for other tasks which cannot be performed by computer such as the selection of further samples and the interpretation of the results already obtained. It also enables more samples to be processed because computers do not require coffee-breaks or sleep. In addition it will make processes such as heating a sample to 100°C more reproducible, partly because the reaction time of a computer is faster (and more reproducible) than that of a human being and partly because computers are less easily distracted from what they are supposed to be doing. The disadvantages of computers are that they cannot cope with the unexpected and that if there is an electrical disturbance such as a thunderstorm or a voltage change in the power supply they may get confused and do the wrong thing. While, in principle, computer systems can be designed to fail-safe, so that for example the heater is switched off if there are any problems, there is always a slight danger that the fail-safe mechanism will also fail and in the given example the sample will overheat. Archaeomagnetic intensity determinations can now be carried out under microprocessor control[25] and a system is also being developed to control and process the measurements involved in TL dating.[26] Many techniques also use computers to turn the initial measurements into a form easily interpreted by the operator. For example NMR spectroscopy is normally carried out using a technique known as Fourier transform spectroscopy because this enables better results to be obtained. However, the initial measurements are produced in a form in which it is not possible to identify the organic molecules present in the sample. To enable this to be done, complex mathematical calculations have to be carried out to turn the measurements into a form that is easily interpreted by the operator. (The technique is known as Fourier transform spectroscopy because the initial measurements are the Fourier transform, i.e. a mathematical function, of the final result.)

The other big role of computers in the laboratory is the statistical analysis of the results obtained. In particular, as was discussed in Chapter 7, elemental analysis of pottery and other materials are frequently only of use once they have also been subjected to statistical analysis to make clear the relationships, if any, between the different samples. Although this process has been in use for many years there is still much discussion as to the best technique to use, with different laboratories using different techniques. The techniques used are sometimes chosen more because they are readily available, rather than because they are the best ones for the problem being considered.[27] The use of microcomputers rather than mainframes for such tasks may well make it easier to compare the results of analysing a data set using more than one statistical technique to check that they do all produce the same groups or to see which produces the clearest classification of the samples.

Notes

1. I. Scollar, 'Some techniques for the evaluation of archaeological magnetometer surveys', *World Archaeology*, vol. 1 (1969), pp. 78–89; I. Scollar and F. Krückeberg, 'Computer treatment of magnetic measurements from archaeological sites', *Archaeometry*, vol. 9 (1966), pp. 61–71.

2. Anthony Clark, 'Archaeological prospecting: a progress report', *Journal of Archaeological Science*, vol. 2 (1975), pp. 297–314.

3. M.A. Kelly, P. Dale and D.G.B. Haigh, 'A microcomputer system for data logging in geophysical surveying', *Archaeometry*, vol. 26 (1984), pp. 183–91.

4. J.G.B. Haigh, 'Practical methods for the rectification of oblique aerial photographs', *Abstracts, 22nd Archaeometry Conference* (Bradford, 1982).

5. A.H.A. Hogg, 'The anchored tape method: an alternative to tacheometry', *Science and Archaeology*, vol. 26 (1984), pp. 9–14.

6. Gary Lock, 'Some archaeological uses of the PICASO computer graphics package', *Science and Archaeology*, vol. 22 (1980), pp. 16–24.

7. B. Booth, R. Brough and F. Pryor, 'The flexible storage of site data', *Journal of Archaeological Science*, vol. 11 (1984), pp. 81–90.

8. Ian Graham, 'Computer recording of archaeological excavations', *Bulletin of the Institute of Archaeology*, vol. 19 (1982), pp. 123–59.

9. M. Fletcher and G.R. Lock, 'Computerized pattern perception within post hole distributions', *Science and Archaeology*, vol. 23 (1981), pp. 15–20.

10. M. Fletcher and G.R. Lock, 'A mathematical model to predict patterning within post hole distributions', *Science and Archaeology*, vol. 26 (1984), pp. 5–8.

11. G.R. Lock, Computer assisted seriation of the pits at Danebury hillfort', *Science and Archaeology*, vol. 25 (1983), pp. 3–8.

12. M.L. Shackley, 'The Danebury project: an experiment in site sediment recording', in D.A. Davidson and M.A. Shackley', *Geoarchaeology* (Duckworth, 1976), pp. 9–22.

13. S. Bishop and J.S. Wilcock, 'Archaeological context sorting by computer. The Strata program', *Science and Archaeology*, vol. 17 (1976), pp. 3–12.

14. Edward Harris, 'Archaeological context sorting by computer', *Science and Archaeology*, vol. 20 (1977), pp. 21–3.

15. G.R. Lock, 'Some archaeological uses of the PICASO computer graphics package', pp. 16–24.

16. R.D. Spicer, 'Stereoscopic representation of archaeological data — a case for drawing conclusions in depth', *Science and Archaeology*, vol. 27 (1985), pp. 13–24; P. Reilly, 'The use of stereoscopy as an aid in interpreting survey data. A burial ground in the Isle of Man', *Science and Archaeology*, vol. 27 (1985), pp. 25–6; G.R. Lock, 'Stereoscopy as an aid in deciphering the results of a resistivity survey', *Science and Archaeology*, vol. 27 (1985), pp. 27–8.

17. J.M. Duncan and P.L. Main, 'The drawing of archaeological sections and plans by computer', *Science and Archaeology*, vol. 20 (1977), pp. 17–21.

18. K. Flude and D. Charles, 'The automatic production of archaeological plans by computer', *Abstracts, 22nd Archaeometry Conference* (Bradford, 1982).

19. J. Barto Arnold III, 'Archaeological applications of computer graphics', in Michael B. Schiffer, *Advances in Archaeological Method and Theory*, vol. 5 (Academic Press, 1982).

20. F.S.C. Celoria and J.D. Wilcock, 'A computer-assisted classification of British Neolithic axes and a comparison with some Mexican and Guatemalan axes', *Science and Arachaeology*, vol. 16 (1975), pp. 11–29.

21. D. Smith, 'Scandinavian Bronze Age razors: the computer analysis', *Abstracts, 22nd Archaeometry Conference* (Bradford, 1982).

22. M.F. Kaplan, G. Harbottle and E.V. Sayre, 'Multi-disciplinary analysis of

Tel El Yahudiyeh ware', *Archaeometry*, vol. 24 (1982), pp. 127–42.

23. G.F. Carter and B.G. Carter, 'Simulated operation of a Roman mint by computer', *Abstracts, 22nd Archaeometry Conference* (Bradford, 1982).

24. Clive Orton, *Mathematics in Archaeology* (Collins Archaeology, 1980).

25. M.J. Aitken, P.A. Alcock, G.D. Bussell and C.J. Shaw 'Archaeomagnetic determination of the past geomagnetic intensity using ancient ceramics: allowance for anisotropy', *Archaeometry*, vol. 23 (1981), pp. 53–64.

26. D.C.W. Sanderson, 'A microcomputer for control and processing in a TL dating system', *Abstracts, 22nd Archaeometry Conference* (Bradford, 1982).

27. A.M. Pollard, 'A criticial study of multivariate methods as applied to provenance data', *Abstracts, 22nd Archaeometry Conference* (Bradford, 1982).

SUMMARY TABLE OF ANALYTICAL TECHNIQUES

This table is intended to help the archaeologist find a technique to solve a particular problem. Some of the less widely used techniques have been omitted.

Information required	Possible techniques		Comments
Provenance	Elemental analysis	NAA	Expensive, but can measure very low concentrations of elements.
		AAS	Less sensitive than NAA but widely used.
		XRF	Cannot detect light elements. Surface analysis can be carried out non-destructively.
		Microprobe	Can be used to study how elemental concentrations vary over surface of artefact.
		PIXE	
	Mineral composition	XRD	Minerals need to be crystalline.
		Mössbauer	
	K/Ar dating		Some stone artefacts only.
	Magnetic properties		Not widely used, but non-destructive.
	Isotope analysis		Only small sample required, but cannot solve all problems.
Firing temperature/ temperature to which sample has been heated	ESR		Useful for organic remains.
	TL		Low temperatures only.
	Magnetic analysis		Low temperatures only.
	Thermal analysis		Can also be used to detect post-burial weathering of fired materials.
	XRD		Useful for pottery
	Mössbauer spectroscopy		Useful for pottery
	SEM		Used to detect use of high temperatures in pottery and other materials.
	IR spectroscopy		
Ancient diet	Elemental analysis		See comments under provenance
	Isotope analysis		Useful for detecting changes in diet
Identification of organic remains	NMR Mass spectroscopy IR spectroscopy Chromatography		Can identify a very wide range of organic compounds. Requires only a very small sample. Non-destructive for liquids and gases. Can also be used to seperate mixtures of compounds.

SUMMARY TABLE OF DATING TECHNIQUES

This table covers the main techniques discussed in this book. Before choosing a technique the archaeologist should read the relevant chapter to check for any problems.

Technique	Age Range	Accuracy	Sample size	Sample material	Destructive	Knowledge of burial conditions	Comments
C–14 or radiocarbon	present to 50,000 BP	± 200 years	2 g of carbon e.g. 30 g of charcoal to 1 kg of bone	charcoal, bone wood, shell	yes	no	For dates in calender years measurements have to be calibrated. Higher accuracy (± 20 years) can be achieved or smaller samples (1 mg of carbon) used in special circumstances
amino acid racemis- ation	present to 100,000 BP	± 15 %	10 g	bone	yes	Temperature	Should only be used if sample cannot be dated by other method. Has to be calibrated using measurements on sample of known age
ESR	present to 500,000 BP	± 20 %	1 g	bone calcite	not always	yes	Alternative to conventional TL dating
TL	present to 500,000 BP	± 8 %	10 g plus soil samples	pottery, calcite loess, burnt flint	yes	yes	If only approximate date required can use smaller samples
K/Ar or potassium/ argon	100,000 BP to before man	± 10 %	10 g	volcanic lavas and igneous rocks	yes	no	Normally cannot date archaeological sites directly

Technique	Age Range	Accuracy	Sample size	Sample material	Destructive	Knowledge of burial conditions	Comments
Uranium series	12,000 to 350,000 BP	± 10 %	100 g	calcite bone	yes	no	Dates archaeological sites directly. Calcite is probably a better sample than bone
Fission track	20 to 1 billion years BP	± 10 %	100 cm²	Volcanic lavas, igneous rocks, glass pottery	yes	no	Obtaining accurate dates is time consuming, so this technique should only be use if other techniques such as TL dating are impossible
Obsidian hydration	500 to 100,000 BP	± 5 %	thin slice	obsidian	yes	Temperature	Determining hydration rate may increase uncertainties in date. Cheap and quick to do
Magnetic	0 to 10,000 BP for direction. Early Man for reversals	± 20 years for direction	25 mm diameter disk	pottery, burnt stones and hearths sediments	yes	no	Need to know orientation of the samples in the ground. For directional dating also need calibration curve for area of interest. Intensity dating still being developed
Uranium, fluorine and nitrogen dating of bone	Relative dates only		100 mg	bone	uranium not always, others yes	no	Appear to be some problems in using nitrogen for more recent samples

SELECTIVE LIST OF LABORATORIES

This list contains some of the more important laboratories involved in archaeometry in the United Kingdom with an indication of the fields in which they are particularly involved. However, because archaeometric techniques are developing all the time it is not possible to list all the techniques available at each laboratory. Further names of laboratories where individual techniques are used can be obtained by consulting recent papers in the relevant field.

Research Laboratory, British Museum, Great Russell St., London WC1B 3DG. Involved in C-14 and TL dating, relative dating of bone, provenance and other artefact studies.

Ancient Monuments Laboratory, 23 Savile Row, London W1X 2HE. Provides scientific back-up for excavations funded by the Department of Environment. Techniques include geophysical surveying, magnetic dating and artefact studies.

Research Laboratory for Archaeology and the History of Art, 6 Keble Rd, Oxford OX1 3QJ. Important centre for the development of new techniques. Research interests include TL and magnetic dating and provenance studies. Also the home of the United Kingdom radiocarbon accelerator unit.

School of Archaeological Sciences, University of Bradford, Bradford BD7 1DP. Provides both under- and postgraduate courses in scientific methods in archaeology on which the students have to carry out projects using the techniques. Techniques available include provenance studies using a variety of techniques including neutron activation analysis, geophysical surveying and TL dating.

Nuclear Physics Division, AERE Harwell, Oxfordshire OX11 ORA, have minicounters for the C-14 dating of small samples.

Palaeoecology Centre (Radiocarbon Dating Research Unit), The Queen's University of Belfast, Belfast BT7 1NN provides high precision and wiggle matched C-14 dates.

C-14 dating is also carried out at the Scottish Universities Reactor Centre at East Kilbride, Strathclyde and at the universities in Cardiff, Birmingham and Cambridge.

A TL dating service for pottery is provided by Durham University and TL dating is also carried out at: Paisley College of Technology, Physics Department, High Street, Paisley; National Museum of Antiquities, West Granton Rd., Edinburgh; and The Godwin Laboratory, University of Cambridge, Free School Lane, Cambridge.

This list contains a small selection of the laboratories outside the United Kingdom involved in archaeometry.

General.
Brookhaven National Laboratory, Upton, NY 11973 USA
Smithsonian Institution, Washington, DC 20560, USA
Groupe d'archéologie nucléaire d'Orsay-Saclay (CNRS), 91406 Campus Orsay, Orsay, France

C–14 dating.
Australian National University Radiocarbon Dating Laboratory, Research School of Earth Sciences, Box 4, Canberra, Australia 2600
Gakushuin University Radiocarbon Laboratory, Mejiro, Toshimaku, Tokyo 171, Japan
Laboratorium voor Algemene Natuurkunde, Afdeling Isotopen, Fysica, Westersingel 34, Groningen, Netherlands
Geochron Laboratories, Krueger Enterprises Inc., 24 Blackstone Street, Cambridge, Mass. 02139, USA
^{14}C and ^{3}H Laboratorium Niedersächsishes Landesamt für Bodenforschung, D3000 Hannover-Buchholz, Postfach 230153, W. Germany
Teledyne Isotopes, 50 Van Nuren Avenue, Westwood, New Jersey 07675, USA
Radiocarbon Dating Laboratory, National Museum, 10 Ny Vestergade, Copenhagen K, Denmark

Radiocarbon Dating Laboratory, Department of Quaternary Geology, Tunavägen 29, S–223 63 Lund, Sweden
Institute of Nuclear Sciences, Private Bag, Lower Hutt, New Zealand

TL dating.
Research Establishment Ris, P.O.B. 49, Roskilde, Denmark
Centre des Faibles Radioactivités, C.N.R.S., Gif-sur-Yvette, France
Laboratoire d'Archéometrie, Université de Rennes, Rennes, France
Max-Planck-Institut für Kernphysik Saupfercheckweg, Heidelberg, West Germany
Universität zu Köln, Institut für Kernchemie, Zülpicher Str.47, Cologne, West Germany
University of Patras, Physics Laboratory II, Patras, Greece
Laboratorio di Termoluminescenza Applicata all'Archeologia, Istituto di Scienze Fisiche, Gruppo Solidi, Via Celoria 16, Milan, Italy

THE PERIODIC TABLE

Legend: atomic number Z | A approximate atomic weight | X symbol | element name

transition elements

Z	A	Symbol	Name
1		H	hydrogen
2	4	He	helium
3	7	Li	lithium
4	9	Be	beryllium
5	11	B	boron
6	12	C	carbon
7	14	N	nitrogen
8	16	O	oxygen
9	19	F	fluorine
10	20	Ne	neon
11	23	Na	sodium
12	24	Mg	magnesium
13	27	Al	aluminium
14	28	Si	silicon
15	31	P	phosphorus
16	32	S	sulphur
17	35	Cl	chlorine
18	40	Ar	argon
19	39	K	potassium
20	40	Ca	calcium
21	45	Sc	scandium
22	48	Ti	titanium
23	51	V	vanadium
24	52	Cr	chromium
25	55	Mn	manganese
26	56	Fe	iron
27	59	Co	cobalt
28	59	Ni	nickel
29	59	Cu	copper
30	64	Zn	zinc
31	65	Ga	gallium
32	70	Ge	germanium
33	75	As	arsenic
34	79	Se	selenium
35	80	Br	bromine
36	80	Kr	krypton
37	85	Rb	rubidium
38	88	Sr	strontium
39	89	Y	yttrium
40	91	Zr	zirconium
41	93	Nb	niobium
42	96	Mo	molybdenum
43	98	Tc	technetium
44	101	Ru	ruthenium
45	103	Rh	rhodium
46	106	Pd	palladium
47	108	Ag	silver
48	112	Cd	cadmium
49	115	In	indium
50	119	Sn	tin
51	122	Sb	antimony
52	128	Te	tellurium
53	127	I	iodine
54	131	Xe	xenon
55	133	Cs	caesium
56	137	Ba	barium
57	139	La	lanthanum
72	178	Hf	hafnium
73	181	Ta	tantalum
74	184	W	tungsten
75	186	Re	rhenium
76	190	Os	osmium
77	192	Ir	iridium
78	195	Pt	platinum
79	197	Au	gold
80	200	Hg	mercury
81	204	Tl	thallium
82	207	Pb	lead
83	209	Bi	bismuth
84	209	Po	polonium
85	210	At	astatine
86	222	Rn	radon
87	223	Fr	francium
88	226	Ra	radium
89	227	Ac	actinium

lanthanides or rare earth elements

Z	A	Symbol	Name
58	140	Ce	cerium
59	141	Pr	praseodymium
60	144	Nd	neodymium
61	145	Pm	promethium
62	150	Sm	samarium
63	152	Eu	europium
64	157	Gd	gadolinium
65	159	Tb	terbium
66	163	Dy	dysprosium
67	165	Ho	holmium
68	167	Er	erbium
69	169	Tm	thulium
70	173	Yb	ytterbium
71	175	Lu	lutetium

actinides

Z	A	Symbol	Name
90	232	Th	thorium
91	231	Pa	protactinium
92	238	U	uranium

INDEX